Orange County, Virginia

Will Abstracts

1821–1838

Ruth and Sam Sparacio

HERITAGE BOOKS
2020

HERITAGE BOOKS

AN IMPRINT OF HERITAGE BOOKS, INC.

Books, CDs, and more—Worldwide

For our listing of thousands of titles see our website
at
www.HeritageBooks.com

Published 2020 by
HERITAGE BOOKS, INC.
Publishing Division
5810 Ruatan Street
Berwyn Heights, Md. 20740

International Standard Book Number
Paperbound: 978-1-68034-309-0

pp.
1-
5

Mr. JOHN URIEL and ROBERT TERRILL'S account as trustees for the estate of OLIVER TERRILL. Account begins in 1820 and into 1821. Credits $226.54. Amount due estate $158.14 made 5 October 1821 by Geo. W. Spotswood, Benj. Hume, Jackson Morton. Returned into court 22 October 1821.

pp.
5-
6

Appraisal of all the slaves and personal estate of JACOB WATTS, dec'd, that was presented to view .. 27th Septr. 1821 .. value not totalled .. made by appraisers James Early Junr., Joab Early, William Cox. Returned into court 22nd October 1821.

pp.
6-
7

A list of an appraisement of the estate of DANIEL THORNTON, dec'd .. value $190.12 1/2, made by appraisers Jno. A. Porter, John Crump, Law. Taliaferro, Luke Thornton. Returned into court 26th November 1821.

pp.
7-
8

An inventory and appraisal of the estate of JACOB WATTS, dec'd .. some entries: Benjamin Fickler for sermon; Warner Cox for coffin; to Doctor D. Whitelaw .. nine representatives to divide $41.58 .. made by appraisers Wm. A. Bradford, Tho. Wood, James Clarkson. Returned into court 26th November 1821.

pp.
8-
10

Inventory and appraisement of the estate of HAY TALIAFERRO, dec'd, lists 29 slaves .. value $7250 .. total value $8668.55 .. made by Catlett Conway, Benja. Hume, Wm. Quarles on 29th June 1821, Hay Taliaferro, executor. Returned into court 28th June 1822.

pp.
11-
12

Will of THOMAS JENKINS. .. I hereby authorize and empower my wife, hereinafter named, executrix .. (will discusses power of wife to sell estate for maintenance of family, to divide estate when child reaches age 21, or her share of the estate if she remarries) .. authorize my wife to bind out my sons as apprentices .. this 17th day of November 1821.
In the presence of   (signed)
   Wm. Johnson, Thacker y. Webb   Thos. Jenkins
  Codicil: .. It is hereby understood to be my wish that the executrix, Elizabeth G. Jenkins, should not be compelled to give security .. this 17th day of November 1821. (same witnesses)
  At a court held .. 28th January 1822 .. proved .. oaths Wm. Johnson, Thacker O. Webb .. bond without penalty ten thousand dollars . . . .

(NB - Compiler's note. In a suit brought in 1834 or 1835, the plaintiffs are George G. Taliaferro and Sarah, his wife, late Sarah Jenkins, and guardian of George G. and Robert T. Jenkins, v. Charles Taylor. The children of Thomas and Elizabeth Jenkins were Sarah, the plaintiff, Robert T. and George G., also plaintiffs. Also William T., Edward, Charles T. and James M. Jenkins.

Elizabeth, Thomas Jenkins' wife, died in November 1823 and Dr.
Charles Taylor became executor of Elizabeth Jenkins and Thomas
Jenkins. He died in 1826 or 1827, Ralph Edmonds was his adminis-
trator. William T. Jenkins, a son, became administrator of his
father and mother. The sum of $7865, the value of the slaves
belonging to Doctor Charles Taylor, was divided into 9 parts:
William Milburn, Thomas Jenkins, Robert Taylor Junr., Charles
Taylor, Catlett Conway Jr., Martha S. Taylor, George Francis
Taylor, Matilda R. Taylor and Eveline M. Taylor.

p.   A Schedule of David P. P. Sholes estate. No value assigned
12   slaves or property .. made 18th January 1822 .. Robert C. Johnson,
     D. S. for Valentine Johnson, Sheriff. Returned into court 28th
     January 1822.

(NB - Compiler's note. In a suit brought in 1834 Solomon Sholes,
Charles Geer and Elizabeth, his wife, formerly Elizabeth Sholes,
and Fanny Sholes v. David Sholes. David Sholes, Margaret (Peggy)
Sholes, who married William Taylor, and Mary (Polly) Sholes, who
married Benson Henry, were children of David P. P. Sholes and
his first wife. Solomon Sholes, Elizabeth Sholes, who married
Charles Geer, and Fanny Sholes, were children of David P. P.
Sholes and his second wife. Subpoena served on Solomon Sholes
Charles Geer and Elizabeth, his wife, in Rockingham County, Virginia, 31 January 1834. The papers show David Sholes died while
the suit was being tried.)

pp.   An inventory and appraisal of the estate of BENJAMIN WRIGHT,
13- deceased, appraised by John Dedman, William Herndon and Tandy
15   Collins, the fourth day of December 1821 .. value $4072.14 1/2.
     Returned into court 28th January 1822.

pp.   Inventory and appraisal of the estate of JOSEPH REYNOLDS,
16- dec'd, taken 30th day of October 1821 .. items valued but no
17   total .. made by George Quisenberry, Daniel Quisenberry, Vivion
     Quisenberry. Returned into court 28th January 1821.

pp.   Inventory and appraisal of the estate of ISAAC JOHNSON, dec'd,
17- .. value $202.59 .. made Octr. 10th 1821 .. by appraisers E. Row,
18   Jas. Saunders, Willis Overton, James Jones. Returned into court
     25th March 1822.

pp.   Will of DABNEY MINOR. .. my wife as executrix and my friends,
18- Dabney Herndon of Fredericksburg and Doctor James Minor, and
20   my son in law, Garritt Meriwether, executors .. authorized to
     sell tract of land purchased of Joseph Alcocke's estate ..(grants
     estate to wife) .. condition ample and confortable support (to
     mother) .. property already given my daughter, Mary Ann Meri-
     wether .. confirmed .. I earnestly desire no expense be spared
     to give my children best education which estate can afford ..
     (includes) son, James Lewis Minor, when he arrives at age of

twenty one (an executor) .. (mentions Dr. James Minor is of
Louisa County) .. wishes no appraisal of estate .. that no security be required of executors .. this 29th day of December 1821.
(no witnesses)   Dabney Minor
   At a court held .. 25th March 1822 .. there being no subscribing witnesses, Yelverton Cowherd and Robert King were sworn ..
whereupon same was ordered to be recorded .. Dabney Herndon
and James Minor bond in penalty of thirty thousand dollars (no
security).

pp.   The estate of LAW. TALIAFERRO, dec'd, with Baldwin Talia-
21-   ferro, executor .. value £ 885.18.6 .. presentation in court
22   mentions William Brooke and Heeling Terrile are dead .. settle-
           ment by William C. Willis, Law. T. Dade, Reynolds Chapman. Re-
           turned into court 25th March 1822.

pp.   The estate of WILLIAM LUCAS, dec'd, in account with ROBERT
23-   CAVE and JNO. LUCAS, executors. Balance due legatees $355.71 ..
25   settlement by T. Bowcock, John Williams, Robt. Mansfield made
           25th January 1822. Returned into court 25th March 1822.

pp.   An appraisal of the estate of OLIVER TERRILL, deceased ..
25-   value not totalled .. made by appraisers Jackson Morton, Wm.
28   Stevens, Benja. Hume .. Returned into court 25th March 1822.

p.   A list of the appraisement of the estate of DAVID P. P.
29   SHOLES, dec'd, taken second day March 1822 .. value $1201.25 ..
           made by appraisers James Finks, James P. Sims, John Sims. Re-
           turned into court 27th May 1822.

pp.   Will of JAMES SCOTT. .. lend to my beloved wife, Mildred
29-   Scott, the whole of my estate .. at her death or marriage, I
30   give to my three children, Mary Ann Lewis Scott, John Thompson
           Scott and James Scott .. I give to my two oldest sisters, Mary
           Lowrie and Martha Goff .. appoint my wife, Mildred Scott, my
           executrix .. this 21st day of January 1821.
           In the presence of: (signed)
              Thos. Row   James Scott
              E. Row, Absolom Row
             Codicil .. wife not be compelled to give neither bond nor
           security .. 6th April 1822 ..
           Witnesses: (signed)
              Thos. Row, Absolom Row   James Scott
             At a court held 27 May 1822 .. proved .. certificate granted
           Mildred Scott . . . .

pp.   Will of JAMES WILLIANS. .. my executors recover the claims
30-   which I have derived from my sons, William and James Williams
33   being all their right, title and interest in the suits and claims
           in favour of the Hites, Greens and McKays against the repre-
           sentatives against the late Thomas Lord Fairfax and others ..

also one half of the interest of Samuel B. Green .. from George
F. Strother to be paid out of monies derived to his wife .. also
one hundred and eighty four acres in Ohio .. to be laid off out
of my land called Cedar farm in the county of Culpeper .. equally
among my seven children to wit: William Williams, Charles B.
Williams, William Bruce Williams, Sally G. Strother, Lucy Ann
Williams & Elizabeth L. Williams (only six are listed) .. to my
son, William Williams .. sixty acres and land called Cedar farm
now adjoining the lands of my said son and the lands of the late
General Edward Stevens .. to my grandson, James F. Strother ..
(in list of children again, Philip Williams appears) .. nominate
.. Isaac H. Williams, John W. Green, Charles B. Williams and
William B. Williams executors .. this 30th day of November 1821.
In the presence of   (signed)
     Jeremiah Pannill   James Williams
     George Morton, Jackson Morton
     At a court held .. 27th May 1822 .. proved .. motion of Charles
B. Williams .. with John Mallory, James Farish, Jackson Morton
and William B. Williams, his securities .. bond in the penalty
of forty thousand dollars.

p.   An inventory of the estate of WILLIAM PAYNE, dec'd, which
33   was put in the hands of the sheriff .. no value shown .. made
April 16th 1822 by R. C. Johnson, D.S. for Val. Johnson, Shff.
Returned into court 30th May 1822.

pp.   Will of WILLIAM EDWARDS. .. I give unto my son, John, one
33-   moiety of the tract of land whereon I live .. if he dies without
35   issue, moiety to my son, Joseph .. devise to my son, Joseph ..
other moiety .. Joseph and his heirs should pay annually to my
daughter, Rachel Paul .. twenty dollars .. to my daughter, Polly
.. to my daughter, Franky Holly .. to my daughter, Sally Langdon
.. appoint my son, Joseph, executor .. this 5th day of July 1817.
In the presence of   (signed)
     Baldwin Taliaferro   William Edwards
     Hay Taliaferro Jr., Paul Verdier
     Codicil .. increase of female slaves since will written to go
to child whom mother devised .. this 11th day of December 1820.
In the presence of   (signed)
     Reynolds Chapman, William M. Chapman   William Edwards
     At a court held .. 24th June 1822 .. proved .. ordered to be
recorded .. motion Joseph Edwards .. with Edmund D. Langdon, his
security .. bond in the penalty of five thousand dollars.

p.   Will of HENRY THOMAS. .. to my loving wife, Mary Thomas,
35   all my whole estate .. after her death to my four brethren viz.
Edward, Nancy, Catharine and Lucy .. I have my friend, Walter
Gambrel and Edward Thomas .. executors .. this 15th day of
February 1822.
In the presence of   (signed)
     Pemberton Claughton   Henry Thomas

At a court held .. 24th June 1822 .. proved .. ordered to be recorded .. motion of Walter Gambrel .. with John Farish, his security .. bond in penalty of five thousand dollars.

pp.   An appraisal of the estate of JAMES SCOTT, dec'd .. value
36- $4067.50 .. made 13th July 1822 by appraisers Thos. Row, Thos.
37   Robinson, E. Row. Returned into court 22nd July 1822.

pp.   Will of JOHN STEVENS JUNR. .. (proceeds of the sale of es-
37-   tate) .. I give to my daughter, Sarah McCaffrey .. to my daugh-
38   ter, Ann S. Stevens .. whatever property which may come to my
estate at the death of my father, John Stevens .. appoint my brother, William Stevens, my nephew, Landon Lindsay, and my friends, Jacob Graves and William T. Burrus, executors .. this 8th day of January 1821.
In the presence of   (signed)
    John Daniel, Ludwell Lindsay,   John Stevens Junr.
    Wm. Brockman Junr.,
    Joseph M. Porter, Hezekiah Quisenberry
   At a court held .. 26th August 1822 .. proved .. ordered to be recorded .. William Stevens with Thomas Woolfolk and Claibourn Graves, his securities .. Landon Lindsay with William Brockman Junr. and James Nelson, his securities . . . .

(NB - Compiler's note. The complete will of John Stevens Junr. may be found on pages 285/286 of PAMUNKEY NEIGHBORS OF ORANGE COUNTY, VIRGINIA. John Stevens Junr., son of John and Sarah Mountague Stevens, married Mary Smith, daughter of William and Ann Stevens Bowker Smith (his cousin). They separated 19 October 1815 and she moved to Clark County, Kentucky. Their older daughter, Ann Smith Stevens was born before 1792 and married John Stevens (called the "Younger" or "Minor.") Their younger daughter , Sarah Mountague Stevens, married William Mc Caffrey 28 January 1819 in Clark County, Kentucky. When he died about 1832, she married second Edward W. Stuart.)

pp.   Report on the estate of JOHN HASKEW, deceased, as adminis-
39-   tered by the executors, Edmund and Haskew Foster .. mentions
41   legacy paid Mary Lucas .. seven legatees mentioned, Edmund Foster, Haskew Foster, George Taylor Senr., Henry Foster's descendants, John Foster, Sary Taylor's descendants, Lewis Hensley .. subscribed 23 August 1822 by Valentine Johnson, T. Bowcock, William Douglass. Returned into court 27th August 1822.

pp.   Will of THOMAS SAMPSON. .. bequeath to my beloved wife,
41-   Margaret Sampson, the tract of land whereon I live .. give and
42   bequeath to my daughter, Mary Sampson, wife of James Yowell .. appoint John Jackson, Obediah Anderson and William Dulaney executors .. this 3rd day of November 1817.
Teste: James Taylor Junr.   (Signed)
    Fielding Smith   Thomas Sampson

At a court held .. 26th August 1822 .. will offered by William Dulaney and being opposed by James Clarke, same continued to next court ..

At a court held .. 23rd September 1822 .. court heard testimony .. concluded will was Thomas Sampson's .. ordered to be recorded .. motion of William Dulaney .. with Obediah Anderson, his security .. bond in the penalty of five thousand dollars.

pp. 42-43   An appraisal of the estate of THOMAS JENKINS, dec'd .. value $4441.64 .. made by appraisers Augustine Webb, Thomas Newman, T. V. Webb. Returned into court 25th November 1822.

pp. 43-48   A list of appraisement and inventory of the estate of THOMAS SAMPSON, deceased, taken on the 9th day of October 1822 .. (inventory includes nearly two pages of books in his library) .. made by appraisers Dabney Herndon and Js. Minor. Returned into court 25th November 1822.

p. 49   The estate of JEREMIAH WHITE, dec'd, in account with Richard White and Jacob Graves, administrators .. account shows a balance of $628.33 for division .. settled 23rd November 1822 by George Shearman, Geo. Stevens Jr., Thomas Eddins, Joel Rucker. Returned into court 25th November 1822.

pp. 49-52   Inventory and appraisal of the property belonging to the estate of EDWARD COLLINS, dec'd, this 1st September 1822 .. value $5043 with $860.59 outstanding .. Lewis D. Collins, executor .. made by appraisers Richd. Rawlings, Claibourn Graves, Wm. Stevens. Returned into court 25th November 1822.

pp. 52-53   Estate of WILLIAM B. HANCOCK to William Hancock Senr. and Mary Hancock, admors .. value $133.75 .. examined by James D. Dillard, Robert Taylor Junr., Joseph Clarke. Returned into court 25th November 1822.

pp. 53-54   An inventory and appraisement of the estate of JOHN STEVENS JUNR., dec'd, taken this 5th day of October 1822 .. value $403.68 made by appraisers Richd. Johnson, Jonathan Graves, Brockman Bell. Returned into court 25th November 1822.

pp. 54-59   Estate of NATHANIEL SMITH, dec'd, in account with Paul Verdier, executor .. covers period 1817-1822 .. balance due estate 22nd November 1822 .. $10,007.37 owed by Paul Verdier .. account given by Wm. Quarles, Baldwin Taliaferro 23rd November 1822. Paul Verdier and James Craig certified they consented to settlement. Returned into court 25th November 1822.

pp. 59-60   The division and alloting of slaves belonging to the estate of JEREMIAH WHITE, dec'd .. William Piper; heirs of Mary Burton; Richard White, Willis White, Jacob Graves, Garrett White, William White, heirs of Nancy Roberts .. made 17th January 1821 by

Thomas Eddins, George Stevens Jr., George Shearman. Returned
into court 23rd December 1822.

pp.   Will of JAMES SMITH. .. land to my daughter in law, Sarah
60-   Smith .. a negro girl .. (after her death).. to be divided among
62   the children she had of Coleby Smith .. to my daughter, Milly
      Cooper .. to my daughter, Dilley Adams .. to my daughter, Polly
      Smith .. I lend to my son in law, William Nelson .. children he
      had by my daughter, Salley .. to my daughter, Agnes Wright .. my
      son, Owen Smith .. management of my property .. keep it out of
      hands of Isaac Wright .. to my son, Tartan Smith .. to my son,
      James Smith .. appoint my two sons, Owen Smith and Tartan Smith,
      with my two friends, James Nelson and William Collins, executors
      .. this 23rd day of March 1821.
In the presence of   (signed)
      Robert S. Spindle   James Smith
      Alexander Chandler
      William Jackson, Wm. M. Daniel.
      NB. It is my will and desire that Jacob Jackson and his wife
have a life estate in one half acre of land where he has built a
house .. with no power to dispose of it (same witnesses).
      At a court held .. 23rd December 1822 .. proved .. ordered to
be recorded .. motions of James Nelson and Tartan Smith .. with
Walter Gambrel and John Terrill, their securities .. bond in the
penalty of twenty thousand dollars.
      At a court held .. 23rd February 1823 .. depositions of James
Nelson & William Collins purporting to be a codicil .. of James
Smith, deceased, was established .. ordered to be recorded as follows: The undersigned do hereby declare that four days before
the decease of James Smith he called upon them to witness that
in consideration of the inconvenience as loss his son, Tatton,
had incurred by moving from Staunton and in further consideration
of his filial care and attention to him in his last days, it was
his will and desire that he (Tatton) should remain in his estate
for one year after his decease .. and that his estate should be
charged with the expenses and loss his son incurred in moving from
Staunton.   James Nelson
                                         William Collins

p.   An inventory of the estate of SYLVESTER LANGDON, deceased,
62   taken -- day of December 1822 .. no value of items shown .. made
      by Geo. Holloway, D. S. for Val. Johnson, Shff. Returned into
      court 23rd December 1822.

pp.   An account of sales of the estate of SYLVESTER LANGDON, de-
62-   ceased, made -- day of December 1822 .. value not totalled ..
63   made by Geo. Holloway, D. S. for Val. Johnson, Shff. Returned
      into court 23rd December 1822.

pp.   Will of ADAM LINDSAY. .. I lend unto my loving wife, Betty
63-   Lindsay, all my estate .. give to my darter, Saley Thompson .. to
64   my son, Reuben Lindsay .. my dec'd darter, Sukie Payne .. appoint

.. my wife, Betty Lindsay, executrix, and my son, Reuben Lindsay, executor .. this 24th day of October 1813.
In the presence of   (signed)
   James Terrill   Adam Lindsay
   Obed Gregory, Maurice C. Webb
  At a court held .. 23rd December 1822 .. proved .. ordered to be recorded .. motion Reuben Lindsay .. with William Stevens, his security .. bond in penalty of thirty thousand dollars.

pp.   Will of WILLIAM C. WEBB. .. I give to my son, William B.
64-   Webb, my surveying instruments and the tract of land he lives
66   on .. to my two sons, Jesse and Richard B Webb .. tract of land I live on .. tract of land in Kentucky in the county of Montgomery .. I lend to my daughter, Ann Perry .. that Mary Grasty, Morton & Delilah Perry to have twenty five pounds .. at their mother's death of the part alloted my daughter, Ann Perry .. appoint my two sons, Jesse and Richard B. Webb, executors .. this 7th day of September 1822.
In the presence of   (signed)
   George Proctor, Thomas Proctor,   Richd. C. Webb
   Ezekiah Richards, Edmund Lancaster
  At a court held .. 27th January 1823 .. proved .. ordered to be recorded .. Richard B. Webb .. came into court and refused .. motion of Jesse B. Webb .. with Richard B. Webb, James Nelson and Richard Richards, his securities .. bond in the penalty of fifteen thousand dollars.

p.   Appraisal of the slaves and other personal property of PHIL-
66   LIP SLEET, deceased .. value $1095.00 .. made by appraisers Hay Taliaferro, Geo. W. Spotswood, Curtis Brockman. Returned into court 24th February 1823.

pp.   Will of MARY RUCKER. .. bequeath to my two daughters, Milley
66-   Head, the wife of Marshall Head, and Mary Graves, the wife of
67   Waller Graves .. land .. bounded on the southeast by Edward Cason and Robert Cave, on the south by Joel Rucker, on the west by said Rucker and Thomas Eddins, on the north by the lands of John Rucker, deceased, it being land formerly claimed by John Rucker, deceased, called the Hamilton land, since proved to be the land of Ann Fathergale, which I have since bought of her attorney for two dollars per acre with my own money .. all the claim I have now arising from my father's estate (to daughters) .. appoint my sons in law, Marshall Head and Waller Graves, executors .. this 23rd day of September 1820.
In the presence of   (signed - her mark)
   John White   Nancy Rucker
   William Collins, William H. Mansfield
  Codicil signed October 8th 1821. Attest Wm. H. Mansfield, Benjamin Cason.
  At a court held .. 24th February 1823 .. proved .. ordered to be recorded.

pp.
68-
69
Estate of RICHARD LANCASTER in account with Benjamin Lancaster, the administrator. Thomas Coleman, blacksmith account; Nathaniel Dickinson repairing dwelling house; Larkin Lancaster the full of his legacy; Washington Hutchinson the full of his legacy; Richard Lancaster the full of his legacy; Jonathan Lancaster the full of his legacy; Thomas Lancaster the full of his legacy; Richard Richards guardian for Mason Lancaster the full of his legacy; James Lancaster the full of his legacy; Bartlett Lancaster the full of his legacy; John Lancaster in part of his legacy; cash paid legatees $4995.25 .. settlement by Reuben Lindsay, John W. Sale, James Nelson. Returned into court 24th February 1823.

pp.
69-
70
REUBEN BOSTON estate to Valentine Johnson, Committee. Account examined by Edmund Henshaw, Wm. Campbell, T. Bowcock 22nd February 1823. Returned into court 24th February 1823.

pp.
70-
73
Estate of THOMAS Y. PARROT to Wm. & Chs. Parrott. Account begins Jan. 9, 1815 through 1819. Settlement made by Tho. Sorrille, Sanford Beasley, William Dulaney. Returned into court 24th February 1823.

pp.
73-
74
Estate of NATHAN MALLORY, deceased, to Charles Mallory and Charles Parrot, executors. Each legatee's portion $500.86 1/2 .. settlement made by Jas. G. Blakey, George S. Blakey, Tho. Sorrille. Returned into court 24th February 1823.

pp.
74-
76
A list of the personal property of every description belonging to the estate of the late GEORGE W. THORNTON in county of Stafford together with the valuation of the appraisers appointed by the County Court of Orange .. lists 45 slaves .. value $13,760 .. total value $17,825.17 .. made 27th October 1817 .. by John Gray, Alexr. Morson, Wm. C. Beale. Returned into Orange Court 24 March 1823.

pp.
76-
77
Will of WILLIAM F. TAYLOR of county of Limestone in the state of Alabama .. my desire that my slaves (names three) not be sold bur remain in my father's possession and at his house .. presuming my child will live with him until arrives at age or marries .. two carriage horses be kept for the use of my mother and friend, Deborah Howard .. (bequeaths one thousand dollars to Deborah Howard) .. my child, Pernello (?) E. H. Taylor .. appoint my father, John Taylor of the county of Orange and state of Virginia. executor .. this 5th day of September 1822.
In the presence of   (signed)
   Charles P. Howard   Wm. F. Taylor
   Lucinda A. Taylor
   Jane F. Taylor, Sarah F. Adams.
At a court held in Orange County at the courthouse 24th March 1823 .. proved .. ordered to be recorded .. motion of John Taylor .. bond without security in the amount of forty thousand dollars.

pp.   Appraisal of the estate of Capt. RICHARD C. WEBB, deceased,
78-   value not totalled .. made 1st day of February 1823 by appraisers
79   Ezekiah Richards, Tandy Collins, Thomas Robinson. Returned into
           court 24th March 1823.

pp.   Appraisal of the estate of OVARRILLA WOOD, dec'd .. value
79- $154.00 .. made by appraisers Edward Cason, Wm. Martin, John Wil-
80   liams. Returned into court 25th March 1823.

pp.   A memorandum of the personal estate of GEORGE BRADLEY, dec'd,
80-   taken the 5th September 1820 .. value $4745.88 .. (appraisal has
83   a number of other items listed after the total value shown with-
           out a value assigned) .. made by appraisers John Williams, T. V.
           Webb, Robt. Mansfield. Returned into court 28th April 1823.

pp.   The estate of GEORGE W. THORNTON, Esqr., deceased, in account
83-   with James F. Maury and Mary, his wife, late Mary Thornton, for
92   transactions previous and subsequent to their marriage .. paid
           James G. Taliaferro board and tuition of H. R. Thornton from
           Apl 1817 to Apl 1818 .. paid G. F. Washington account .. paid
           Mrs. Hackley board and tuition for Lucy Thornton, August and
           September .. Doctor William Burrus account .. credit guardian-
           ship accounts of the children of Geo. W. Thornton to wit: Henry
           R. Thornton, Lucy W. Thornton, Mary G. Thornton, Seth B. Thorn-
           ton (each $115.11) .. account examined by Thomas Seddon, John
           Gray, Murray Forbes. Commissioners noted "it appears .. the
           widow and executrix of Geo. W. Thornton, dec'd, kept the estate
           together for several years after the decease of her husband and
           previous to her intermarriage with Mr. Maury. (This detailed
           account of settlement has many interesting details and also in-
           cludes the suit initiated by James F. Maury and Mary, his wife,
           regarding the division of the slaves.) Returned into court 28th
           April 1823.

pp.   Will of JAMES WHITE. .. my beloved wife, Susanna White, for
92-   the natural affections I bear for her, my mansion house and one
94   hundred and fifty acres of land, together with Patrick, Rachel,
           her child, and Mariah .. to my son, Crenshaw White .. to my son,
           Willis .. to my son, Anderson .. lend to my daughter, Susanna
           Stephens .. to my daughter, Nancy .. to my son, Overton .. to my
           son, Early .. to my daughter, Polly .. to my daughter, Kitty ..
           appoint my sons, Willis and Anderson, my executors .. this 2nd
           day of April 1823.
In the presence of   (signed)
     Wm. Catterton, Wm. Cave,   James White
     Ewall Mason, D. Whitelaw
   At a court held .. 28th April 1823 .. proved.. ordered to be
recorded.
   At a court held .. 26th May 1823 .. motion Willis White and
Anderson White .. with Crenshaw White and Overton White, their
securities .. bond in the penalty of ten thousand dollars.

pp.   An inventory and appraisement of the estate of WILLIAM EDWARDS,
94-   deceased .. value not totalled .. made by appraisers Wm. Quarles,
95   John Taylor, Richard Cave, Richd. H. Taliaferro. Returned into
           court 26th May 1823.

pp.   Amount of sales of the personal property belonging to the es-
95-   tate of ISAAC JOHNSON, deceased .. eleventh October 1821 .. sold
96   by Fielding Jones as administrator .. amount of sale $253.31.
           Returned into court 26th May 1823.

pp.   Account of sales of THOMAS ADAMS, deceased, by Henry Tandy
96-   Senr, administrator, October 13, 1820, November 14, 1820 and
97   September 28, 1821... value of sale $277.10. Returned into court
           23rd June 1823.

pp.   Will of WILLIAM VAWTER. .. give to my daughter, Frances
97-   Vawter .. and fifty acres of land including my dwelling house ..
98   to my daughter, Melinda Hilson .. to my daughter, Mary Lower ..
           to my son, Benjamin .. I leave my son, Benjamin Vawter, and my
           friend, Claibourn Graves, for my executors .. (no date).
           Teste   (signed - his mark)
               Benjamin Cooper   William Vawter
               Claibourn Graves, Henry Day
             At a court held .. 23rd June 1823 .. proved .. ordered to be
           recorded .. Benjamin Vawter .. with Christian F. Kinzer and Daniel
           Hord, his securities .. bond in penalty of two thousand dollars.

pp.   An inventory of property belonging to the estate of WILLIAM
98-   F. TAYLOR, dec'd, this 9th day of April 1823 .. value $430 ..
99   Returned into court 28th July 1823.

p.   An account of sales of the estate of PHILIP SLEET, dec'd ..
99   value $355.29 .. Weedon Sleet, executor. Returned into court
           28th July 1823.

pp.   Appraisal of the estate of ELIZABETH SAUNDERS, dec'd .. value
99- $201.50 .. appraisers John Mallory, William Graves, Benj. Hume.
100   Returned into court 28th July 1823.

pp.   Estate of JAMES PIERCE, deceased .. debits $2132.41 .. credits
100- $1798.57 .. received of Elizabeth Pierce, $321.40 .. examined,
102   stated and settled accounts of Minor Rucker .. by William Parrott,
           Thomas Eddins, David Whitelaw, Thos. Sorrille. Returned into
           court 25th August 1823.

pp.   Appraisal of the estate of JAMES BEASLEY SENR., dec'd ..
102-   presented to view .. value not totalled .. made by appraisers
104   Isaac Davis Jr., Thomas Davis, Thos. Sorrille, Edward Ancell
           15th September 1821. Returned into court 25th August 1823.

pp.
104-
106
Will of SAMUEL TWYMAN. .. executors should proceed to sell my whole estate .. put two thousand dollars out to interest for the use of my beloved wife, Frances Twyman .. to my son, Iverson Twyman, when he arrives to age twenty one .. executors to bind my son, Iverson, to the carpenter's trade until he comes to the age of twenty one .. (one eighth part of the estate to) .. my son, John Twyman .. my son, Elijah Twyman .. my son, Paschal Twyman .. my son, Mordecai Twyman .. my son, Iverson Twyman .. my daughter, Judah White .. my daughter, Nancy Thornton .. in trust to my daughter, Frances Rogers .. empower my executors .. buy a piece of land somewhere in the western country for the benefit of my daughter, Frances Rogers .. (to her children after her death) .. appoint my son in law, Anthony Thornton and Isaac Davis Junr., my executors .. this 21st day of March 1823.
In the presence of

                              (signed)

Isaac Davis, Jonathan Twyman,
                   Samuel Twyman
William Rucker, Robt. Mitchell,
William Shearman, Douglass Dickinson, John Beasley,
James Dennison, William White, Henry Marr, John Rucker.
At a court held .. 27th October 1823 .. proved .. ordered to be recorded .. with Isaac Davis and John Head, their securities .. bond in the penalty of twenty thousand dollars.

pp.
106-
107
A list of sundry papers produced by Thomas Sorrille, administrator of WILLIAM HERRING, dec'd, on 5th day of August 1819 .. settled account 28th August 1819 by John (X) Hainey, John Mallory, John (X) Shiflett. Returned into court 27th October 1823.

pp.
107-
110
Will of MARK HORNSEY. .. give and bequeath to my executors .. all my bank stock, to say, thirty shares in the Bank of Virginia, twenty six in the Bank of Potomac and eight shares in the Farmers Bank of Virginia .. in trust for my nephew, Christopher Hornsey .. in trust also .. to pay eight legacies to my relatives in England of one hundred dollars each .. to Robert Hornsey of Southampton Court, Queens Square, Bloomsburg, London .. to Willim Hornsey, the father of the aforesaid Christopher of Oversby near Castor in the county of Lincoln .. to John Hornsey near Gainsborough in the said county of Lincoln .. to Susan Hornsey, Sarah Hornsey, Mary Hornsey and Ann Hornsey by whatever name and place of abode my said four sisters may be identified .. to James Milson of the city of Lincoln .. all the legatees save James Milson are my brothers and sisters, are all of them the children of Christopher and Elizabeth Hornsey, deceased, and were all born on the Oversby farm .. James Milson is the only child of my deceased sister, formerly Elizabeth Hornsey .. give my executors two shares each of turnpike stock .. to my god son, William L. Terrill, my surveyors instruments, staff, chain and pins, also an elegant set of plotting instruments .. an elegant box of colours presented me many years ago by his grandfather, Lovell .. to Doc-

tor Uriel Terrill, my watch .. my old sea chest and its contents
.. to Mrs. Susan Terrill, widow of Oliver Terrill, deceased, my
spectacles and case .. Mrs. Jane Terrill .. except the sheets in
which to wrap my body .. to Miss Mary Ann Terrill, a gold buckle
which I have worn in my bosom for 46 years in small acknowledg-
ment of her kind attentions to me during the absences of Mrs.
Jane Terrill .. appoint William Lovell, esquire, of the county
of Culpeper, John Yates, esquire, of the county of Jefferson,
and Captain William Mallory of the county of Madison, executors
.. this 20th day of August 1823.

In the presence of   (signed)
    Daniel M. Smith   Mark Hornsey
    John Farish, Robert Terrill Jr.

(In a codicil, he notes bank stock would be sold at a sacri-
fice at this time, and since his nephew, Christopher, expressed
a desire to come to America even before he knew of his inheri-
tance, his relatives should help him.)

At a court held .. 24th November 1823 .. proved .. ordered to
be recorded .. with Uriel Mallory Jr. and Philip Mallory, their
securities .. bond in the penalty of twelve thousand dollars.

pp.   Will of HOPEFUL WOOD. .. I give to my daughter, Alby Harvey
110- .. all reversionary rights .. estate of brother, Zebidiah Wood's
111   estate .. bequeath to my daughter, Nelly Mitchell .. to my daughters, Nancy Dickinson, Sally Taylor and Polly Herndon .. to each
of my sons, Richard, Hisiciah, William and James .. appoint Wm.
Harvey and Latin Harvey, my executors .. (no date) ..

Teste   (signed - his mark)
    David Whitelaw   Hopeful Wood
    R. C. Clayton, Laton Harvey

At a court held .. 24th November 1823 .. proved .. ordered to
be recorded.

pp.   Will of LEWIS G. POWELL. .. desire all the perishable part
111- of my estate be immediately sold .. sell so much of my real es-
113   tate necessary settle debts .. lend to my wife, Sally Powell,
.. land purchased of John Shelor whereon I now live .. to my
youngest daughter, Rhody, after the death of her mother, Sally
Powell .. (land lent mother) .. to my son, James Powell .. already given to my daughter, Joice, who intermarried with James
Walker .. to my daughter, Elizabeth Seal .. to my daughter, Sally
Riddle .. to my son, Lewis G. Powell .. also tract of land purchased of Thomas Thornton and his father, George Thornton .. to
my daughter, Polly Powell .. to my son, William Powell .. also
tract of land whereon William Exton formerly lived on east side
of Swift Run .. the tract of land whereon Fielding Powell now
resides .. to be sold .. to my grandson, Lewis Riddle .. appoint
my friends, William Dulaney, Charles Parrot, and my son, Lewis
G. Powell, executors .. this 15th day of October 1823.

In presence of   (signed)
    Thos. Sorrille   Lewis G. Powell
    John Fleak, St. Clair Smith.

-14-

3 Orange County Will Book 6

At a court held .. 24th November 1823 .. proved .. ordered to
be recorded .. with William Early, his security .. bond in penalty
of ten thousand dollars.
(On margin. Admin. de bonis non with the will annexed granted
to Thos. G. Garth, May 25, 1846.)

pp.
113-
114

1

Will of WILLIAM CAMPBELL. .. I appoint my wife, Susanna
Campbell, executrix .. not to be required to give security, to
make no inventory or have a sale unless she may think it necessary
for the payment of my debts .. wish my real property in city of
Richmond to be disposed of .. I give my lands and my claims to
lands in Kentucky to my four sons and my son in law, Hill Maury,
but in the division Hill Maury is to retain the part I have already given him .. (property lent wife)) .. to all my daughters
except Virginia Maury .. my sons, Joseph, William and Woodson ..
this 1st day of October 1823 (no executors shown).
In the presence of   (signed)
    James Barbour, William S. Acre   Wm. Campbell
    At a court held .. 24th November 1823 .. proved .. ordered to
be recorded.
    At a court held .. 22nd December 1823 .. Susan Campbell granted
probate certificate.

pp.
114-
115

Appraisal of the estate of MARY RUCKER, dec'd .. value $47.50
.. made by appraisers Edward Cason, Wm. H. Mansfield, William
Herndon. Returned into court 22nd December 1823.

pp.
115-
117

Estate of DABNEY MINOR, dec'd, in account with D. Herndon,
Excor. Account from 3 April 1822 to 27 December 1822. Balance
in hand of excor $33.56 .. examined and settled account of Dabney
Herndon 17 June 1823 by J. F. Ford, Reuben T. Thom, William I.
Roberts of Fredericksburg. Returned into Orange Court 22nd
December 1823.

pp.
117-
121

Inventory of the perishable property and appraisement of the
estate of THOMAS JENKINS, dec'd .. value of slaves $2700.00 ..
value of other property $495.25 .. made by appraisers Robt. Wil-
son, John Williams, Robert Mansfield. Returned into court 22nd
December 1823.

pp.
121-
122

Will of JOHN WRIGHT SENR. .. I lend unto my beloved wife,
Sarah Wright .. (slaves) .. land on which I live .. to my son,
William Wright .. to my son, John Wright .. to my son, Alexander
Wright .. at his death to be divided between his three sons,
John H. Wright, William W. Wright and Thaddeus S. Wright .. to
my daughter, Frances Lancaster .. for the support of my daughter,
Mary Wright .. my grandsons, Jefferson Wright and Booker W.
Wright .. appoint my sons, John Wright and Alexander Wright, execu-
tors .. this 30th day of August 1823.
In the presence of   (signed)
    Richard Richards   John Wright
    Richard Richards Junr., Vivion Quisenberry

At a court held .. 22nd December 1823 .. proved .. ordered to
be recorded .. with William Peacher, Richard Richards and Thomas
Robinson, their securities .. bond in penalty of ten thousand
dollars.

pp.   Examined and settled administration accounts of Richard
122-   Richards upon the estate of ROBERT LANCASTER, dec'd .. paid one
125   ninth part of $188.88 to William Lancaster, Thos. Lancaster,
Reuben Lancaster, John Lancaster, Ricd. Lancaster, Robert Lancaster, John Conner right of his wife, Mary; Steven Adams in
right of his wife, Elisabeth; James Nelson in right of his wife,
Ann .. made by Benj. Hume, Edmd. Row, Tandy Collins. Returned
into court 22nd December 1823.

pp.   Will of JANE MORTON. .. bequeath to my granddaughter, Sarah
125-   Terrill .. devise and bequeath to Sarah Terrill, George Terrill,
127   William H. Terrill and Jane Pilcher, children of my daughter,
Jane Terrill, dec'd .. to my daughter, Frances Mallory .. my lands
left by my husband, George Morton .. now therefore, not unto
Susannah Terrill, but 5thly unto the children of Susannah Terrill
.. appoint William Morton Junr. and Jackson Morton, trustees
(bequest) to children of Susannah Terrill and so much .. given
Elisabeth Terrill, Nancy Terrill and Claibourne Terrill (children of Susannah Terrill) .. residue of estate divided equally
between my granddaughters, Sarah Terrill, Jane Pilcher, Sarah
Street Mallory, Hannah Mallory, Elisabeth Terrill, Nancy Terrill,
Catherine Terrill and Sarah Mallory, wife of Philip Mallory ..
appoint my grandsons, William Morton Jr., Jackson Morton and
George Terrill, executors .. this 8th day of November 1823.
In the presence of   (signed)
    Philip Mallory,   Jane Morton
    Tartan Smith, Charles M. Morton,
    George Morton
    At a court held .. 22nd December 1823 .. proved .. ordered to
be recorded .. with William Morton and John Mallory, their securities .. bond in penalty of ten thousand dollars.

pp.   An inventory and appraisement of the estate of MARY PORTER,
127-   dec'd .. value not totalled .. Benj. F. Porter, administrator
129   of Mary Porter .. made by appraisers 21 January 1824 Robert Taylor Junr., James Marshall, Cudden Davis. Returned into court
26th January 1824.

pp.   A list of property appraised on Saturday the 10th day of
129-   January 1824 belonging to the estate of Capt. JOHN WRIGHT, dec'd
133   .. value not totalled .. subscribers William Herndon, Tandy Collins, Ezekiah Richards. Returned into court 23rd February 1824.

pp.   Appraisal of the slaves and other personal property of JANE
133-   MORTON, deceased .. produced by Wm. Morton Jr. and Jackson Mor-
135   ton, executors .. value not totalled .. made by appraisers Wm.

T. Burrus, Thos. Coleman, John Terrill, John W. Sale .. Returned
into court 23rd February 1824.

pp.   ' An inventory and appraisement of the estate of JAMES ROACH,
135-   deceased, Nov. 12, 1823 .. value not totalled .. William Roach,
139   administrator .. Thomas Graves, Thos. Row, Benj. Sanders, appraisers. Returned into court 23rd February 1824.

pp.   Will of BENNETT BEASLEY. .. my beloved wife, Mary Beasley,
139-   is to have one third part of all my land including my mansion
140   house and orchard .. my will that at her death, my negro man,
Bob, be free .. other part of land .. to Brother, James Beasley,
after paying my nephew, Stephen Miller .. appoint William Kite
and Henry Hansbarger, executors .. this 31st day of May 1823.
In the presence of   (signed – his mark)
     William Kite, John Clark,   Bennett Beasley
     Sarah Kite, Melinda Kite.
     At a court held .. 23rd February 1824 .. proved .. ordered to
be recorded.
     At a court held .. 22nd March 1824 .. William Kite and Henry
Hansbarger, executors named in the will came into court and refused .. on motion of Mary Beasley .. with James Longher and James
Beasley, her securities .. bond in penalty of one thousand dollars.

pp.   This 6th day of December 1823 appraised following property
140-   belonging to the estate of MARK HORNSEY, dec'd, being all the
141   property we know of .. value $126.23 1/2 .. made by appraisers
Robert Terrill Jr., Uriel Terrill, Edmond Terrill .. William
Mallory, executor. Returned into court 22nd March 1824.

pp.   Appraisement of the estate of LEWIS G. POWELL, deceased, made
141-   this 9th day of December 1823 .. value $3868.31 .. by appraisers
144   George Price, Michael Mayers, James Melone .. William Dulaney,
executor. Returned into court 22nd March 1824.

p.   An inventory of the property belonging to LUCY W. DANIEL
144   that came into my hands on the thirty first day of December 1823
.. (negroes named) .. made by Coleby Cowherd, guardian for Lucy
W. Daniel. Returned into court 22nd March 1824 and ordered to
be recorded.

pp.   An inventory of the property which has fallen into my posses-
144-   sion from estate of JOHN DANIEL, deceased, as guardian for Susan
145   Ann Daniel, December 31st 1823 .. (5 negroes named and their
children) .. made by John Scott, guardian of Susan Ann Daniel.
Returned into court 23rd March 1824.

pp.   Will of JAMES RIDDLE SR. .. give my wife, Mary Riddle, all
145-   my estate .. (after her death) .. to my children .. my son,
147   James Riddle .. tract of land whereon I now live which I purchased

of Lockly Leonard .. after his death, to his daughter, Mary Riddle .. with condition son, James, to pay daughter, Frances Collins .. to my son, Turner Riddle .. land   purchased by my father
William Riddle, of Daniel Sturgeon .. to my sons, John Riddell,
and Valentine Riddell .. tract of land I purchased of William
Bird .. Mildred Riddell not to be disturbed as long as she wishes
to live where she now resides .. after death of wife (proceeds
of sale to be divided into ten parts) .. to William Riddell ..
James Riddell .. equally divided (a tenth share) between the
heirs of Fielding Riddell, dec'd .. to Ely Oliver and Willis
Oliver, children of my daughter, Winnifred Oliver, dec'd .. to
my daughter, Mary Jones .. son, John Riddell .. son, Valentine
Riddell .. daughter, Frances Collins .. son, Taverner Riddell ..
and remaining tenth to my daughter, Lucy Goodall .. appoint my
wife, Mary Riddell, and my son, Taverner Riddell, executrix and
executor .. this 16th day of October 1821.
In the presence of   (signed)
     Charles Hagish   James Riddell Sr.
     Geo. S. Blakey, Richard (X) Goodall
     At a court held .. 25th October 1824 .. on motion of Edmond
Jones .. with James Riddle, Valentine Riddle and John Riddle,
his securities .. bond in penalty of ten thousand dollars ..
it being proved to the satisfaction that the persons named as
executors in the said will have refused the executorship.

pp.   Will of JULIUS OLIVER. .. I hold Minor Rucker's bond for
147-   two hundred dollars now due which I give to Blyfil Rucker .. give
149   to Nancy Rucker, wife of Blyfil Rucker .. to my two brothers,
       Durrett and James Oliver .. accounts of Doctor Whitelaw and Doc-
       tor Briggs paid .. to my brother, James, my watch .. appoint my
       friend and cousin, Blyfil Rucker, my executor .. this 30th day
       of April 1824.
       Teste   (signed)
           Robert Cave   Julius Oliver
           Wm. H. Mansfield, Joel Rucker
         At a court held .. 26th April 1824 .. proved .. ordered to be
       recorded.
         At a court held .. 24 May following .. Blyfil Rucker, executor,
       with Minor Rucker, his security .. bond in penalty of three thou-
       sand dollars.

pp.   Appraisal of the estate of BENNETT BEASLEY, deceased ..
149-   value $709.30 .. made by appraisers William Kite, Jasper Smith,
150   George Dear. Returned into court 26th April 1824.

pp.   An inventory and appraisement of the estate of JAMES SMITH,
150-   dec'd .. value not totalled .. made by appraisers John W. Sale,
153   Landon Lindsay, John Fisher .. certified a true inventory by
       Tartan Smith and James Nelson, executors. Returned into court
       24th May 1824.

pp. 153- 154   Appraisal of the estate of WILLIAM VAWTER, dec'd, at his dwelling house .. value not totalled .. made by appraisers Lewis D. Collins, Benj. Cooper, Thos. Woolfolk .. certified a true inventory by Benjamin Vawter, executor. Returned into court 24th May 1824.

pp. 154- 155   An inventory of the Negro property belonging to JOHN F. DANIEL which fell into the hands of Buckner Terrill, his guardian, December 31st 1823. Returned into court 24th May 1824.

pp. 155- 156   An inventory of the appraisement of the estate of JOSEPH HAM, dec'd .. value $80.96 .. made by appraisers Michael Mayers, William Melone .. bonds belonging to the estate .. value $253.00 .. by John Goodall. Returned into court 28th June 1824.

pp. 156- 158   Will of SAMUEL THOMPSON. .. to my son, Reuben Thompson, all the tract of land I purchased of my father's estate .. to each of my daughters, Suckey, Salley and Elizabeth Thompson .. to my son, William Thompson .. land I purchased of Alexander Whitelaw and his adjoining to the land I live on .. my will and desire that my said son, William, be raised and educated out of my estate without any expense to him .. lend to my beloved wife, Sally Thompson .. appoint my son, Reuben Thompson, and my friend, Reuben Lindsay, my executors .. this 1st day of January 1824.
In the presence of   (signed)
    John Mallory, John Farish,   Samuel Thompson
    Elias Faulconer, Charles Boswell
  At a court held .. 28th June 1824 .. proved .. ordered to be recorded .. Reuben Lindsay came into court and refused .. Reuben Thompson with Reuben Lindsay and Charles Boswell, his securities .. bond in penalty of twenty thousand dollars.

(A note. Samuel Thompson was the son of Samuel Thompson (will probated 22 July 1793). He married Sarah (Sally) Lindsay, daughter of Adam and Elizabeth Garnett Lindsay 29 October 1801. Their son, Reuben L. Thompson (executor of this will) was born in 1803. Reuben Lindsay, the other executor, was Sally Lindsay Thompson's brother. Charles Boswell, mentioned as a witness and security, was the husband of Lucy Thompson, Samuel's sister. The children of Samuel Thompson Senr. and Samuel Thompson are shown in the appendix of PAMUNKEY NEIGHBORS OF ORANGE COUNTY, VIRGINIA.)

pp. 158- 159   Will of LEWIS SHIFLETT. .. unto my beloved wife, Sally Shiflett .. all my whole estate .. to my son, Joel Shiflett, after the death or marriage of his mother .. I give to my daughter, Sally Miller Shiflett .. to my son, John .. to my son, Lewis .. to my son, Linsy Shiflett .. to my daughter, Nancy Sanders .. to my grandson, Benjamin Sanders .. ordain my beloved wife and my son, Joel Shiflett, jointly executors .. this 29th day of March 1824.
In the presence of   (signed)
    George Bingham, Enoch Seamonds,   Lewis Shiflett
    Martin D. Harvey, James Harvey

At a court held .. 26th July 1824 .. proved .. ordered to be recorded .. Joel Shiflett .. came into court and refused .. Sarah Shiflett .. with John Shiflett and Joel Shiflett, her securities .. bond in the penalty of four thousand dollars.

pp. 159-162   Appraisal of the estate of Mr. GEO. STEPHENS, dec'd .. value $3928.44 .. Geo. Stephens, adm. of Geo. Stephens .. made by appraisers Richd. White, Joel Rucker, Geo. Shearman on 24th March 1824. Returned into court 26th July 1824.

pp. 162-164   An inventory of the estate of JAMES EARLY, dec'd, made this eleventh day of October 1822 .. value not totalled .. by appraisers Isaac Davis Jr., Charles Parrott, Edward Ansell. Returned into court 23rd August 1824.

pp. 164-166   NANCY LINDSAY, administratrix of the estate of Wm. Lindsay, dec'd .. amount $359.68 .. settled by John W. Sale, John Terrill, Geo. W. Morton, commissioners, who were sworn before George Morris 23rd August 1824. Returned into court 23rd August 1824.

pp. 166-167   LANDON LINDSAY, administrator of the estate of Wm. Lindsay, dec'd .. account settled 20th August 1824 by commissioners John W. Sale, John Terrill, Geo. W. Morton. Returned into court 23rd August 1824.

pp. 167-169   REUBEN LINDSAY, administrator of the estate of Wm. Lindsay, dec'd .. account settled 20th August 1824 by commissioners John W. Sale, John Terrill, Geo. W. Morton. Returned into court 23rd August 1824.

pp. 169-171   A list of the property appraised belonging to the estate of JOHN LANCASTER, dec'd, on 28th day of August 1824 .. amount of appraisement $1423.61 .. made by appraisers Tandy Collins, John Dedman, William Herndon. Returned into court 27th September 1824.

pp. 171-175   Estate of WILLIAM C. WEBB in account with Thacker V. Webb, executor. Debit amount 5 Aug 1824 $3333.72 3/4 .. same credit amount .. settled by Richd. M. Chapman, William Smith, Reuben Newman. Returned into court 25th October 1824.

pp. 175-181   A list of the amount of sales of the estate of WILLIAM C. WEBB, dec'd, together with the names of the purchasers taken Feby 21st and 22nd, 1816, and 18th March .. to Augustine Webb; to Thacker O. Webb; to William C. Webb; to Charles Webb; John V. Webb; Cornelius Devenney; Emanuel Henshaw; Edward Winslow; Henry Mitchel; William Acre; Joseph Cave; Jno. Priddy; Hord Watts, William Watts; Major William B. Branham; William Wood, John Turner; Joshua Long; Reuben Morris; Newman Faulconer; Thomas Hutchinson; Samuel Allen; Jacob Bell; Robert King; Charles Newman. Returned into court 22nd November 1824.

pp.   A list of appraisement of the personal estate of JONATHAN
181-   HERRING, deceased .. value $277.42 1/2 .. made 19th October 1824
182   by appraisers Jeremiah Pannill, Philip Mallory, George Pannill.
        Returned into court 22nd November 1824.

pp.   Will of SAMUEL ESTES. .. to my loving wife, Jane Estes ..
182-   to Warner Cox .. appoint my loving wife, executrix .. this 29th
183   day of September 1824.
        Teste   (signed)
             Charles Parrott, George A. Gentry,   Saml. Estes
             Elizabeth Early, Jeremiah Roberts,
             Augustine Snow, Thomas (X) Shiflett
        At a court held 22nd November 1824 .. proved .. ordered to be
        recorded .. Jane Estes .. with James Ogg and George A. Gentry,
        her securities .. bond in penalty of three thousand dollars.

        (A note. In a suit filed in 1835 or 1836, George A. Gentry, Jane
        Estes (formerly Ogg), widow of Samuel Estes, and Susan Ogg, are
        plaintiffs against David Goodall. Sarah Ogg, widow of John Ogg,
        qualified as his administratrix with David Goodall as her secur-
        ity. David absconded with the proceeds of the sale of the es-
        tate. In a deposition sworn 23 October 1837, he was declared not
        to be a resident of Virginia. Sarah Ogg died in 1828. The child-
        ren of John and Sarah Ogg were Janes (Estes) and Susan.

pp.   Will of JOHN BEADLES SENR. .. I give to my son, William
183-   Beadles, the plantation on which I now live .. (description of
186   the land) .. to my daughter, Jane Maupin .. (description of the
        land) .. to my son, James Beadles .. to my grandchildren, namely
        Madison Beadles, Elizabeth Beadles, James Beadles, Lucinda Bea-
        dles, Lurancy (?) Beadles and Catherine Elliott Beadles, children
        of my son, John Beadles .. (description of land) .. to my daugh-
        ter, Clairey Shelton .. three of my daughters and one of my daugh-
        ters and one of my grandsons, namely, Nancy Winslow, Clairey
        Shelton, Lurancy Mayers and Winslow Beadles .. appoint my sons,
        James Beadles and William Beadles and William Dulaney, my execu-
        tors .. 15th September 1824.
        In the presence of   (signed)
             Moses Winslow   John Beadles
             William L. Powell, John Offield.
          Codicil .. requires son, William Beadles, to pay to son, James,
        Beadles and Jane Maupin each seventy five dollars .. 9 November
        1824.
        In the presence of   (signed)
             William Dulaney   John Beadles
             John Offield, William Taylor
        At a court held 22nd November 1824 .. proved .. ordered to be
        recorded .. separate bonds .. William Beadles with James Beadles
        and William Wayland, his securities .. William Dulaney with John
        Offield, his security .. bond in penalty of six thousand dollars.

pp.   Will of THOMAS CHILES. ... to my beloved niece, Elisabeth
186-   Chiles, and my beloved nephew, James Chiles, all my property ..
187   appoint my said nephew, James Chiles, executor .. this 2nd day
of November 1824.

    In the presence of   (signed - his mark)
      Jo. Atkins   Thomas Chiles
      Theresa Garton, Thomas Atkins
    At a court held .. 22nd November 1824 .. proved .. ordered to
be recorded.

pp.   Will of JOHN BROCKMAN. .. to my dear and beloved wife should
187-   she survive me .. all the property of which I may die possessed
188   .. at her death, to my son, Oswald .. to my son, Asa .. to my
son, Jacob Brockman ...to my son, Stephen .. to my daughter, Molly,
and to my daughter, Rebecca .. proceeds equally divided between
my sons, Samuel, Elijah, John and Thomas, and my daughter, Eleanor
.. appoint my son, Oswald to be the sole executor .. this 25th
day of September 1823.

    In the presence of   (signed)
      Ben. Coleman   John Brockman
      Robert Newman, Mildred Coleman
    At a court held .. 27th December 1824 .. proved .. ordered to
be recorded .. with Benjamin Coleman, William Stevens and Brockman Bell, his securities .. bond in penalty of twelve thousand
dollars.

pp.   Will of NICHOLAS COLLINS. .. give and bequeath to my son,
188-   John Collins, all that part of my land on the east side of Berry's
190   Run .. to my daughter, Lucy Collins Long .. west side Berry's
Run .. ten acres to be subject to the use of Ann Collins .. laid
off around the house where she now resides .. knowing it is in
the power of my loving wife to take a sufficient part of my estate .. for her support .. I therefore make no provision for her
.. appoint Reuben Lindsay, executor .. this 25th day of January
1819.

    In the presence of   (signed - his mark)
      Pierce Sanford   Nicholas Collins
      Elizabeth Sanford, Sally Collins
    At a court held .. 27th December 1824 .. proved .. ordered to
be recorded.

pp.   Will of URIEL MALLORY. .. give and bequeath to my son, Wil-
190-   liam Mallory in trust all the land I purchased of John McCoull
191   whereon my son, Robert Mallory, now resides .. to be occupied
and cultivated by my son, Robert, and Elizabeth, his wife ..
(after their deaths) .. to my son, William Mallory, and my son,
John Mallory .. equally divided .. to my daughter, Mary Welch ..
to my daughter, Elizabeth Welch ... to my son, John Mallory's four
children, Sarah, Hannah, John and George .. to my son, Philip ..
appoint my sons, William and Philip, my executors .. this 1st day
of November 1821.

In the presence of   (signed)
    Wm. Morton, Jackson Morton,   Uriel Mallory Senr.
    George Morton, Wm. Morton Junr.
    At a court held .. 27th December 1824 .. proved .. ordered to
be recorded .. with Uriel Mallory and Oliver Welch, their securities .. bond in pendalty of ten thousand dollars.

pp.   An inventory and appraisement of the estate of JAMES RIDDLE
191-   SR., dec'd, taken this 21st day of January 1825 .. value $2892.25
192   .. made by appraisers Samuel Ham, Reuben Golding, George S. Blakey. Returned into court 24th January 1825.

pp.   An inventory and appraisement of the estate of JOHN R. BRAD-
193-   LEY, deceased, commenced the 20th day of August 1824 and con-
195   cluded the 25th of November 1824 .. value $805.03 .. made by
appraisers Michael L. Eheart, Joseph Snell, Austin Gaines. Returned into court 28th February 1825.

pp.   A list of the property of JOHN R. BRADLEY, dec'd, sold by
195-   Pollard Bradley, administrator .. 4th day of December 1824 ..
196   sold to William M. Amos, Jacob Walters, Augustine Gaines, Robert
Brooking, Ezekiel Wilhoit, Littleton Canady .. total amount of
sale $386.69 .. returned into court 28 February 1825.

pp.   An inventory and appraisement of the estate of JOHN BEADLES,
196-   dec'd, made the 26th day of November 1824 .. value $3900.41 ..
200   made by appraisers Thomas Davis, James Melone, Joseph Eddins ..
William Dulaney and William Beadles, executors .. returned into
court 28th February 1825.

pp.   List of sales of the property of GEORGE BRADLEY, dec'd, the
200-   24th November 1820. Some purchasers: Pollard Bradley, Robert
206   Cave, John Bradley, Joshua Gee, Benjamin Scott, John Thomas, William Bradley .. sales amount $308.68 .. returned into court 28th
February 1825.

pp.   An inventory and appraisement of the estate of JULIUS OLIVER,
206-   dec'd .. taken 24th day of February 1825 .. two slaves .. value
207   .. $270 .. commissioners Ezekial Lucas, Thomas Eddins, W. H.
Mansfield. Returned into court 28th February 1825.

pp.   Estate of GEORGE W. THORNTON, deceased, in account with
207-   James F. Maury and Mary, his wife, late Mary Thornton, for trans-
217   actions previous and subsequent to their marriage .. children
of Geo. W. Thornton: Henry R. Thornton, Lucy W. Thornton, Mary
G. Thornton, Seth B. Thornton .. Murray Forbes, John Gray, Thomas Seddon settled acout 23rd February 1825 (account contains
long statement by commissioners regarding the handling of the
estate). Returned into court 28th February 1825.

pp.   Estate of DR. CHARLES TAYLOR, deceased, in account with Ro-
217-   bert Taylor, executor .. amount $7094.05 with $2510.85 1/2 owed
223   estate .. settled 24th January 1824 by Reuben Conway, Reynolds
         Chapman, Richd. H. Taliaferro. Returned into court 28th Febru-
         ary 1825.

pp.   The estate of ELIZABETH BUTLER, deceased, in account with
223-   Reuben Newman, administrator .. sum received by deceased of my
227   father, Jas. Newman .. May 9, 1822 .. to cash paid George Newman
         Jr., who intermarried with Elizabeth Twyman, one of the distribu-
         tees on account of his share on the 26th October 1819 .. cash
         paid Henry T. Philips, guardian of Thomas and Wm. Twyman, dis-
         tributees .. cash paid John Twyman one of distributees .. cash
         paid Reuben Thom, guardian of Lewis H. Pearson .. James Newman
         the father and testator of the said Reuben .. commissioners Coleby
         Cowherd and John Henshaw, sworn before Thos. Row, 28th February
         1825. Returned into court 28th February 1825.

pp.   An inventory and appraisement of the slaves and other per-
227-   sonal estate of CHAS. S. STERN, dec'd .. value not totalled ..
230   made by appraisers Richd. M. Chapman, Cuddin Davis, James Shep-
         herd. Returned into court 28th March 1825.

pp.   Appraisal of the estate of JAMES SCOTT, dec'd .. shown by
231-   Henry Thompson, administrator de bonis non with will annexed of
233   James Scott, dec'd .. value not totalled .. made 18th December
         1824 by appraisers Thos. Row, John Sanders, Edmd. Row. Returned
         into court 28th March 1825.

p.   An inventory and appraisement of the estate of JOHN B. JOHN-
234   SON, dec'd .. value not totalled .. made by appraisers John San-
         ders, Eliphalet Johnson, William Graves, Edmd Row. Returned into
         court 28th March 1825.

pp.   An inventory and appraisement of the estate of JAMES WHITE,
234-   dec'd, made July 21st 1823 .. value not totalled .. appraisers
239   George Bingham, Josiah Huckstep, Charles Parrott. Returned into
         court 28th March 1825.

pp.   An inventory and appraisement of the estate of JOHN BROCKMAN,
239-   dec'd .. value $4361.50 .. certified by Oswald Brockman, 12th
240   Jany 1825 .. appraised by Jacob Graves, Richd. Johnson, Isaac
         Graves Senr., commissioners. Returned into court 28th March
         1825.

pp.   Will of JAMES DENNISON. .. bequeath unto Nancy Dennison during
241-   her life all the land I purchased from the heirs of Zachariah Lucas,
242   deceased .. after her death I wish it left to Marcus Dennison and
         James Dennison, sons of Mathew Dennison of the state of Ohio emi-
         grated from Harford County, Maryland .. money arising from said
         slaves to be given to Marcus Dennison, son of John M. Dennison,

deceased, formerly of Baltimore ... all the stock and crops to be
left with my wife, Nancy Dennison ... I also leave Sims Brockman,
overseer for Colonel Barbour, and James Willis of Madison, executors .. this 12th day of September 1823.

                                        Adieu   James Dennison

At a court held 28th March 1825 ... there being no subscribing
witnesses to the same, Robert Cave, William Douglass and Jonathan
Twyman sworn .. whereupon ordered to be recorded .. Henry Herndon .. with David Whitelaw, his security .. bond in penalty of
six thousand dollars.

pp.   An inventory and appraisement of the personal estate of ROGER
242-   SLAUGHTER, dec'd, made the 8th day of Novr. 1823 .. value not
244   totalled .. administrators Gabriel Long and James Long .. sub-
        scribed 15th December 1823 by appraisers Wm. Stevens, Wm. Collins,
        Jacob Graves, John Fisher. Returned into court 28th March 1825.

pp.   Appraisal of the estate of JOHN WRIGHT, dec'd .. this 11th
244-   day of May 1819 .. value $305.79 .. made by appraisers Geo. Mason,
245   James Jones, Francis Jones .. Benjamin Sanders, executor. Re-
        turned into court 28th March 1825.

pp.   An inventory and appraisement of the estate of SAMUEL THOMP-
245-   SON, dec'd .. taken and appraised this 30th day of December 1824
249   .. value not totalled .. made by appraisers Wm. C. Webb, Uriel
        Terrill, Walter Gambrel .. Reuben Thompson, executor. Returned
        into court 29th March 1825.

pp.   List of property of CHAS. S. STERN, dec'd, sold this 9th De-
249-   cember 1824. Some purchasers: Marshall P. Richards, Jeremiah
257   Dowell, Hugh S. Darby, John P. Coons, Conway C. Macon, Henry
        Stubblefield, Abraham Webster, Joseph Atkins, Smith Stubblefield,
        Robert Willis, James Marshall, James Willis, Tartan Smith, Joshua
        Willis, Maria Stern, Atwell Dowell .. value not totalled .. Jo-
        seph Atkins, clerk, 10th December 1824. Returned into court 29th
        March 1825.

pp.   Will of WILLIAM SHEPHERD. .. bequeath to my niece, Jennett
257-   Blair .. to Maria Louisa Shepherd, daughter of my brother, James
260   Shepherd .. lend to my sister, Ellen Blair .. plantation whereon
        she now lives called Woodville .. my brother, Alexander Shepherd,
        deceased .. whereas James Madison, esqr. agreed to pay five
        hundred dollars towards purchasing the said slaves for Elizabeth
        C. Shepherd, widow of my said brother .. whereas my brother, Ro-
        bert, is indebted to me a very large sum of money .. appoint my
        brother, James Shepherd, and my friend, Reynolds Chapman, execu-
        tors .. this 17th day of March 1825.
In the presence of   (signed)
    Paul Verdier   William Shepherd
    James Marshall, Smith Stubblefield
    At a court held .. 23rd May 1825 .. proved .. ordered to be
recorded.

pp.   An appraisement of the slaves and other personal property of
260-   JAMES DENNISON, dec'd .. value not totalled .. Henry Herndon,
261   administrator with will annexed of James Dennison, dec'd .. Returned into court 23rd May 1825.

pp.   Appraisal of the estate of MILDRED SCOTT, dec'd .. value
261- $236.87 1/2 .. made by appraisers Thos. Row, John Sanders, Edmd.
262   Row .. 9th December 1824, Henry Thompson, administrator. Returned
into court 27th June 1825.

pp.   Will of FRANCES BURNLEY. .. bequeath to my granddaughter,
262-   Frances Ann Taylor .. my executors to purchase for her the cabi-
264   net which belonged to my daughter, Lucy Burnley .. to my granddaughter, Sarah Adams .. to my grandson, Thomas Adams .. to my
granddaughter, Jane Taylor .. to my granddaughter, Hardema (?)
Taylor .. my son in law, William D. Taylor .. my son in law,
Thomas B. Adams .. my executors not be held to give security ..
appoint my brother, John Taylor, and my friend, Charles P. Howard,
to be executors .. this 19th day of January 1825.
Witnesses: (signed)
  Robert Taylor   Frances Burnley
  Edmd. P. Taylor, June Howard
  At a court held .. 27th June 1825 ... proved .. ordered to be
recorded .. bond in penalty of ten thousand dollars without se-
curity.

p.   Noncupative will of DOCTOR DAVID WHITELAW, who died the 8th
264   day of April 1825 of a sudden illness at Mrs. Dennison's in
Orange County. He desired that his estate should be kept together
until his children come of age .. law made provision for his wife
.. he wished his children to receive the best education that the
country would afford and to be brought up in the fear of the God
.. made in the presence of us, Wm. T. Banks, Alexander Whitelaw.
  At a court held .. 27th June 1825 .. depositions established
as the will of David Whitelaw and ordered to be recorded .. on
motion of Isaac Davis Jr. .. with Isaac Davis Senr., his security
Mary Whitelaw, widow, having waived her right to the administration.

pp.   Appraisal in current money the slaves and other personal
264-   estate of THOMAS CHILES, dec'd .. 13th May 1825 .. value $237.25
265   .. made by appraisers Wm. T. Burrus, Benjamin Cooper, Claibourne
Graves. Returned into court 27th June 1825.

p.   An inventory and appraisement of the estate of JOHN EDDINS,
265   deceased, taken this 29th day of April 1825 .. (two bonds total-
ling $1150.70) .. made by Blyfil Rucker, Minor Rucker, Joel Rucker.
Returned into court 27th June 1825.

pp.   Will of JAMES COLEMAN. .. estate to be kept together for
265-   the benefit of my beloved wife, Elizabeth L. Coleman, and my
266   daughter, Elizabeth F. Coleman .. appoint my wife, Elizabeth

Coleman as executrix, and my friends, John W. Sale and William
Stevens, executors .. this 10th day of April 1825.
In the presence of   (signed)
   Joseph Coleman Jr.   James Coleman
   John Humphreys, John T. Moore
   At a court held .. 25 July 1825 .. proved .. ordered to be re-
corded .. bond in penalty of ten thousand dollars without se-
curity.

(A note. In a Bill filed October 1, 1834, it is noted that James
Coleman was the son of Elizabeth Coleman. He married Elizabeth
Coleman, daughter of Joseph Coleman of Albemarle County. They had one
daughter, Elizabeth F. Elizabeth married second Robert Terrill,
who died without issue.)

pp.   Appraisal of all the slaves and other personal estate of
266-   SAMUEL ESTES, dec'd, presented to our view 22nd Decr. 1824 ..
269   Joseph Huckstep, James Early, Joab Early .. value not totalled.
Returned into court 27th July 1825.

pp.   A list of an appraisement of the medicine and other property
269-   belonging to the estate of DOCTOR DAVID WHITELAW taken on Fri-
271   day the 5th Augt. 1825 .. value $8922.15 .. made by appraisers
Robt. Cave, Henry Herndon, Edward Cason, R. Thomas Jr. Returned
into court 22nd August 1825.

pp.   Will of REUBEN NEWMAN. .. the residue of my perishable
271-   property, if any .. I give to Henry Hill .. also gives slaves to
272   Henry Hill .. John and Judy should be restored to their freedom
.. but since they must leave the state and separate from their
children, bequeath to Henry Hill .. appoint my friend, William
Morton Junr., executor .. this 7th day of August 1819.
In the presence of   (signed)
   Jackson Morton, George Morton   Reuben Newman
   At a court held .. 22nd August 1825 .. proved .. ordered to be
recorded .. with Henry Newman, his security .. bond in the penalty
of four thousand dollars.

pp.   The estate of NATHL. GORDON, dec'd, to Charles Beale, adminis-
272-   trator .. balance due estate $1157.81 .. made 24th June 1825 by
276   appraisers James Lindsay, Henry Richards, Jno. T. Thornton. Returned into court 22nd August 1825.

pp.   Estate of NATHL. GORDON in account with Nathl. Gordon, ad-
276-   ministrator .. balance due estate $921.54 .. Gordonsville 24th
279   June 1824 .. made by commissioners Henry Richards, Jno. T.
Thornton, James Lindsay. Returned into court 22nd August 1825.

p.   A list of an appraisement of the property belonging to the
279   estate of BENJAMIN ATKINS, dec'd, this 9th day of October 1824 ..
value $43.12 1/2 .. made by appraisers Richd. Johnson, Wm. Stevens,
Jacob Graves. Returned into court 22nd August 1825.

p.   Examination of executor's account of the estate of ISAAC
280   GRAVES, dec'd .. they find it stands as they did at a settlement
           of same .. 9 January 1822 .. made by Landon Lindsay, James Wil-
           son Jr., John M. Goodwin. Returned into court 22nd August 1825.

pp.   Inventory of the estate of FRANCES BURNLEY, dec'd, made by
280-   Charles P. Howard, Executor, 1 August 1825 .. no value assigned
284   items. Returned into court 24th October 1825.

pp.   Will of JOSEPH BICKERS. .. to my beloved wife, Agness Bic-
284-   kers .. my household and kitchen furniture to give to who she
285   will after her death .. (remaining estate) .. (no executor) ..
           this 25th day of April 1816.
           Teste   (signed - his mark)
               Wm. Mallory, Benjamin C. Bickers   Joseph Bickers
             At a court held .. 22nd September 1817 .. proved oath of Wm.
           Mallory .. at a court held .. 24th October 1825 .. proved oath
           of Benjamin C. Bickers .. and ordered to be recorded.

pp.   An inventory and appraisement of the estate of THOMAS MILLER,
285-   dec'd, made 21st June 1825 .. by John Miller, administrator ..
287   value $2356.54 .. appriasers W. H. Stanard, George Thornton, Wil-
           liam Dulaney. Returned into court 24th October 1825.

p.   Will of JOSEPH EDDINS. .. lend unto my beloved wife, Sarah
287   Eddins, the tract of land whereon I now live .. at my death my
           executor to seel the whole of my real and personal estate ..
           except the land heretofore lent to my beloved wife .. and proceeds
           divided equally between all my children namely, Theophilus,
           Abraham, John, Churchill, Joel, Elizabeth, Thomas, Elijah, Blar-
           key, Jinny, Nancy, Sally, Joseph and Polly .. at death of wife
           remainder of estate to be sold and proceeds divided (as before)
           .. appoint Theophilus Eddins, Abraham Eddins, Joel Eddins,
           Thomas Eddins, and my son in law, John Graves .. executors ..
           this 17th day of February 1808.
           In the presence of   (signed)
               Merry Walker, Miles Goodall,   Joseph Eddins
               Isaac Goodall, Sim Banks, Thos. Miller.
             At a court held .. 24th October 1825 .. proved .. ordered to
           be recorded .. on motion of Thomas Eddins .. with Abraham Eddins,
           his security .. bond in the penalty of ten thousand dollars.

pp.   Will of MARY EDDINS. .. give and bequeath to my nephew,
288-   William Dulaney, son of my brother, John Dulaney, the land
289   whereon I now live .. and land I bought of Benjamin Long .. all
           my slaves being twenty five in number .. (and remainder of es-
           tate) .. appoint my nephew, William Dulaney, executor .. this
           22nd day of August 1811.
           In the presence of   (signed - her mark)
               Isaac Davis, Benjamin Burton,   Mary Eddins
               Simon Graves, Valentine Johnson
             At a court held .. 24th October 1825 .. proved .. ordered to
           be recorded .. with Isaac Davis, his security .. bond in penalty
           of twenty thousand dollars.

pp.   Memorandum of all the estate that came unto my hands of
289-   ROBERT BEAZLEY, dec'd, delivered me by Sanford Beazley, late ad-
290   ministrator of said Beazley .. bonds on Anner Beazley; bond on
         Reuben Daniel .. given 26th November 1825 .. John Head .. Teste
         Tho. Sorrille. Returned into court 28th November 1825.

pp.   Will of WILLIS WHITE. .. give and bequeath my rifle gun unto
290-   my brother, Overton White .. my sorrel horse to my brother, Early
291   White .. all my plantation utensils except my waggon unto my
         mother, Susanna White .. bequeath my watch to my sister, Susanna
         Stephens .. my side saddle to my sister, Polly White .. (from sale
         of items) .. to my two sisters, Nancy and Kitty White .. my land,
         saw mill and slaves to be sold .. proceeds to my brothers and
         sisters (those already named listed) .. to my brother, Crenshaw
         White .. my brother, Anderson White .. make and ordain Mr.
         Charles Parrott and my brother, Early White, executors .. this
         2nd day of September 1825.
         In the presence of   (signed)
             George Bingham   Willis White
             James Ogg, Josias Bingham
           At a court held .. 28th November 1825 .. proved .. by James
         Ogg and ordered to be recorded .. Charles Parrott refused the
         executorship and Early White, the other executor named, is under
         age .. motion of Anderson White .. with Valentine Head, his se-
         curity .. bond in penalty of two thousand dollars .. letters of
         administration granted .. during minority of the said Early White.

pp.   Estate of MARK HORNSEY in account with William Mallory, exe-
291-   cutor .. cash paid Henry Stubblefield for coffin... cash paid
293   Dr. Uriel Terrill .. J. C. Gibson Lawyer fees .. account examined
         by James Shepherd, Richard Cave, Reynolds Chapman, Richd. M.
         Chapman. Returned into court 28th November 1825.

pp.   An inventory and appraisement of the slaves and other per-
293-   sonal estate of Uriel Mallory, dec'd .. value $5517.32 .. made
297   18th January 1825 by Benj. Walker, Jackson Morton, Thomas Graves ..
         William Mallory and Philip Mallory, executors. additional items
         listed .. no value assigned .. submitted by executors. Returned
         into court 28th November 1825.

pp.   Appraisement of the estate of OLIVER TERRILL, dec'd .. value
298- $7584.37 1/2 .. made by appraisers John W. Sale, Wm. Stevens,
301   Benj. Hume. Returned into court 28th November 1825.

pp.   Estate of OLIVER TERRILL, deceased, in account with Uriel
301-   Terrill, administrator; balance due estate $1773.97 1/4 .. made
302   by subscribers Jackson Morton, Benj. Hume, Wm. Stevens, John W.
         Sale .. who note .. bond of Hay Taliaferro Senr, dec'd, with
         Lawrence Taliaferro, his security, not made payable until death
         of Lucy Taliaferro, the widow of said Hay Taliaferro, dec'd.
         Returned into court 28th November 1825.

pp.
302-
303

Will of JAMES DENNISON. I James Dennison of the County of Orange being in sound mind and memory have taken up my pen to make the very last will I will ever make leaving my effects in the following manner. I lend to my beloved wife 1/3 of all I have after the payment of my just debts. The balance I give to Marcus Dennison, son of John, and James Dennison and Marcus Dennison, sons of Mathew & children of Cinuattie state of Ohio. Orange 1st Sept. 1824   James Dennison

(Except for the last two lines of the foregoing will, remainder of page 303 is blank.)

p.
304

The following property of LUCY W. DANIEL, orphan of John Daniel, deceased, has come into my possession as guardian since the inventory of her property was returned by me to court.
One negro girl named Sarah.

Coleby Cowherd
Decr. 20th, 1825

Returned into court 26th December 1825.

pp.
304-
306

Appraisal of the estate of WILLIAM GRADY, dec'd, made 31st December 1823 by appraisers Thos. Row, Geo. Grasty, Edmd. Row .. William Grady and Alexander Grady, administrators... value $6031.08 3/4. Returned into court 26th December 1825.

pp.
306-
312

List of property sold at the sale of Capt. URIEL MALLORY's, deceased, 18th January 1825 .. account of Major Jackson Morton, $769.37 1/2; of Philip Mallory, $921.19 1/2; of John Brown, $58.00; of Uriel Smith, $108.09 1/4; of Fielding Jones, $10.50; of Doctor George Morton, $207.52 1/2; of John Sleet, Benjamin Sisson, James Farish, Doctor Charles S. Waugh, Benjamin Walker, Lewis Alexander, John Newman, Lewis Lindsay, Abner Sisson, William Roach, Sarah M. Terrill, Lancelot Burrus .. whole amount of sale $3915.82, signed by R. Richards Junr. Returned into court 26 December 1825.

pp.
312-
316

An inventory of the estate of JOSEPH EDDINS, dec'd, taken 15th November 1825 .. value $6076.90 .. made by S. Graves, Clk. Estate appraised by Isaac Goodall, Robt. Miller, Jas. G. Blakey, James Melone .. Thomas Eddins, executor. Returned into court 26th December 1825.

pp.
316-
317

Estate of Capt. JOHN WRIGHT, dec'd, in account with John Wright and Alexander Wright, executors .. balance due estate $1,000 .. account examined by Richard Richards, Ezekiah Richards, Richard Richards Junr. Returned into court 26th December 1825.

pp.
317-
319

A last inventory and appraisement of the property belonging to the estate of JAMES COLEMAN, dec'd, this 27th day of August 1825 .. value $4979.25 .. Elizabeth L. Coleman, executrix of James Coleman, deceased .. appraisers Jacob Graves, Tartan Smith, William Collins. Returned into court 26th December 1825.

pp.   A list of ESTER HILMAN'S property sold the 15th November
320-   1825 .. amount of Ester Hilman's estate $231.12 1/2 .. amount of
322   Joseph Hilman's estate, $530.63.. Richard Richards Junr., Clk.
       Returned into court 23rd January 1826.

pp.   A list of property sold at the sale of JOSEPH HILMAN, dec'd,
322-   the 14th day of November 1825 .. amount of sale $3530.63 ..
325   Richard Richards Junr., clerk. Returned into court 23rd January
       1826.

pp.   January 11th 1824. The appraisement of Will. Lee, dec'd,
325-   estate .. value $678.10 .. made by appraisers William Clarke,
326   Joshua Willis, William S. Berry. Returned into court 23rd Janu-
       ary 1826.

pp.   A list of appraisement of slaves and other perishable property
326-   of James Dennison, dec'd .. value $3411.66 .. made by appraisers
329   Joel Rucker, Richd. White, Blyfil Rucker. Returned into court
       23rd January 1826.

pp.   An inventory and appraisement of the estate of MARY EDDINS,
329-   made the 25th day of November .. 1825 .. value $11474.50 .. made
331   by appraisers Catlett Conway Junr., Michael Mayer, Thomas Davis,
       William Dulaney. Returned into court 23 January 1826.

pp.   Appraisal of the property of WILLIAM STEPHENS, dec'd, and
331-   have appraised the same to the amount of four hundred and thirty
332   dollars and twenty nine cents .. 17th January 1825 .. by ap-
       praisers D. Whitelaw, George Parrott, Geo. Payne .. value $529.29.
       Returned into court 27th February 1826.

pp.   Appraisal on the 30th August in current money the slaves and
332-   other personal estate of REUBEN NEWMAN, deceased .. value not
333   totalled .. signed by Wm. Morton Junr, executor of R. Newman,
       dec'd .. appraisers Benjamin Walker, Philip Mallory, Benj.
       Beckham. Returned into court 27th February 1826.

pp.   Appraisal of the estate of THOMAS GRAVES, dec'd, as shown
334-   us by William Graves, administrator .. value $3194.87 1/2 .. made
335   21st February 1826 by appraisers Edmd. Row, John Gibson, William
       W. Hume. Returned into court 27th February 1826.

pp.   Will of BENJAMIN WINSLOW. .. I give to my son, Edward Wins-
335-   low .. (description of property including plantation house) ..
337   unto my daughter, Susannah Winslow, all that tract of land I pur-
       chased of William Winslow .. to my son, Moses Winslow .. balance
       of tract of land I inherited from my father .. land lying between
       the lands of Edward Winslow, George and Elias Newman .. to my
       grandson, Benjamin Winslow Beadles .. beach spring tract and dog-
       wood hollow .. to my son, Valentine Winslow .. my son, Fortunatus
       Winslow .. daughter, Elisabeth Beadles .. my granddaughter, Ann
       Winslow, daughter of my son, Edward Winslow .. my granddaughter,

Columbia Henley .. appoint my son, Edward Winslow, and my neighbor, John Walker, executors .. court not require security .. this
20th day of December 1825.
In the presence of   (signed)
    Thos. Scott   Benjamin Winslow
    George Newman Junr., Robert Willis.
  At a court held .. 27th March 1826 .. proved .. ordered to be recorded .. bond without security .. in penalty of twenty thousand
dollars.
    At a court held 26th March 1827 .. motion of Moses Winslow ..
with Valentine M. Houseworth and William H. Stanard, his securities .. bond in the penalty of ten thousand dollars .. John Walker, the other surviving executor .. having by note addressed
to the court refused the executorship.

pp.   A list of the appraisement of EDMOND TERRILL, deceased ..
337-   value $1430.27 .. made 23rd March 1825 by appraisers William W.
339   Reynolds, Washington Reynolds, George Quisenberry .. Nancy Ter-
        rill, administratrix of Edmond Terrill, deceased .. Returned
        into court 24 April 1826.

pp.   Estate of Dr. CHARLES TAYLOR in account with Robert Taylor,
339-   Executor .. paid Martha F. Taylor, her proportion of money now
341   in hand arising from sale of land .. to Matilda R. Taylor (same)
        .. to Evelina M. Taylor (of whom I am guardian) (same) .. to Cat-
        lett Conway Jr. in right of his late wife, Harriett (same) ..
        cash loaned to James Shepherd for the benefit of Mrs. Elizabeth
        G. Jenkins .. paid George F. Taylor .. paid William Milburn in
        right of his wife, Sarah T. Milburn through the W. States branch
        bank at Louisveille, Kentucky .. made by Renolds Chapman, Richard
        Cave, Richd. M. Chapman. Returned into court 22nd May 1826.

pp.   A list of property sold at the sale of JAMES BECKHAM, dec'd,
342-   October 28th 1819 .. some purchasers: Landon Allan Sr., Joel W.
352   Brown, William Clarke, William Robertson, William G. Allan,
        Robinson Brown, John Sleet, Thomas Hawkins, Fayette Smith, Henry
        Jones, Camp Beckham, John Mallory, Eliphalet Johnson, John Mit-
        chell, Isaac Johnson, Humphrey Hume, William H. Hume, Weedon Sleet,
        Daniel Dougherty, George Watson, Gabriel Gray Jr., Edward Ste-
        vens, John Oaks, William Thornton, Augustine Weedon, William Mills,
        Wm. G. Zimmerman, Benjamin Wiltshire, George Scott, Benjamin
        Beckham, John Farish, Benjamin Hawkins, John Cole, Alexander
        Robertson, William Smithers, Lawrence Taliaferro, Ambrose Cole-
        man, Henry Taliaferro, Wm. Davis, Thomas Robinson, William Morton,
        Edward Ryal, John Finnell, Dudley Gatewood, James Coleman, Henry
        Clarke, John Guard, James Beckham, John Thornton, Luke Thornton,
        Thomas Beckham, Wm. West, George Collins, William Boswell, John
        Faulconer, Anthony Stipes, Wm. Weaglesworth, Robert Kendall,
        Elijah Hudson, Tandy Collins, Wm. Cox, John S. Barbour, John Col-
        lins, George Porter, James Collins, John Porter Jr., Nathaniel
        Yager, John Foushee, Wm. Beckham, James Stubblefield .. certified

22nd April 1820 by Wm. G. Zimmerman, clerk at sale in October
1819 .. certificate of Camp Beckham .. certify and state that my
father, James Beckham .. 7th March 1821 .. certificate from Madison County. Returned Orange Court 26th June 1826.

pp.   An account of sales of the estate of THOMAS JENKINS, deceased,
352-   December 18th, 19th and 20th, 1823. Some purchasers: Wm. Bradley,
357   Jno. V. Webb, Thomas Yater, Hord Watts, Ambrose Henderson, James
         Marshall, Jonathan Pratt, Conway C. Macon, James M. Macon,
         Christopher Crigler, Sims Brockman, Charles T. Graves, Jacob
         Walters, Alexander Leathers, Moses T. Ham. Returned into court
         26th June 1826.

pp.   Will of LEWIS DAVIS. .. I lend to my wife, Dosha Davis ..
357-   all my real and personal estate .. the estate my wife had when
358   we were married .. to be disposed of as she thinks proper .. es-
         tate not be appraised until after the death of my wife .. to my
         son, Absolom Davis .. (proceeds from the sale of estate) .. to
         balance of my children .. viz. Mary Snow, Anny Morris, Sukey
         Shiflett, Ezekiah Davis, John Davis, William Davis, Pleasant
         Davis, Bartlett Davis, Nancy Meadows, Elisabeth Hicks, Sarah
         Morris .. appoint John Head and Joseph Cave joint executors ..
         4th August 1819.
         In the presence of   (signed - his mark)
            Tho. Sorrille   Lewis Davis
            John N. Sorrille, P. Samuel
           At a court held .. 26th June 1826 .. proved .. ordered to be
         recorded.

p.   List of appraisement of the estate of THOMAS BROCKMAN, dec'd
358   .. value $47.25 .. given 7th day of July 1826, certified by
         Oswald Brockman .. appraisers Brockman Bell, James Daniel, Isaac
         Graves. Returned into court 24 July 1826.

pp.   An inventory and appraisement of the estate of WILLIS WHITE,
358-   dec'd .. value $868.75 .. given 22nd July 1826 by appraisers
359   George Bingham, Josiah Huckstep, James Simms. Returned into
         court 28th August 1826.

p.   Will of JOHN TAYLOR. .. I lend my carriage and carriage
360   horses to the families of my two sons .. direct estate not be
         appraised .. selling my negroes as much as possible in families
         and allowing them as much as possible to choose the master they
         may wish to be sold to .. that my negroes be sold at private sale
         .. instead of giving it to my son, John M. Taylor, I give to be
         equally divided between such children as he may leave at his
         death .. other portion I give to my son, Gilbert D. Taylor ..
         appoint my brother, Robert Taylor, and my friend, William Quarles,
         my executors .. they shall not be bound to give security ..
         this 3rd day of March 1824. The whole of the above was written
         with my own hand.   (signed)
                                            John Taylor

At a court held .. 28 Aug 1826 .. there being no subscribing witnesses .. Lawrence T. Dade, Hugh A. Darley, Joseph Atkins and Richard H. Taliaferro were sworn .. whereupon writing was established and ordered to be recorded as last will and testament of John Taylor.

pp.   Estate of ROGER BELL, dec'd, in account with Wm. B. Bell
361-   Jr., excutor, and Catherine Bell, executrix of Roger Bell, dec'd
363   .. balance of $369,34 due said Catherine and William B. Bell .. given 14 August 1826 by Joseph Atkins, Daniel Hord, Lewis D. Collins. Returned into court 28th August 1826.

p.   Inventory of the property of WILLIAM MASON, dec'd, and
363   appraised by us on the 12th day of August 1826 .. Samuel Mason, Richd. Richards, William Peacher, Elisabeth Mason. Returned into court 28th August 1826.

pp.   Will of JOHN FAULCONER. .. to my grandson, William Faul-
363-   coner Junr., son of my son, William Faulconer, who now lives
367   with me .. appoint my son, John Wright, a guardian to my said grandson .. if grandson dies before age 21 to go to his father .. to my son, Spencer, .. give upon loan to my daughter, Nancy Jacobs .. I loaned some years ago to my daughter, Sarah Grant, wife of Jesse M. Grant .. (negroes) which Jesse M. Grant has carried to Kentucky .. to my son, Thomas Faulconer .. I loaned some years ago (negro) my daughter Catharine Wright, who has several children .. to my son, Hugh M. Faulconer in trust for the support and maintenance of my daughter, Elisabeth Scott .. also bond given me by her husband, Larkin Scott .. to my son, John Faulconer .. to my son, Thomas Faulconer .. to my son, Nicholas Faulconer .. to my granddaughter, Elisabeth Wright, the daughter of my daughter, Lucy Wright, deceased .. appoint my son in law, John Wright, guardian to Elisabeth Wright, my granddaughter .. to my grandchildren, Lucy Roads, William Roads and John Roads .. appoint my sons, Spencer Faulconer, Nicholas Faulconer, and son in law, John Wright, and Benjamin Jacobs, executors .. this 3rd day of January 1826.
In the presence of   (signed)
    Reuben T. Clarke, Fleming T. Wells,   John Faulconer
    Thomas Stubblefield, John Bledsoe,
    Edwin E. Gibson, William W. Hume.
Codicil .. my wish and will that my neighbor, George Pannelle, and my in law, John Wright, be one or the other that it may suit guardian to my grandchildren, Lucy Roads, William Roads and John Roads .. this 7th day of January 1826.
    At a court held .. 28th August 1826 .. proved... ordered to be recorded .. Hugh M. Faulconer and John Wright .. with Richard Richards, George Grasty, William Peacher, William Wright and Ezekiah Richards, their securities .. bond in penalty of twenty thousand dollars.

pp.   Will of JOHN STEVENS. .. I give one acre of land I purchased
367-   of Dillard Collins to my son, William .. I give to my son,
369   John, all that tract of land whereon he now lives .. claims to
       lands in Kentucky which I will dispose of .. give my son,
       William .. equally divided among all my children to wit, James,
       John, William, Nancy Duncan, Elisabeth Burrus and Sally Lind-
       say .. appoint my two sons, James and William Stevens, execu-
       tors .. this 9th day of October 1819.
       In the presence of   (signed)
           Thomas Woolfolk   John Stevens
           John Moore, Wm. T. Burrus.
         At a court held .. 28th August 1826 .. proved .. ordered to
       be recorded .. William Stevens .. with William T. Burrus and
       James Daniel, his securities .. bond in penalty of ten thousand
       dollars.

       (A note. John Stevens is of the ancestral Stevens family in
       PAMUNKEY NEIGHBORS OF ORANGE COUNTY, VIRGINIA. He was the son
       of James Stevens of Caroline County, and married Sarah Mountague,
       daughter of Peter and Anthorit Mountague.)

pp.   Examined and settled Wm. Grady's administration account
369-   upon the estate of WM. GRADY SENR., dec'd 29 July 1826 by Thos.
372   Row, John Gibson, Edmd. Row. Returned into court 30th August
       1826. Examined and settled Alexander Grady's administration
       account upon the estate of WM. GRADY SENR., by Thos. Row, John
       Gibson, Edmd. Row. Returned into court 30th August 1826.

p.   Oswald Brockman, administrator to the estate of THOMAS
372   BROCKMAN, dec'd. Account examined 25th September 1826 by Wm.
       Stevens, Brockman Bell, James Daniel. Returned into court 25th
       September 1826.

p.   Inventory of the slaves belonging to the estate of FRANCES
373   BURNLEY, dec'd, which were omitted in the return made the 1st
       of August last .. thirteen slaves all that have come into pos-
       session of Charles P. Howard, executor of F. Burnley, dec'd,
       Orange, October 17th 1826. Returned into court 23rd October
       1826.

pp.   Will of LEWIS DAVIS. (The will on these pages is the same
373-   as the one on pages 357-358.) At a court held .. 23rd October
374   1826 .. further proved by the oath of John N. Sorrille, a wit-
       ness thereto and as relates to real estate, ordered to be
       recorded.

pp.   ROBERT BEAZLEY estate to John Head, administrator .. given
374-   12th August 1826 by James Melone, Geo. W. Price, Tho. Sorrille.
375   Returned into court 23rd October 1826.

p.   ROBERT T. MOORE estate in account with James D. Dillard,
375   admr. de bonis non .. settled 19th October 1826 .. Waller Holla-
       day, Ben. Coleman, Coalby Graves. Returned into court 23rd
       October 1826.

p.   The estate of PHILIP SLEET, deceased, in account with Weedon
376   Sleet, administrator .. settlement approved and ordered to be
        recorded .. 23rd October 1826.

pp.   A bill of sales at publick auction affected on the seven-
376-   teenth day of October 1822 of the property of ROGER BELL, dec'd
379.   .. certified by Garrard Atkins, Clk., October 20th 1826. Re-
        turned into court 27th November 1826.

pp.   Sale of the property of WILLIAM GRADY, deceased, commenced
379-   October 15th 1823. Sale continued 18th December 1823. Sale
380   continued January 1, 1824. Sales account certified by William
        and Alexander Grady. Returned into court 27th November 1826.

p.   Jeremiah Jarrell Williams and John Sims, executors of
386   WILLIAM SIMS, dec'd .. in account with William Sims, deceased,
        estate .. given January 1826 by James Finks, James Clark, J.
        Booton. Returned into court 28th November 1826.

pp.   Allot and divide the slaves of the estate of DOWNING SMITH,
386-   dec'd, each part by valuation amounting to $405, first to
387   Elisabeth Smith .. to Downing Smith .. to Thomas Smith .. to
        pay Lewis G. Powell .. William Cave .. made the 4th of November
        1826 by Thos. Davis, George S. Blakey, William Dulaney. Re-
        turned into court 28th November 1826.

pp.   The executor of the estate of JULIUS OLIVER, deceased,
387-   account settled (executorship of Blyfil Rucker) by Thomas Ed-
388   dins, Ezekiel Lucas, Geo. Stephens. Returned into court 28th
        November 1826.

pp.   Estate of ABNER PETTY, deceased, in account with Thomas
388-   Petty, the administrator, for cash paid sundry persons. Cre-
389   dits and debits balanced at $179.37 1/2 by Baldwin Taliaferro,
        Wm. C. Willis, John Mallory. Returned into court 28th November
        1826.

pp.   The estate of JOHN LUCAS in account with Henry Houck and
389-   John Doling, executors .. This sum received by John Lucas as
390   guardian for my wife, Mildred Houck, then Mildred Lucas ..
        accounts examined 18th December 1826 by W. White, Robt. Cave,
        P. C. Cave. Returned into court 25th December 1826.

pp.   Will of WILLIAM ADAMS. .. my desire that my loving wife,
391-   Nancy Adams, shall remain upon my farm and have the sole con-
392   trol and profits thereof .. allot to my daughter, Elizabeth
        Howard ($300) .. my children, Robert and William Adams, Lucy
        White, Nancy Herndon, Catharine and Polly Adams .. appoint my
        friend, Edmond Row, my sole executor .. this 1st day of March
        1826.
        In the presence of   (signed - his mark)
            Samuel Mason   William Adams
            Thomas Rhodes, Elijah McKenny

Codicil .. my wife to have the whole of the crop of corn fodder together with the stock of bacon .. pay my daughter, Polly Adams, twenty dollars more than her other brothers and sisters on account of her affection and that John Herndon account for forty dollars which he had by way of advancement .. this 1st day of March 1826.
In the presence of   (no signature
    Samuel Mason   entered in record)
    Thomas Rhodes, Elijah McKenny
    At a court held .. 25th December 1826 .. proved .. ordered to be recorded .. Edmund Row .. with Richard Richards, Ezekiah Richards, William Beazley and William Roach, his securities .. bond in penalty of four thousand dollars.

pp. 392-393
Examine, state and settle Nancy Mason's administration account upon the estate of JAMES MASON, dec'd .. given 7th December 1826 by Thos. Row, Benj. Sanders, Edmd. Row, William Peacher. Returned into court 25th December 1826.

p. 394
Appraisal of the slaves and other personal estate of ALEXANDER SMITH, dec'd, John H. Gordon, administrator .. no property or assets have come into his hands .. since a bond on Edmund Terrill amounting to seventy five dollars (with interest) and that he knows of no property of the decedent to be appraised .. submitted 29th July 1826 by Jeremiah Pannill, George Pannill, W. Davis .. John H. Gordon, administrator of Alexander Smith, dec'd. Returned into court 25th December 1826.

pp. 394-395
The estate of ALEXANDER SMITH in account with John H. Gordon, administrator .. account examined and settled 19th December 1826 by Philip Mallory, John A. Porter, Jeremiah Pannill. Returned into court 25th December 1826.

pp. 395-396
Appraisal of all of the property of WILLIAM ADAMS, deceased, presented to our view 17th day of January 1827 .. value not totalled .. Edmond Row, executor .. appraisers Thomas Row, Eliphalet Johnson, James Jones, William Graves Jr. Returned into court 22nd January 1827.

pp. 397-399
A list of the appraisement of the property of JOHN FAULCONER, deceased, September 27th 1826 .. value $9136.25 .. made by appraisers William W. Hume, Jeremiah Pannill, John Gibson. Returned into court 22nd January 1827.

pp. 399-400
1824. August 12th. Anderson White, executor of JAS. WHITE, dec'd .. executorship account examined by Charles Parrott, George Bingham, Josiah Huckstep. Returned into court 26th February 1827.

pp. 400-401
May 7, 1825. Willis and Anderson White, executors of JAS. WHITE, dec'd. Executorship account examined by Charles Parrott, George Bingham, Josiah Huckstep. Returned into court 26th February 1827.

pp.   The estate of Mrs. FRANCES WEBB, deceased, in account with
401-   William C. Webb, administrator thereof .. account examined,
402   stated and settled 30th July 1825 by John W. Sale, Washington
           Reynolds, William Reynolds. Returned into court 26th February
           1827.

pp.   The estate of MARY RUCKER, dec'd, in account with Waller
402-   Graves, executor .. William Eddins for making coffin, $5 .. 3
403   gallons of whiskey for sale, $2 .. Dr. Whitelaw's account for
           attendance while sick, $45.75 .. account settled 19th November
           1825 by Robt. Cave, Joseph Cave, Thomas Eddins. Returned into
           court 26th February 1827.

pp.   Tartan Smith, executor of JAMES SMITH, deceased .. account
403-   examined and settled by Lewis Lindsay, John W. Sale, Geo. W.
404   Morton. Returned into court 26th February 1827.

pp.   The estate of THOMAS JENKINS and ELIZABETH G. JENKINS in
404-   account with Charles Taylor, administrator .. (some entries)
408   April 1824 Mrs. Lucy Conway laid out in Richmond for the child-
           ren .. cash advanced to Charles Jenkins .. Wm. Jenkins in re-
           covery of a runaway slave .. cash advanced to Madison Jenkins
           for pocket money and to pay his expenses to Rockingham ..
           Adam Darby for board and tuition of George and Sarah Jenkins,
           children of Thomas and E. G. Jenkins in 1825 .. account settled
           May 25, 1825, by Richard Cave, Wm. Quarles, Richard H. Talia-
           ferro. Returned into court 26th February 1827.

pp.   List of the names and amount of what each man bought of the
408-   estate of GEO. STEPHENS, dec'd .. total amount of sales $1012.26
409   .. (Stephens mentioned in the list -- Hugh, George, Joseph,
           William, Elias, Richard, Mary) .. settlement of George Stephens'
           administration account of the estate of George Stephens, dec'd,
           made 22nd March 1826 by William Dulaney, Anthy. Thornton, James
           Melone. Returned into court 26th February 1827.

pp.   Vivion Quisenberry, administrator of the estate of BENJAMIN
409-   WRIGHT, dec'd, and administrator de bonis non of the estate of
411   BENJAMIN HALEY, dec'd .. settlement of Benjamin Wright's execu-
           torship account with said Haley's estate $204.71 1/2 .. account
           examined and settled by Reuben Lindsay, Tandy Collins, Thos. Row.
           Returned into court 26th February 1827.

pp.   John Terrill executor's account against the estate of G. L.
411-   GRASTY, dec'd .. 23rd July 1824 - 19th August 1826 .. settled
416   19th August 1826 by Jacob Graves, Wm. Stevens, Landon Lindsay.
           Returned into court 26th February 1827.

pp.   William Stevens and Landon Lindsay, executors, estate of
417-   JOHN STEVENS, deceased .. (some entries) .. cash paid Beverley
418   Daniel, attorney in fact, for Nancy Stevens and her children ..

Capt. Jacob Graves for coffin .. Dr. Fackler .. Lancelot Burrus store account .. paid William McCaffrey for legacy .. account settled 28th December 1824 by Reuben Lindsay, Jacob Graves, Geo. W. Morton, Brockman Bell. Returned into court 26th February 1827.

pp. 418-420
Reuben Thompson, executor, estate of SAMUEL THOMPSON, dec'd .. settled 28 A 1826 by Reuben Lindsay, John W. Sale, Walter Gambrel. Returned into court 26th February 1827.

pp. 420-421
The estate of Capt. RICHARD C. WEBB, dec'd, in account with Jesse B. Webb .. settled by Thos. Row, Benj. Hume, Tandy Collins. Returned into court 26th February 1827.

pp. 421-422
The estate of THOMAS ADAMS, dec'd, in account with Henry Tandy Senr., dec'd .. account settled 1st day of December 1824 by Thos. Coleman, John W. Sale, Reuben Lindsay. Returned into court 26 February 1827.

pp. 422-423
Estate of GEORGE BELL, dec'd, to Elijah Bell and Richard Richards .. account settled by Thos. Row, Tandy Collins, Edmd. Row. Returned into court 26th February 1827.

pp. 423-425
Estate of ZAC. LUCAS, dec'd, admr. of Z. Lucas, dec'd, to Nancy Dennison .. examined 21st February 1825 by Isaac Davis, Thomas Eddins, Tho. Sorrille .. estate of Zac. Lucas, dec'd, to Anthony Thornton, admor .. settled 21st May 1825 by Isaac Davis, Thomas Eddins, Tho. Sorrille. Returned into court 26th February 1827.

pp. 425-428
Joseph Maury as executor in account with the estate of THOMAS MAURY, dec'd .. examined 3rd March 1825 by George Gilmer, Saml. H. Lewis, Layton Yancey. Returned into court 26th February 1827.

pp. 428-431
Inventory and appraisement of the estate of JOHN STEVENS, dec'd .. value $5645.07 .. made by appraisers Jacob Graves, Claiborne Graves, John W. Sale, Geo. W. Morton .. Wm. Stevens, executor of John Stevens, dec'd. Returned into court 26th February 1827.

pp. 432-433
Estate of RICHARD C. WEBB in account with Jesse B. Webb, executor .. account of Jesse B. Webb upon the estate of his father, R. C. Webb .. examined 17th February 1827 by Thos. Row, Benj. Hume, Edmd. Row. Returned into court 26th February 1827.

pp. 433-434
Inventory and appraisement of the perishable property of WM. HERRING, dec'd .. value $512.43 .. certified true inventory by William Herring .. inventory made 7th November 1826 by appraisers John A. Porter, George Pannill, Philip Mallory. Returned into court 26th February 1827.

pp.   Estate of JACOB PAUL, dec'd, to James Beazley, dec'd ..
434-   sum of $1162.01 to be divided between 5 legatees gives to each
435   the sum of $232.40 1/5 .. made 1 April 1823 by Isaac Davis,
           Isaac Davis Jr., Tho. Sorrille. Returned into court 26th
           February 1827.

pp.   Estate of JAMES BEASLEY, dec'd, to Sanford Beasley ..
435-   (some entries) .. paid Mary Beasley one saddle left her by the
436   will which cost $12.00.. tuition of Martha Whitelaw one year
           $10.00 .. paid Mary Beasley eight hundred dollars for the sup-
           port of Durrett Beasley left him by the will .. paid the heirs
           of Jacob Paul .. made 14th June 1824 by Charles Parrott, Thos.
           Sorrille. Returned into court 27th February 1827.

pp.   Estate of ROBERT BEASLEY, dec'd, to Sanford Beasley ..
436-   Capt. John Head, administrator de bonis non of Robert Beasley
437   .. bond on Anner Beasley .. settled by W. H. Stanard, George W.
           Price. Returned into court 27th February 1827.

p.   Estate of JAMES BEAZLEY, dec'd, to James Beazley, administrator
438   (some entries) .. paid John Beazley as legatee .. Tandy Collins
           as legatee .. Nicholas Whitelaw as legatee .. Willis Huckstep
           as legatee .. James P. Sims as guardian of the heirs of Robert
           Beazley, dec'd .. Sanford Beazley as legatee .. James Beazley
           as legatee .. each legatee $215.08 .. James Sims $264.73 ..
           sum due estate Ann Sanford .. settled 23rd February 1827 by
           George W. Price, William Dulaney, Jas. G. Blakey. Returned
           into court 27th February 1827.

pp.   Account of the sales of the estate of BENJAMIN WINSLOW,
438-   deceased .. N. Faulconer, clerk for Edward Winslow, executor.
444   of Benjamin Winslow, dec'd. Returned into court 28th March 1827.

pp.   Estate of THOMAS SAMPSON, dec'd, to William Dulaney ..
445-   account examined and settled 16th February 1827 by George W.
446   Price, Charles Parrott, Thos. Sorrille. Returned into court
           28th March 1827.

pp.   An account of the sale of property belonging to the estate
446-   of SAMUEL ESTES, deceased, Decr. 28th 1824 .. amount $1396.09.
450   Returned into court 28th March 1827.

pp.   A list of bonds and notes due the estate of SAMUEL ESTES,
450-   deceased, November 24th 1826 .. amount not totalled .. returned
451   into court 28th March 1827.

p.   Estate of SAMUEL ESTES, deceased, to Jane Estes, executrix
451   of said estate .. examined and settled 22nd February 1827 ..
           W. H. Stanard, William Dulaney, James Melone. Returned into
           court 28th March 1827.

p.
452

List of the appraisement of the negroes of Mrs. MILDRED SCOTT, dec'd .. 3 in number .. value $974.00 .. appraised by Wm. Frazer, Jno. Payne, John Sleet. Returned into court 28th May 1827.

pp.
452-
453

An inventory of the goods and chattels of JOHN FAULCONER, deceased .. 598 acres, 2 roods, 32 poles of land .. 17 negroes .. etc., given 1st December 1826 by Hugh M. Faulconer, John Wright Junr. Returned into court 28th May 1827.

pp.
453-
454

Account of sales of the personal property belonging to the estate of NICHOLAS FAULCONER, dec'd .. on 29th day of November 1826, sold by William Faulconer, administrator of said estate .. amount $73.80 1/4 .. Fielding Jones, clerk at sale. Returned into court 28th May 1827.

p.
454

Jonathan Claiborne and Jacob Graves, executors in account with the estate of ISAAC GRAVES, dec'd .. (some entries) .. paid George Boxly as part of his legacy .. Coalby Graves .. Francis Graves .. Lewis Graves .. Isaac Graves .. Spotswood D. Crenshaw .. Nancy Cason for purchase of a saddle .. settled 24th February 1827 by Landon Lindsay, John M. Goodwin, James Wilson Jr. Returned into court 29th May 1827.

pp.
455-
456

Estate of SAMUEL TWYMAN, dec'd .. met at the house of Robert Cave 12 November 1825 and settled the executorship account of Anthony Thornton .. Robert Cave, Henry Herndon, Geo. Stephens, Thomas Collins. Returned into court 25th June 1827.

pp.
456-
458

Benjamin Lancaster, administrator with the will annexed of RICHARD LANCASTER, dec'd, in account with said estate .. legacies paid Jonathan Lancaster, Richd. Lancaster .. account settled 27th September 1821 by John W. Sale, James Nelson, Washington Reynolds, Reuben Lindsay. Returned into court 25th June 1827.

pp.
458-
459

Estate of JAMES EARLY in account with William Early, administrator .. November 19th 1824 .. commissioners made partial settlement of the account of William Early .. Isaac Davis Jr., James Melone, Geo. W. Price. Returned into court 25th June 1827.

pp.
459-
460

Benjamin Wright in account with the estate of BENJAMIN HALEY .. Returned into court 25th June 1827.

pp.
460-
461

Estate of WILLIAM PEACHER in account with William and Edward Peacher .. examined and settled 3rd November 1824 by Thos. Row, James Nelson, Tandy Collins. Returned into court 25th June 1827.

pp.   John Terrill's executor's account with the estate of G. L.
461-   GRASTY, dec'd .. from 3 March 1821 - July 24, 1822 .. settled
470   executorship account of Capt. James Terrill on the estate of
        Goodridge L. Grasty, dec'd .. given 24th day of July 1824 ..
        commissioners Wm. Stevens, Landon Lindsay, Reuben Lindsay, Jacob
        Graves. Returned into court 25th June 1827.

pp.   Estate of THOMAS WHITELAW in account with James Whitelaw,
470-   one of the executors .. examined 1st December 1823 by Robert
474   Cave, Joel Rucker, Edward Cason. Thomas Whitelaw in account
        with David Whitelaw, executor .. February 11, 1819 .. (an entry
        shows) .. schooling Ellen and Thomas .. examined 1st December
        1823 by Wm. Stevens, Landon Lindsay, Reuben Lindsay, Jacob
        Graves. Returned into court 25th June 1827.

pp.   Estate of GEORGE BRADLEY in account with George and Wm.
474-   Bradley, executors .. amount due legatees $2222.88 1/2 ..
476   examined and settled 4th August 1823 .. Joseph Cave, T. V.
        Webb, Robt. Mansfield. Returned into court 25th June 1827.

pp.   The estate of HAY TALIAFERRO, deceased, in account with
476-   Robert Taylor, exor .. examined and stated 2nd February 1824 ..
480   and the admission of Mrs. Milley Taliaferro of the supplies
        furnished to her and family thru the said Robert Taylor,
        that the estate is indebted to the said Robert Taylor in the
        sum of seven hundred eighty two dollars and forty two and
        one half .. commissioners Wm. C. Willis, Wm. Quarles, Richd. M.
        Chapman. Returned into court 27th June 1827.

pp.   The estate of DANIEL THORNTON, dec'd, in account with Luke
480-   Thornton, admor .. account examined .. agreed to by widow for
481   her support she being entitled to the property of the estate.
        Given 15th January 1824, made by John Crump, Benjamin Walker.
        Returned into court 25th June 1827.

pp.   Jonathan Claibourne and Jacob Graves, executors, to the
481-   estate of ISAAC GRAVES, dec'd .. 1820 legacy to Joel Graves'
482   heirs .. amount remaining for distribution among legatees
        $29,038.42 .. account examined 7th January 1822 by Thos. Cole-
        man, Landon Lindsay, James Nelson Jr. Returned into court 25th
        June 1827.

pp.   Estate of JOHN R. BRADLEY, dec'd, with Pollard Bradley, the
482-   administrator .. given 23rd February 1827 by Joseph Cave, Joseph
484   Snell, Augustine Gaines. Returned into court 25th June 1827.

pp.   A list of property of JOHN R. BRADLEY sold by Pollard Brad-
484-   ley, administrator of said John R. Bradley, deceased, this 9th
485   day of February 1827 .. to Lewis Bradley .. to Reuben H. Bradley
        .. to William Bradley .. to George Bradley. Returned into
        court 25th June 1827.

pp.   The estate of JAMES SCOTT, dec'd, in account with Henry
485-   Thompson, admor. de bonis non .. paid Samuel Garland, attorney
486   .. divident on 24 shares Virga. stock .. account examined 12th
           October 1825 by Hugh M. Patton, E. P. Cady, A. Walker. Returned
           into court 25th June 1827.

p.   Names of negroes who came in my possession on the 4th day
486   of May 1827 belonging to SUSAN ANN DANIEL .. made by John
           Scott, guardian .. sworn to before Edmund Henshaw 25th June
           1827, Returned into court 25th June 1827.

pp.   The estate of THOMAS ELLIS, dec'd, in account with John and
487-   James H. Ellis, executors .. commissioners Leroy Chandler and
490   John W. Sale credited estate of decedent with the amt recd for
           sales of crops, debts collected, cash, etc., and have debited
           said estate with amt of various disbursements and two debts
           due the executors by their testator anterior to his death ..
           29th day of January 1825. Returned into court 25th June 1827.
           Wm. Stevens and Thomas Coleman, who were also appointed com-
           missioners to examine and settle the said account were present
           and assented to the settlement . . . .

pp.   Amount of property sold belonging to the estate of THOMAS
490-   ELLIS, dec'd, the 1st of November 1816 .. amount of sale $247.25
491   .. made by John Ellis and James H. Ellis, executors. Returned
           into court 25th June 1827.

pp.   Inventory and appraisement of the real and personal property
491-   of JOHN TAYLOR, deceased .. value $17,024.58 .. given 5th July
494   1827 by appraisers Wm. Quarles, C. P. Howard, Richd. H. Talia-
           ferro, Richard Cave.

pp.   Inventory of the debts due estate of JOHN TAYLOR, dec'd,
495-   and money in his possession at the time of his death .. cash
496   in Virginia and United States B notes $415.00 .. cash in gold,
           silver and cents, $230.84 .. of 23 bonds listed, 9 are noted
           as bad, 5 as doubtful .. bonds in hands of Major William Taylor
           of Kentucky for collection on persons unknown, about $250.00
           .. made by J. M. Taylor, admr. of John Taylor, dec'd, with the
           will annexed. Returned into court 23rd July 1827.

pp.   The estate of URIEL MALLORY, deceased, in account with
497-   William Mallory and Philip Mallory, executors .. stated, settled
499   and reported May 2nd 1827 by commissioners Richd. M. Chapman,
           Richard Cave, John Walker. Returned into court 23rd July 1827.

p.   Will of ROBERT SNELL. .. give and bequeath to my wife, Lucy
499   Snell, all my estate .. after the death of my wife, I wish the
           same to be equally divided between my son, Joseph Snell, and
           my daughter, Katharine Spicer .. appoint my friends, Joseph
           Snell, Joseph Cave and William Porter, executors .. this 13th
           day of September 1825.

Teste   (signed)
   John Williams,   Robert Snell
   Joseph Williams, William Williams.
   At a court held .. 27th August 1827 .. Joseph Cave by note
refused the executorship .. at same court continued 29th of
same month .. will was proved .. by witnesses thereto and ordered to be recorded.

pp.   Will of CATLETT CONWAY SENIOR. .. direct my executors ..
500-   to sell all my personal estate, except my slaves, and apply the
501   proceeds thereof .. to the payment of my debts .. (if more
money is needed) from sale of land .. then sale of slaves ..
sell all my lands, as well those in Virginia and those in the
state of Kentucky .. I direct, however, that in the sale and
conveyance of the land on which I reside, my executors reserve
one eighth of an acre, including the family burying ground, and
that they have as much thereof inclosed with brick or stone
wall reserving also the privilege at all times of a road to and
from the same .. to my four sons and two daughters to be equally
divided between them, namely Francis, John F., Catlett and
Reuben Conway, Elizabeth C. Fitzhugh and Susanna Taliaferro ..
appoint my four sons .. and my sons in law, Henry Fitzhugh and
Hay Taliaferro, executors .. this 29th day of December 1826.
In the presence of   (signed)
   Thomas Brown,   Catlett Conway
   Bushrod W. Brown,
   Andrew B. Samuel, Joshua Willis.
   At a court held .. 24th September 1827 .. proved .. ordered
to be recorded .. Francis Conway, Catlett Conway, Reuben Conway
and Hay Taliaferro, executors named .. came into court and
refused the executorship .. on motion of John F. Conway ..
together with Francis Conway, Catlett Conway, Reuben Conway and
Hay Taliaferro, his securities .. bond in penalty of forty
thousand dollars.

pp.   Will of ELIZABETH RUCKER. .. all the property which my four
501-   children now has in possession (namely Ezekiel Rucker, Sarah
502   Farneyhough, Molly Herndon and Tabitha Lloyd) I do hereby give
to them in fee simple .. constitute Joseph Cave actor to this
my last disposition of property .. this 26th day of April 1826.
Teste   (signed)
   Alexr. Bradford, Henry Herndon   Elizabeth Rucker.
   At a court held .. 24th September 1827 .. proved .. ordered to
be recorded .. Joseph Cave .. by note addressed to the court
refused the executorship .. on motion of William Herndon ..
with Henry Jr., his security .. bond in penalty of five thousand
dollars.

pp.   Return of sale of the goods and chattels of JOHN FAULCONER,
502-   dec'd, sold on the 28th of September and 28th of November, 1826
504   .. certified 24th August 1827 by Hugh M. Faulconer and John
Wright, executors of John Faulconer, dec'd, of Orange County.
Returned into court 24th September 1827.

pp.   The estate of WILLIAM SHEPHERD, dec'd, in account current
504-   with James Shepherd .. (some items) .. paid (Dec. 16, 1825) Mrs.
511   Darby this sum being Int. on money left in hands of testator
       by father .. John Evans for making shoes .. Mrs. Laurie (Feb.
       16, 1826) amt. of Int. due on a/c of money left in hands of
       testator by father .. Dr. Edward Carmichael medical acct .. cash
       paid (Sep. 18, 1826) Jannett Blair on a/c of her legacy left
       by testator .. cash sent (Dec. 21, 1826) to Adam Darby for Mrs.
       Kemper on a/c of a legacy left her in the hands of the testator
       .. to Maria Louisa Shepherd (Feb. 1, 1827) for this sum amt.
       of legacy left her by testator .. paid (same date) J. B. Jones
       amt. of George Shepherd's order, who is a legatee .. to cash
       (same date) paid John M. Shepherd this sum in part of legacy
       left by W.S. .. (Mar. 20, 1827) cash paid George Shepherd, a
       legatee of W.S. .. cash paid Ballard for lock to put on family
       burying ground .. cash paid Wm. Rolls for iron gate for family
       burying ground .. (June 11, 1827) cash paid Adam Darby as lega-
       tee .. (Sep. 13, 1827) to Andrew Shepherd for this sum paid
       Thomas Shepherd as legatee .. amount owed estate $6834.75 ..
       commissioners discuss suit brought by James Fleshman against
       Robert W. Shepherd (Robert largely indebted to his testator)
       which was awarded Fleshman and paid from estate .. there is a
       balance due from the executor, after retaining in his hands the
       legacy left by the testator to his daughter, Maria Louisa
       Shepherd .. submitted October 19, 1827 by Philip S. Fry, Sam.
       H. Stout, Edwin Nichols, Cudden Davis. Returned into court
       22nd October 1827.

pp.   Estate of Dr. WILLIAM SHEPHERD, deceased, in account with
511-   Reynolds Chapman, executor .. (some items) .. paid John Gardner
515   on account of wages as overseer for testator .. paid Adam Darby,
       a legatee .. paid John P. Coons in part for walling in the
       family burying ground .. paid Miss Jannet Blair legacy ..
       paid George Shepherd, a legatee .. cash paid Mrs. Catherine
       Darby on account of interest upon money devised to testator
       by his testator .. to Andrew Shepherd in trust for the benefit
       of Mrs. Darby .. the commissioners state "the executor shewed
       us a letter from seven of the legatees under the will to him
       and his coexcutor requesting them to have the family burying
       ground enclosed with a brick wall .." Submitted at Orange
       Courthouse October 19th 1827 by Charles P. Howard, Edwin Nichols,
       Sam. H. Stout, Cudden Davis. Returned into court 22nd October
       1827.

pp.   An inventory and appraisement of the personal property of
515-   the estate of REUBEN SCOTT, dec'd, by order of the County Court
516   of Orange bearing date the 28th May 1827 .. value $3717.94 1/2
       .. made 14th June 1827 by appraisers John Gibson, Philip Mallory,
       William Graves, William W. Hume. Returned into court 22nd
       October 1827.

pp.   WILLIS WHITE, deceased, executor of James White in account
516- with the said James' estate .. account examined and settled by
517   George Bingham, Charles Parrott, James Simms. Returned into
court 26th November 1827.

pp.   The estate of JAMES WHITE, deceased, to Anderson White,
517- executor .. an amount, $200.00, paid James E. White as a legacy
518   .. examined and settled May 4th 1827 by George Bingham, Charles
Parrott, James Simms. Returned into court 26th November 1827.

pp.   The estate of WILLIS WHITE, deceased, to Anderson White,
518- administrator .. examined and settled May 4th 1827 by George
519   Bingham, Charles Parrott, James Simms. Returned into court
26th November 1827.

pp.   Will of WILLIAM SUTTON. .. lend to my beloved wife, Tabytha
519- Sutton, all my real and personal estate .. if she marries to be
520   taken from her and sold at auction and the money to be divided
amongst my children by my executors .. my will that after my
wife's decease my real and personal estate be sold by my son,
William W. Sutton, and my son in law, Christian Kinzer, or
either of them .. give to my son, William W. Sutton, fifty
pounds .. give to Caty Griffey, my daughter, fifty pounds ..
all my children have five pounds apecse .. that Abel Griffey
shall not have one shilling of my estate or the value of it ..
appoint my beloved wife, Tabytha Sutton, whole and sole
executrix .. that Mildred, my daughter, take twenty pounds as a
present of my estate besides an equal share with William and
Elijah .. this 7th day of January 1815.
In the presence of   (signed)
   William Vawter, Monroe B. Hancock,   William Sutton
   Wm. Cole, Eliza W. Trevillian.
   At a court held .. 26th November 1827 .. proved .. ordered
to be recorded .. and at a court held .. 24th December following
.. Tabytha Sutton, the executrix named .. by note addressed to
the court refused the executorship .. on motion of Christian
F. Kinzer .. together with Benjamin Hawkins, Daniel Landrum,
Mallory Martin and William P. Southerland, his securities .. bond
in the penalty of five thousand dollars.

pp.   Will of WILLIAM SNIGHTER. .. I give to Lydia Ham Hall,
520   otherwise Lydia Ham Snighter as I consider my daughter .. I lend
521   to Susannah Hall, otherwise Susanna Snighter, as I consider her
my wife .. if Lydia Ham Hall should die without child .. to
Mary Carroll, daughter of William and Sally Carroll .. appoint
John Woolfolk executor .. this 5th day of October 1827.
In the presence of   (signed — his mark)
   Thos. Woolfolk   William Snighter
   Thos. Woolfolk Jr., Wm. T. Burrus

At a court held .. 26th November 1827 .. proved .. ordered to be recorded.

At a court continued .. 27th November 1827 .. John Woolfolk, named as an executor .. came into court and refused the executorship .. on motion of Lydia Ham Hall otherwise called Lydia Ham Snighter .. together with Susannah Hall otherwise called Susannah Snighter, her security .. bond in penalty of three hundred dollars.

p. 521   Will of WILLIAM SAMPSON. .. to my beloved wife, Sarah Sampson, the land I now live on .. if she sees cause to leave it before her decease, then I also give and bequeath to my son, William Sampson .. all my freehold or tenements, situated lying in the county of Orange .. William Sampson, whom I hereby appoint sole executor .. this 19th day of May 1815.
In the presence of   (signed - his mark)
    Jno. Yowell.   William Sampson
    Jas. Jollett, Peter Marsh.
        At a court held .. 26th November 1827 .. proved .. ordered to be recorded.

pp. 521- 522   An appraisement of the estate of ELIZABETH RUCKER, deceased, taken this 6th day of November 1827 .. value $60.75 .. made by appraisers Edward Cason, Alexr. Bradford, John Thornton. Returned into court 26th November 1827.

pp. 522- 525   Inventory and appraisement of the estate of Capt. JOHN MOORE, deceased, taken and appraised this 2nd day of October 1826 .. value $6691.18 .. James B. Moore, administrator .. made by appraisers Reuben Lindsay, Washington Reynolds, William W. Reynolds. Returned into court 27th November 1827.

pp. 525- 526   Estate of MARY PORTER, dec'd, in account with Benjn. F. Porter, administrator .. examined and settled by James Shepherd, Robert Taylor Junr., Jo. Atkins. Returned into court 27th November 1827.

pp. 527- 528   Proceeded to examine, state and settle Uriel Hilman's administrator's account upon the estate of JOSEPH HILMAN, dec'd, this 4th day of August 1827 .. by Thos. Row, Tandy Collins, Geo. Grasty, Edmd. Row. Returned into court 24th December 1827.

pp. 527- 528   Proceeded to examine, state and settle Uriel Hilman's administrator's account upon the estate of ESTHER HILMAN, dec'd .. by Thos. Row, Tandy Collins, Geo. Grasty, Edmd. Row. Returned into court 24th December 1827.

pp. 528- 529   Proceeded to examine, state and settle up Esther Hilman's executrix accounts upon the estate of JOSEPH HILMAN, dec'd .. made by Tandy Collins, Thos. Row, Geo. Grasty, Edmd. Row. Returned into court 24th December 1827.

pp.   John Moore, executor of the estate of ALEXANDER HOMES, dec'd,
529-   estate .. some items .. cash paid Dr. Charles Taylor ..
533   Garrott Keaton for coffin .. articles furnished Joseph Chandler's
children .. paid Edmund Terrill for tuition of Joseph Chandler ..
paid Pierce Sanford for tuition of Joseph Chandler .. Archibald
Rose for tuition of said Chandler's children .. to Thomas Goodwin
for goods furnished the children of Nancy Chandler .. given
20th October 1826 by Reuben Lindsay, Jacob Graves, Wm. Stevens ..
Returned into court 24th December 1827.

p. .. .   Tartan Smith, executor of JAMES SMITH .. cash paid James
533   Nelson Jr., attorney in fact for Lucy G. Wailer, formerly Lucy
Nelson .. cash paid James Nelson Jr., attorney for Agnes N.
.. cash paid Wm. Smith for Dorcas Smith .. cash paid Wm. Smith
for Elizabeth and Polly Smith .. cash paid Wm. Smith for James
Smith .. settled 29th October 1827 .. by Lewis Lindsay, John W.
Sale, Geo. W. Morton .. Returned into court 24th December 1827.

pp.   John Taylor, executor, in account with the estate of WILLIAM
534-   F. TAYLOR, dec'd .. state of Alabama .. Madison County. I,
536   Samuel Chapman, judge of the county court of Madison County do
hereby certify that I have this day examined the accounts and
vouchers of John Taylor, executor .. of William F. Taylor ..
paid John M. Taylor, guardian of A. G. Taylor $300 in Tennessee
Bank .. Samuel Chapman.
    The State of Alabama. County Court of Madison County this
16th May _eighteen hundred and twenty six. Settlement of the
estate of William F. Taylor, deceased, having this day made with
the executor for the assets in this county. It is ordered by
this court that the same be recorded and certified to the county
court of Orange County, Virginia, for final settlement which is
duly done this 24th day of May 1826 in Will Book No. 3, pages
377 and 78. Thomas Brandon, Clk. Returned into Orange County
Court 24th December 1827.

End of Will Book 6

pp.
1-
3

Thomas Eddins and Benjamin Graves to the estate of WM.
COLLINS, dec'd .. account settled 20th May 1820 by Tho. Sorrille,
Joseph Cave, Benjamin Burton. Returned into court 24th December 1827.

pp.
3-
4

Robert Davis and Isaac Davis, executors, to the estate of
THOMAS DAVIS, dec'd .. sale made on the 1st day of January 1816
.. paid Mildred Simms .. paid Davis Durrett .. paid Thos. Carr
and Joshua Homer .. paid Thomas Durrett .. paid Thomas Durrett
for Elisa Watts .. paid Thomas Davis .. paid Wm. Simms, Susanna
Garth and Winston Durrett .. paid Isaac Davis for Golding's heirs
.. paid Absolom Bostick for Dalton's heirs .. paid D. P. Key for
Durrett's heirs .. paid Francis Durrett for Durrett's heirs ..
paid Isaac Davis for Davis's heirs .. settled 4th August 1821 by
William Parrott, Tho. Sorrille, Sanford Beazley, Charles Parrott.
Returned into court 24th December 1827.

pp.
4-
5

Elijah Morton, administrator of the estate of JOHN MORTON,
dec'd, in account with sd estate .. cash paid George Morton for
his trouble and expenses going to Kentucky and getting a deed of
said Bohannon's tract .. to Mary Morton, the widow .. estate
divided 4th November 1820 by commissioners Thos. Coleman, Reuben
Lindsay, Jacob Graves. Returned into court 24th December 1827.

pp.
5-
6

David Whitelaw to the estate of JAMES McALLISTER .. (Mary
McAllister appears to be widow) .. account examined by Richard
H. Parkes, Edward Cason, Thomas Eddins. Returned into court 24th
December 1827.

pp.
7-
8

George Quisenberry, administrator on the estate of JONATHAN
ATKINS, dec'd .. account begins in 1814 .. balance due estate
of $112.83, one third of which the widow is entitled to, the
other two thirds is left for the son of said dec'd, it being the
only child .. made 11th May 1821 by Reuben Lindsay, Washington
Reynolds, Jesse B. Webb. Returned into court 24th December 1827.

p.
8

Estate of JOHN SCOTT in account with Sarah Scott, administratrix .. sum alloted Mrs. Sarah Scott in the division of the
estate $1095.43 .. $365.14 each to Richard Tyler, John Scott,
Charles Scott, Sarah A. Scott, Mary Scott, Garnett Scott. Returned into court 24th December 1827.

pp.
8-
10

William Sims, executor of ALEXR. OGG, dec'd, to his estate
.. paid Aaron Gentry as per request of will .. Wm. Cave for making
coffin .. cash paid Peter Ogg and Daniel Ogg as legacy .. paid
Jane Ogg as per request of will .. paid Susanna Ogg as per request of will .. paid James Ogg as per request of will .. paid
Saml. Estes as legatee .. paid Saml. Estes for George Gentry ..
account settled 7th April 1821 by George Bingham, Josiah Huckstep, James White. Returned into court 24th December 1827.

pp.   John Head to the estate of ROBERT BEAZLEY, dec'd .. account
10-   examined and settled by Thos. Sorrille, George Stephens, Geo.
11   Payne the 15th day of August 1827. Returned into court 24th
December 1827.

pp.   The estate of ROBERT SANFORD, dec'd, in account with John
11-   Head, administrator with will annexed .. £ 43.15.9 1/4 paid
12   legatees Richard Sanford, Reuben Sanford, Augustine Sanford,
Muse Sanford, James Beazley, William Burton, Henry Head, John
Head, Burwell M. Sanford, Willaby Sanford .. account settled
by Joseph Cave, Edward Cason, Thomas Eddins. Returned into
court 24th December 1827.

pp.   Will of CALEB LINDSAY. .. lend to my dear wife, Sally Lind-
12-   say, during her natural life, my land in Orange County which I
13   purchased of Edmund Rowe .. also six slaves .. also one third
part of my other personal estate .. after death of wife .. desire
.. my executors .. shall make sale of all and singular the
property herein lent to her .. divide the money equally between
all my children .. after my said wife have her allotted part ..
executors sell the remainder of my estate .. and divide the
same equally between all my children .. do hereby appoint my son,
Lewis Lindsay, and my friend, William Stevens, guardian to all
my children until they arrive to lawful age .. I nominate and
appoint my wife, Sally Lindsay, executrix, and my son, Lewis
Lindsay, and my friend, William Stevens, executors .. this fif-
teenth day of October 1822.
In the presence of   (signed – his mark)
    William Stevens, Saml. Brockman,   Caleb Lindsay
    William Brockman, Francis Worehage.
   Codicil .. give to my son, Levingston Lindsay, one negro slave
named Richmond .. this 26th day of February 1823.
In the presence of   (signed – his mark)
    William Stevens   Caleb Lindsay
    Wm. L. Brockman, Samuel Brockman.
   At a court held .. 24th December 1827 .. proved .. and ordered
to be recorded .. on motion of Lewis Lindsay .. together with
Landon Lindsay, John S. Lindsay and Ludwell Lindsay, his secur-
ities .. bond in the penalty of thirty thousand dollars.

(A note. Caleb Lindsay was the son of Joshua and Mary (Polly)
Nichols Lindsay of Caroline County, the grandson of Caleb and
Clare Lindsay of Essex County. He married Sarah (Sally) Mountague
Stevens, daughter of John and Sarah Mountague Stevens on 9 March
1785. After Caleb's death, his wife traveled to Christian
County, Kentucky where she lived with her son, Lunsford, until
her death in 1850 or 1851. Caleb and Sally had the following
children: two daughters, Polly Nichols Lindsay and Sallie
Mountague Lindsay who died in infancy. Sons, Landon, Lunsford,
Lewis, Littleton, Ludwell, John Stevens, Levingston and Lancelot.
The Lindsay genealogy appears in the introduction of the book,
PAMUNKEY NEIGHBORS OF ORANGE COUNTY, VIRGINIA. On the 23rd
October 1777, Caleb Lindsay was appointed First Lieutenant in
the Virginia Militia, and on 23rd day of November 1780, he was
appointed Captain.)

pp.   James Nelson to the estate of HENRY WOOD .. account for
13-   1822-1824 .. one sixth part to be paid each legatee .. 8th Decem-
14   ber 1827 examined and settled by John W. Sale, Richd. Richards,
         Ezekiah Richards. Returned into court 24th December 1827.

p.   Appraisal of the estate of ESTHER HILMAN, dec'd, this 2nd
15   day of November 1825 .. value $176.92 .. Thos. Row, Benj.
         Sanders, Edmd. Row, appraisers. Returned into court 28th Janu-
         ary 1828.

pp.   Being selected commissioners by Elijah Hawkins and Elizabeth,
15-   his wife, formerly Elizabeth Scott, Alexander Hawkins and Ann,
16   his wife, formerly Ann Scott, Henry G. Scott and George Scott,
         who are the legal heirs and representatives of REUBEN SCOTT,
         dec'd, and all of the county of Orange, to lay off and divide
         all the lands and negroes belonging to the sd Reuben Scott,
         dec'd, between them, they being the four legatees and all of
         lawful age .. to Elijah Hawkins one tract of land lying on the
         Russell Run containing 100 acres and land adjoining the land of
         John C. Gordon and three negroes .. allot Alexander Hawkins
         one tract of land containing two hundred acres lying on the Long
         Branch adjoining the lands of Jere. Pannill .. (and negroes) ..
         Henry G. Scott tract of land containing one hundred and thirty
         four acres .. lying on the Mountain Run .. (and negroes) .. George
         Scott tract of land containing one hundred and eighteen acres
         lying on each side of Black Walnut Run adjoining the land of
         James Coleman .. (and negroes) .. division made by Philip Mallory,
         William Graves Senr., John Mallory .. (agreement signed by all
         the legatees). Returned into court 28th January 1828.

p.   A list of the appraisement of the estate of ROBERT B. LONG,
17   dec'd, made this 29th day of January 1828 .. value $100.75 ..
         given 29th January 1828 by Tho. Sorrille, James Beasley, William
         Sims. Returned into court 25th February 1828.

pp.   List of sales of the property of ROBERT LONG, dec'd, Feby.
17-   1st 1828 .. only shows items sold to Susan Long .. value not
18   totalled .. returned into court 25th February 1828.

pp.   This 5th day of January 1828 appraised in current money to
18-   the best of our judgment .. the real and personal estate of
19   WILLIAM SUTTON, deceased, shown to us by his executors .. value
         $2496.31 .. William C. Moore and Wm. Cole. Returned into court
         25th February 1828.

pp.   We, Reuben Conway, William Smith, James M. Macon and Conway
19-   C. Macon .. have appraised the slaves and other personal
22   estate of EDWARD WINSLOW, dec'd, shown to us by the administra-
         trix, Elizabeth Winslow .. value not totalled. Returned into
         court 25th February 1828.

pp.   A schedule of the estate of AMBROSE CLARK, dec'd .. value
22- $270.12 1/2 .. given 6th day of November 1827 by Walt. Gambrel,
23   George Waugh,, Henry Clark. Returned into court 25th February
      1828.

pp.   An inventory and appraisement of the estate of ALEXANDER
23-   HOLMES, deceased, taken this 5th day of January 1818 .. value
24     $1848.04 .. (appraisers not shown). Returned into court 25th
      February 1828.

pp.   Examined and settled William Faulconer's administration
24-   account upon the estate of NICHOLAS FAULCONER, dec'd .. found
25   administrator had only $4.68 1/4 .. settled by Tho. Row, Thomas
      Robinson, Benj. Sanders, Edmd. Row... 22nd March 1828. Returned
      into court 24th March 1828.

pp.   An inventory and appraisement of the negroes and other per-
25-   sonal estate of WILLIAM BECKHAM, dec'd, taken this 15th day of
26   December 1825 .. value $197.00 .. slaves $1200 .. total value
      $1397 .. reported 10th March 1828 by W. Davis, John A. Porter,
      Benjamin Walker. Returned into court 24th March 1828.

p.   An inventory and appraisement of the estate of JOHN DAVIDSON,
26   dec'd, 10th March 1828 .. value $3.06 .. made by appraisers John
      Sleet, W. Davis, Benjamin Walker. Returned into court 24th
      March 1828.

pp.   An inventory and appraisement of the estate of WILLIAM ESTES
26-   SENR., dec'd .. value $3327.02 .. made 12th February 1828 by
30   Charles Parrott, James Early, George Stephens, Joseph Huckstep
      .. Ira B. Brown, administrator of William Estes Senr., dec'd.
      Returned into court 28th April 1828.

pp.   Will of JOHN S. FOX. .. I give and bequeath all that I
30-   possess or may have a right to, that is my negro boy, Larkin,
33   now with me, all my interest in the tract of land in Orange
      County, state of Virginia, whereon my father formerly lived,
      which he received by my deceased mother, all my interest in my
      grandmother's, Mrs. Mary Jones, dower, all my interest in the
      several tracts of land in the state of Kentucky which I claim
      by my late deceased mother, all my interest in the estate of my
      late deceased Aunt Polly Fox as left to me in her last will ..
      to my dear Father, Doctor Stephen Fox .. this 18th day of
      August 1823.
      Teste   (signed)
        J. D. Boyd, James M. Leary,   John S. Fox
        James Hamilton, Lewis Denkins.
      State of North Carolina. Mecklenburg County .. certified in
      court .. proved .. ordered to be recorded .. 10th March 1826 by
      Isaac Alexander, Clerk .. followed by an exchange between Orange
      County and Mecklenburg County.

At a court held .. 22nd May 1826 .. authenticated copy of will
of John S. Fox produced in Orange Court by Stephen Fox.
    At a court held .. 28 April 1828 .. will ordered to be recorded
.. on motion of Stephen Fox .. with Richard Rawlings, his security
.. bond in penalty of five thousand dollars.

pp.   Will of ROBERT OSBORN. .. my will and desire is that the
33-   land whereon I live estimated at five hundred acres more or
34   less be enjoyed by my son, Holland .. and if his wife survives
        him, then by her .. after the death of both it shall go to their
        children .. I give to my grandchildren, children of Holland ..
        to Mildred Osborn .. to Martha Osborn .. to Robert Osborn .. the
        land whereon my son, Braxton lives, estimated at two hundred and
        twenty six acres .. and after his death to go in fee to my grand-
        children, the children of my son, Sinclair .. remainder of my
        negroes I give to the children of my sons, Sinclair and Fielding
        .. having heretofore advanced what I deem sufficient to my son
        in law, Elijah Eddins, and my son, Willis, I intentionally omit
        them in this my will .. appoint my son, Holland, and my neighbors,
        Robert Chewning and Robert Cave, executors .. this 16th day of
        September 1826.
In the presence of   (signed)
        James Barbour   Robert Osborn
        Robert Cave, Robert Chewning.
    At a court held .. 28th May 1828 .. will purported to be last
will and testament of Robert Osborn offered for probate and
James Barbour, who resides out of the state of Virginia, and
Robert Cave and Robert Chewning being the only attesting witnesses .. Robert Chewning came into court and refused .. said
writing was approved .. and ordered to be recorded .. whereupon
the said Robert Cave came into court and refused .. and Holland
Osborn .. also refused .. on the motion of Robert Cave, with
Robert Chewning and James Melone, his securities .. bond in
penalty of five thousand dollars.

pp.   Will of CHARLES MALLORY. .. the plantation whereon I now
34-   live should be rented out .. until my youngest son arrives to the
35   age of twenty one and the rents to be used for the support of all
        my children and then to be sold and the money equally divided
        among them .. my negroes should be hired out .. and the money
        used to support my children until my daughter, Lucy Jane, be-
        comes of age or marries .. until my son, Nathan James, comes of
        age .. I give my son, William Harding .. appoint my friend,
        Charles Parrott, executor .. this 30th day of April 1828.
Teste   (signed)
        Matthew Lamb, Josiah Huckstep   Charles Mallory
    At a court held 27th May 1828 .. proved .. ordered to be re-
corded .. Charles Parrott with Matthew Lamb and Josiah Huckstep,
his securities .. bond in penalty of four thousand dollars.

pp.   The estate of JOSEPH EDDINS, deceased, in account with Thomas
36-   Eddins, executor .. paid Theophilus Eddins as part of his legacy
38   .. paid Joel Eddins as part of his legacy .. paid William Rogers
.. paid Michael Lower .. paid Joseph Eddins .. paid Abraham Graves
for John Graves .. paid Simeon Graves for George Collins ..
settled May 23, 1828, by Joseph Cave, James White, Bleffield
Rucker. Returned into court 28th May 1828.

pp.   Orange County, November 27th 1827 .. we Reuben Newman, John
38-   Williams, Robert Brooking and William Crittenden .. appraise the
44   estate of AUGUSTINE WEBB, dec'd .. John V. Webb, administrator
.. appraisal amount $8285.29 1/2. Returned into court 23rd
June 1828.

pp.   We proceeded on the 13th of February 1828 .. to appraise
44-   so much of the estate of JOSEPH CHANDLER, deceased, as was pro-
45   duced to us .. value $3.25 .. made by appraisers Benjamin Cooper,
John Herndon, Thomas Woolfolk. Returned into court 23rd June
1828.

p.   In addition to the assets of the estate of WM. SUTTON, dec'd
45   .. since received $214.34 according to the weight it being in
gold .. if the banks make it less I shall report. This money
was kept by Mr. Sutton as the legacy of Wisdom's heirs to whom
he (Sutton) acknowledged it belongs and which I shall retain
until I can inform them of their rights and give them time to
apply for it. The money was weighed by Cudden Davis in the
presence of Thomas Woolfolk, June 2, 1828. Christian F. Kinzer.
Returned into court 23rd June 1828.

pp.   An inventory and a list of appraisement of those who pur-
45-   chased and the amount of the estate of WILLIAM SUTTON, deceased
47   .. as sold on this 12th day of October 1827. Some purchasers ..
Lucy Willoughby, Tandy Willoughby, Thomas Gibson, William Dunaway,
Thomas Stephens, William Stephens, Francis Robinson .. whole
amount of estate $281.14 .. Richard Richards. Returned into
court 23rd June 1828.

pp.   An account of the sale of part of the estate of REUBEN SCOTT,
47-   dec'd, on the twenty third day of August 1827, by George Scott,
54   administrator. Some purchasers .. George Scott, Alexander Hawkins, John Farish, Elijah Hawkins, Ambrose Coleman, John Scott,
Thomas Stubblefield, William Ready, John C. Gordon, Richard Rhoades,
Henry Scott .. total of sale $920.43 .. certify by George Scott,
administrator. Returned into court 23rd June 1828.

pp.   Will of WILLIAM WHITE. .. give and bequeath to my son,
54-   Henry White, my two tracts of land lying in the state of Ohio...
55   lying in the county of Fayette, the other .. in Highland County
.. I give my other three tracts of land in the sd state of Ohio
to my son, Jeremiah White .. one lying in the county of Clinton
.. another in Clinton County .. the third in Highland County ..
I also give .. Jeremiah .. two hundred acres to be taken from the

tract I purchased of Wm. Stanard adjoining the Ocktoni line,
George Shearman and James Burton .. to my daughter, Lucy White
.. to my son, William White .. to my son, Daniel White .. to my
son, Washington White .. I wish my wife to own the tract of land
whereon I live or at least the balance of the tract .. after her
decease to my youngest son, John White .. my desire that Patsy
White, my wife .. appoint my brother, Garnett White, George
Shearman, and my son, Daniel White, as executors .. this 8th
day of December 1824.

In the presence of   (signed - his mark)
   R. Cave   Wm. White
   David Whitelaw, George Stephens.
    At a court held .. 28th July 1828 .. proved .. ordered to be
recorded.
    At a court held 25th August 1828 .. George Shearman and Daniel
White .. with Thomas Eddins, William White, John Head, Henry
Herndon, Henry White, Washington White, Jeremiah White and Benja-
min Burton, their securities .. bond in the penalty of twenty
thousand dollars.

p.   Will of HENRY G. SCOTT. .. give and bequeath to my beloved
56   wife, Nancy Scott, all my property of every description .. I
appoint my beloved wife, Nancy Scott, sole executrix .. this
25th day of August 1827.

In the presence of   (signed)
   Robert Mallory,   Henry G. Scott
   J. Farish, William W. Hume
    At a court held .. 28th July 1828 .. proved .. ordered to be
recorded.
    At a court held .. 26th January 1829 .. on the motion of Nancy
Scott .. with William W. Hume, her security .. bond in penalty
of two thousand dollars.

pp.   Inventory and appraisement of the estate of GEORGE GRASTY,
56-   deceased, taken this 28th day of December 1829 (as appears in
57   record) .. value $5594.80 .. made by appraisers John W. Sale,
Richard Richards, Alexander Wright .. George Grasty, administrator de bonis non with the will annexed of George Grasty, deceased.
Returned into court 28th July 1828.

pp.   Inventory and appraisement of the estate of ANN GRASTY taken
58-   the 28th day of December 1827 .. value $919.30 1/4 .. appraisers
61   John W. Sale, Richard Richards, Alexander Wright. Returned into
court 28th July 1828.

p.   MEMORANDUM .. regards a note on John G. Wright given on demand
61   to Ann Grasty .. 16th day of August 1821 .. for $117.00 .. for
notes on the Nashville Bank of Tennessee, received in part of the
estate of Thomas Grasty, dec'd .. one note on Joseph Wiltshire
given on demand and dated the 9th day of February 1828 for $220
due the estate of Ann Grasty, dec'd ..George Grasty, administrator
of Ann Grasty, deceased. Returned into court 28th July 1828.

p.
62

6th December 1827 .. appraisement of the estate of WM. KNIGHTEN, dec'd, of Orange County, Va .. value $120.25 .. appraisers Robert Payne, Claibourne Graves, John Henderson .. by will of Lydda Ham Hall otherwise Lydda Ham Knighten. Returned into court 25th August 1828.

pp.
62-
65

A list of the slaves and other personal estate of ROBT. OSBORNE, dec'd, appraised on the 2nd day of June 1828 .. value $3636.27 .. appraisers H. Houck, George Watters, Jesse Ball. Returned into court 25th August 1828.

pp.
65-
66

An inventory of the estate of CATLETT CONWAY, dec'd .. no value shown for items or total .. John F. Conway executor of C. Conway, dec'd .. Returned into court 25th August 1828.

pp.
66-
69

The estate of FRANCES BURNLEY, dec'd, in account with Charles P. Howard, executor .. Balance of estate above of which I have paid to Thos. B. Adams, guardian of his two sons, Charles and Thomas, and to Garland B. Taylor $158.16 .. to Thomas Garland in right of his wife, Jane, who is a daughter of S. G. Taylor .. signed Charles P. Howard .. settled by Reynolds Chapman, Edmd. P. Taylor, Richard M. Chapman. Report of settlement returned to court 27th August 1828.

pp.
69-
71

Will of WILLIAM HANCOCK. .. to my daughter, Nelly Hancock's children with whom I am not acquainted, I give one hundred and twenty dollars to be equally divided among them having heretofore given my said daughter a negro boy which was to be considered her legacy .. to my son, Monroe B. Hancock, I give one dollar he having received his part of my estate before his death, but land having fallen in value, I give to his little son, William B. Hancock Junr., $100, and to his daughter, Jane Elisabeth Hancock, a good bed worth twenty five or thirty dollars .. to my daughter, Mary Weirhaye, having had a negro girl as her legacy, I give one dollar .. and to her children she already has or may hereafter have by her husband, Francis Weirhaye .. to my granddaughter, Frances Garton, now living with me .. the residue I leave to be divided equally among my other four children, Benjamin Hancock, Mary Garton, Sarah Bradley and Susanna Stephenson .. I constitute and appoint my grandson, Lewis Bradley, executor .. this 25th day of June 1828.
Teste   (signed)
    James Shepherd   Wm. Hancock
    Joseph Stephens.

It is my further will that Rebecca Beckham and her children by her first husband, John Beckham, receive an equal portion of my estate with my other four children before named .. it is my will that my land be equally divided among my five children, Benjamin, Mary, Sarah, Susanna and Rebecca.

At a court held .. 22nd September 1828 .. proved by the oaths of James Shepherd and Joseph Stevens .. Lewis Bradley, executor in will, came into court and refused the executorship .. and on the motion of said Lewis Bradley, who made oath and together with William Bradley, his security .. certificate granted for obtaining letters of administration ..

pp.   Settlement of the estate of MILDRED SCOTT in account with
71-   HENRY THOMPSON, administrator .. expenses to Charlottes to receive
72   four negroes of George Kinsolving, admr. of Mary Thompson .. set-
         tled by Hugh M. Patton, E. P. Cady, N. Walker. Returned into
         court 27th October 1828.

pp.   Sale made this 3rd day of December 1827 of EDWARD WINSLOW,
72-   dec'd, estate .. total amount of $1038.88 .. made by H. Gee ..
74   Returned into court 27th October 1828.

pp.   Estate of REUBEN SCOTT, deceased, to George Scott, administra-
74-   tor .. value $487.60 1/2 .. settled by William Graves, Philip
76   Mallory, Edmd. Row. Returned into court 27th October 1828.

pp.   Estate of Mr. NAT. GORDON, dec'd, to Charles Beale, adminis-
76-   trator .. settled 8th February 1828 by James Lindsay, Jno. Taylor
77   Thornton, Henry Richards .. proportion of estate received and
         receipt given by John N. Gordon, Lucy Gordon, Priscilla C. Gordon,
         Nat. Gordon, Sarah Ann Gordon, Marcia H. Gordon. Returned into
         court 27th October 1728.

pp.   The undersigned was appointed guardian of Sarah Ann and Marcia
77-   H. Gordon by the county court of Orange on the 4th Monday of
78   December 1823. Besides their interest in the real estate of
         Gordonsville, Sarah Ann had in her possession a negro girl named
         Early and an old man named Aaron, also a small quantity of produce
         and being a proportion of the crop made at Gordonsville in 1823
         valued at $539 6/100; and Marcia had in her possession a negro boy
         named Paul, also a small quantity of produce and provisions being
         her proportion of the crop made at Gordonsville in 1823 and valued
         at $69 19/100. Gordonsville the 13th of August 1828. John N.
         Gordon. Sarah Ann Gordon and Marcia H. Gordon certificates.
         Returned into court 27th October 1828.

pp.   Estate of NAT GORDON, dec'd, in account with NATHL. GORDON,
78-   administrator .. settled by James Lindsay, Henry Richards, Jno.
81   T. Thornton .. legatees receipt signed by Chas. Beale, John N.
         Gordon, Lucy Gordon, Priscilla C. Gordon, Sarah Ann Gordon, Marcia
         H. Gordon. Returned into court 27th October 1828.

pp.   List of property sold belonging to the estate of THOMAS ADAMS,
81-   dec'd, the land being sold on the 23rd day of August 1827; the per-
82   sonal property was sold by the administrator with the will annexed
         the 19th day of September 1827 .. value not totalled. Returned
         into court 27th October 1828.

pp.   Will of JAMES FARISH. .. I give to my wife, Rebecca, forever
82-   two small negro girls .. after my debts and funeral expenses are
83   paid, I give to my son or daughter, whichever it may be, all my
         lands and the negro girl, Francis .. should my child die before
         it arrives to the age of twenty one or never comes into existence,
         then it is my wish that my lands shall be sold and the money
         equally divided among my three sisters and brother, viz. Mary S.
         Long, E. Jones and E. S. Farish and Benja. Farish. I appoint

Wm. W. Jones my executor .. this 15th day of July 1828.
                                        (signed)
(no witnesses)   James Farish
    At a court held .. 27th October 1828 .. there being no sub-
scribing witnesses, John Mallory, Jeremiah Pannill and Phillip
Williams were sworn .. on the motion of William W. Jones, the
executor named in the will .. with William B. Long, Benjamin
Farish and Thomas D. Hansbrough, his securities .. bond in the
penalty of five thousand dollars.

pp.   Will of JOHN DOUGLAS. .. all my lands to be equally divided
83-   between my two sons, William Douglas and John Douglas .. the tract
84   on which I live on to my son, William .. my son, John, to have all
        the land on the east side of the said road (Barboursville to
        Fredericksburg) .. I desire the tract of land in Albemarle County
        may be equally divided between him and his brother, John Douglas
        .. my son in law, Tandy Bowcock .. my house servant may be free
        .. appoint my two sons, William Douglas and John Douglas, executors
        .. this 29th day of July 1828 ..
        Witnesses   (signed)
            Wm. H. Johnson   John Douglass
            Ro. C. Johnson, Henry G. George
        At a court held .. 27th October 1828 .. proved by witnesses ..
        John Douglas with John Bowcock, Henry Herndon, Ezekiel Wilhoite
        and Jacob Walters, his securities .. bond in the penalty of five
        thousand dollars .. William Douglas, the other executor, by note
        to the court refused.

pp.   JOHN TERRELL'S executor's account with G. Grasty's estate ..
84-   expenditures total $1515.94 1/3 .. settled by Landon Lindsay,
88   James B. Moore, Tartan Smith .. Returned into court 24th November
        1828.

pp.   The estate of THOMAS GRAVES, dec'd, to WILLIAM GRAVES JUNR.,
88-   administrator thereof .. amount $967.06 .. additional expenditures
90   brings total to $1279.91 .. account examined 1st December 1827 by
        Edmd. Row, Philip Mallory, John Gibson. Returned into court 24th
        November 1828.

pp.   Estate appraisal of the slaves and other personal estate of
90-   WM. WHITE, dec'd .. total value $10913.30 .. amount of mill and
93   plantation, $477.35 .. made by appraisers Robt. Cave, Anthony
        Thornton, George Stephens .. 10th day of November 1828. Returned
        into court 25th November 1828.

pp.   Inventory and appraisement of the personal estate of JOHN
93-   DOUGLASS, dec'd, so far as was showed to us by JOHN DOUGLASS, the
95   executor .. value not totalled .. appraisers John Williams, Robt.
        Mansfield, Valentine Johnson. Returned into court 25th November
        1828.

p.   Will of JASPER HAYNES of the County of Madison .. (property
95   listed) to Mr. John Beadles of Orange County, except Daniel, who
            is hired out to be sold .. and money kept at interest in such man-
            ner that as John Beadles' children that he had by my daughter,
            Lucinda, arrives to lawful age .. children to inherit equally ..
            appoint my friend, James Walker, executor .. this 24th day of
            February 1827.
            Teste   (signed)
              Leroy Canady   Jasper Haynes
              Elijah Harvey, Lewis Harvey
              At a court held .. 22nd December 1828 .. presented .. ordered to
            be recorded.

pp.   Inventory and appraisement of the estate of WILLIAM HERNDON,
95-   deceased, taken the 15th day of November 1828 .. total value
98          $1132.04 1/2 .. appraisers Alexander Wright, John Wright, Richard
            Richards Junr., Owen Cooper. Certified by James Herndon, adminis-
            trator of William Herndon, dec'd. Returned into court 22nd Decem-
            ber 1828.

pp.   The estate of WILLIAM ADAMS, dec'd, to Edmd. Row, executor ..
98-   total value $1482.15 .. settled by Benja. Sanders, Richard Richards,
99   William Graves Junr .. 13th day of December 1828. Returned into
            court 22nd December 1828.

pp.   Inventory and appraisement of the estate of WILLIAM WILLOUGHBy,
99-   deceased, taken the 12th day of October 1827 .. value $325.75 ..
100   appraisers Owen Cooper, William Reynolds, Wm. C. Webb, Richard
            Richards. Returned into court 22nd December 1828.

p.   List of property appraised of MARY EHART, deceased, on the
100   10th of October 1827 .. value $203.75 .. appraisers William Way-
            land, John Farneyhough, August Gaines. Returned into court 26th
            January 1829.

pp.   List of property appraised of ADAM EHART, deceased, on the
100-   8th day of June 1827 .. value $892.00 .. appraisers William Way-
101   land, John Farneyhough, August Gaines. Returned into court 26th
            January 1829.

pp.   Henry Tandy, administrator with the will annexed on the estate
101-   of THOMAS ADAMS, dec'd .. value $228.46 .. appraisers Thomas Cole-
102   man, Reuben Lindsay, John W. Sale. Returned into court 26th Janu-
            ary 1829.

p.   Reuben Thompson in account with the estate of SAMUEL THOMPSON,
102   deceased .. value $21.26 .. appraisers' report 22nd October 1828
            by Reuben Lindsay, John W. Sale, Daniel M. Smith. Returned into
            court 26th January 1829.

pp.   Henry Tandy, an administrator with the will annexed of the
103-   estate of THOMAS ADAMS, dec'd .. in the hands of the administrator
104   for division into 3 parts, $781.23 1/2 .. each legatees' part,
            $260.41 .. the administrator in our presence divided the money

among the respective legatees .. bond of Owen Cooper to remain in the hands of Cooper during the life of Amey Adams .. Richard Richards, attorney for Lucy Willoughby, her one third part of the division which was due to her from her first husband, Waller Stevens, dec'd, under the will of her father, Thomas Adams. Given this 5th day of October 1828 by Reuben Lindsay, Jonathan Graves, Jacob Graves. Returned into court 26th January 1829.

pp. 104-105   William Stevens, executor, in account with the estate of John Stevens, dec'd .. paid various amounts to James Stevens, Nancy Duncan, Thomas Burris, Sarah Lindsay, John Stevens (minor), Wm. W. McCaffrey .. cash paid Lewis Lindsay, Sarah Lindsay and Dr. J. M. Goodwin .. settled 21st October 1828 by John W. Sale, Geo. W. Morton, Thos. Coleman. Returned into court 26th January 1829.

pp. 105-106   Lewis Lindsay .. estate of CALEB LINDSAY, dec'd .. to amount of sale, $2495.65, charges to Landon Lindsay, Lunsford Lindsay, Lewis Lindsay, Jno. S. Lindsay, Ludwell Lindsay, Levingston Lindsay, Lancelot Lindsay (charged to each in the lifetime of their testator) .. $15054.00 .. balance due estate, $904.50 .. settled 24th October 1828 by Wm. T. Burrus, John W. Sale, Geo. W. Morton. Returned into court 26th January 1829.

pp. 106-107   Amount of property sold by the administrator of JAMES DENISON, dec'd, on the 10th January 1826 .. total sale, $597.75. Returned into court 26th January 1829.

p. 107   An inventory of the money, goods and chattels found with the negro man, Reuben, upon the inquest of JAMES DENISON taken on the 4th day of November 1824 .. value not totalled .. Henry Herndon, administrator of Jas. Denison, dec'd. Returned into court 26th January 1829.

pp. 108-115   The estate of ROGER SLAUGHTER, dec'd, in account with Gabriel Long, one of the administrators .. to Mrs. Lucy Slaughter .. paid Mildred Slaughter .. fee for dividing land among the legatees .. the sum received of Christopher Johnson, executor of Henry T. Slaughter, dec'd, as a legacy .. settled 29th November 1828 by John W. Sale, Wm. Campbell, Geo. W. Morton. Returned into court 26th January 1829.

pp. 115-118   A list of the perishable property of Col. WM. WHITE, dec'd, sold on the 17th day of November 1828 .. purchasers include Martha White, Daniel White, William White Junr., Jeremiah White, William White, Washington White, Layton D. Eddins, William Dean .. total $2478.96. Returned into court 26th January 1829.

pp. 118-119   Inventory and appraisement of the estate of WILSON COLEMAN, dec'd, taken the 19th of December .. value $6217.25 .. given 22nd June 1829 by John W. Sale, Wm. Stevens, Jacob Graves. Returned into court 26th January 1829.

p.   Estate of WILSON COLEMAN .. additional settlement .. value
120         $702.86 .. made 22nd January 1829 by John W. Sale, Wm. Stevens,
            Wm. T. Burrus.

pp.   Richard Richards, administrator of the estate of WILLIAM
120-   WILLOUGHBY, dec'd .. value $564.04 .. services rendered as over-
121   seer, as guardian for the orphans and admr. of the estate .. $150.
            Returned into court 26th January 1829.

pp.   Estate of WILLIAM WILLOUGHBY dec'd in account with Richard
121-   Richards, admr. .. settled 3rd January 1829 by Thos. Row, Geo.
123   Grasty, Benj. Sanders, Edmd. Row.
                Richard Richards, administrator of ROBERT LANCASTER, dec'd,
            settled 3rd January 1829 by Thos. Row, Geo. Grasty, Benj. Sanders,
            Edmd. Row.
                Estate of WILLIAM MASON, dec'd, with Elisabeth Mason, adminis-
            tratrix .. value $271.44 .. settlement returned into court 26th
            January 1829.

p.   Estate of ROBERT LANCASTER, dec'd, in account with Richard
123   Richards, administrator .. paid back to James Jones, $6.90, for
            two acres and thirty six poles of land as sold to him but since
            found to belong to Vivion Quisenberry. Returned into court 26th
            January 1829.

pp.   Elisabeth Mason, administratrix to the estate of WILLIAM MASON,
123-   dec'd .. for power of attorney to authorise an agent to collect
125   money due the estate in the state of North Carolina .. (later
            shown as James Mason) .. stated and settled 22nd January 1829 by
            Geo. Grasty, Edmd. Row, George Proctor. Returned into court 26th
            January 1829.

pp.   Estate appraisal of the property of JOHN EUBANK, deceased,
125-   shown to us by his administrator, William Smith .. value $139.38
126   .. appraisers Thacker V. Webb. Rob. B. Long, Jas. M. Macon.
                Returned into court 26th January 1829.

p.   List of the appraisement of the estate of JOHN PLUNKETT, dec'd
126   .. value $943.75 .. given 8th day of December 1828 by appraisers
            Anthony Thornton, Benjamin Anderson, Thomas S. Thornton. Returned
            into court 26th January 1829.

p.   Michael L. Eheart, administrator to the estate of ADAM EHEART,
127   deceased .. settled 20th January 1829 by Robt. Mansfield, John
            Williams, Joseph Cave. Returned into court 23rd February 1829.

pp.   Estate of WILLIAM ACRE, deceased, to Robt. Acre .. settled
128-   11th November 1828 by Buckner Terrell, T. V. Webb, John V. Webb.
129   Returned into court 23rd February 1829.

p.   Michael L. Eheart, administrator to the estate of MARY EHEART,
129   deceased .. settled 20th January 1829 by Robt. Mansfield, John
            Williams, Joseph Cave. Returned into court 23rd February 1829.

pp.   Account of sales of the estate of JAMES FARISH, dec'd, made by
130-   William W. Jones, his executor, on the 10th day of December 1828
133   .. purchasers include William Porter, John Gibson, Thomas S.
Hansbrough, Benjamin Farish, Eliphalet Johnson, William B. Long,
Philip Williams, Peter Hansbrough, Thomas Wharton, John Martin,
Uriel Hilman .. total of sale $3144.58. Returned into court 23rd
February 1829.

pp.   Inventory and appraisement of the estate of WILLIAM LEE, de-
133-   ceased .. value $202.25 .. made the 3rd day of February 1829 by
134   appraisers Francis Conway, George C. Porter, Law. H. Taliaferro.
Returned into court 23rd February 1829.

pp.   Will of NELLY MADISON. .. I give and bequeath one sixth
134-   part of my slaves to my granddaughter, Nelly Conway Willis, wife
138   of Doctr. John Willis, and daughter of my deceased son, Ambrose
Madison .. of the remaining five sixth of my slaves, I give one
fourth part to my son, James Madison, and his heirs and one fourth
part to my son, William Madison, and one fourth part thereof I
give and bequeath to my son, James Madison .. in trust for my daughter, Sarah Macon, during her life and at her death in trust for
such children as my said daughter shall leave .. one fourth part
(same manner) .. for my daughter, Frances T. Rose .. slaves to
choose legatee .. that each of my sons, James and William, shall
pay to my granddaughters, Kitty and Fanny Madison, daughters of my
deceased son, Francis .. my will my estate not be appraised .. executors not be held to give security .. appoint my sons, James and
William Madison, executors .. this 28th day of November 1807 ..
In the presence of   (signed)
    Robert Taylor   Nelly Madison
    Robert Taylor Junr.
  Codicil revokes one sixth part devised to her granddaughter,
Nelly Conway Willis and instead gives her one hundred dollars ..
made the 16th day of September 1808 ..
In the presence of   (signed)
    Robert Taylor   Nelly Madison
    Robert Taylor Junr.
  Codicil .. in addition to James as trustee, she names son, Wil-
liam, and my friend, Abraham Eddins .. and mentions son in law,
Robert H. Rose .. made the 8th of January 1817 ..
    Witness   (signed)
     Robert Taylor   Nelly Madison
  Codicil .. re slaves .. and children of daughter, Sarah Macon,
James Madison, Ambrose, Edgar, Henry and Reuben ..
  At a court held 25th March 1829 .. proved will and codicils ..
  At a court held 22nd June 1829 .. James Madison, William Madison
and Abraham Eddins, executors named refused .. on motion of Rey-
nolds Chapman, with James and William Madison, his securities,
certificate granted for obtaining probate.

p.   Appraisal of Charles, a negro fellow belonging to the estate
138   of AUGUSTINE WEBB at three hundred dollars. Given 25th day of
December 1828 .. by John Williams, Wm. Crittendon, Robert W.
Brooking. Returned into court 27th April 1829.

pp.
138-
139
Appraisal of the estate of JOHN LEATHERS, deceased, and also the real estate of the said Leathers which by his will is subject to the authority of his administrator .. have appraised the tract of land upon which the said Leathers resided in the county of Orange adjoining William Quarles and others .. no other estate shown to us .. given the 9th day of March 1829 by Peyton Grymes, Garland Ballard, Cuddin Davis. Returned into court 27th April 1829.

pp.
139-
142
Estate of ANN KEY, dec'd, to John White, administrator .. legatees William B. Key, James Key, Judith Key, daughter of James Key; Thomas Key; Walter Key; Elisabeth Daniel ; Tandy Key; Strother, son of John Key, dec'd; Richard W. Key, another son of John Key, dec'd; Jesse Key, another son of John Key, dec'd; John C. Blaydes, who represents his wife, a daughter of John Key, dec'd .. John Key, another son of John Key, dec'd; Joshua Key; Henry Key .. estate settled 23rd April 1829 by Edmd. Row, Benj. Sanders. Returned into court 27th April 1829.

pp.
142-
143
Will of JOHN GOODALL. .. unto my wife, Sarah Goodall, the whole of the tract of land on which I live .. after her death to be divided equally between my two children, Mary Cudding Goodall and Margaret McKenny Goodall .. no executors shown .. this 5th day of March 1829.

Witnesses   (signed)
    Parks Goodall   John Goodall Senr.
    Thomas Harvey, Emanuel Runkel.

At a court held .. 25th May 1829 .. proved .. ordered to be recorded .. motion of Sarah Goodall .. with Cudden Davis and Emanuel Runkel, her securities .. bond in the penalty of two thousand four hundred dollars ..

pp.
143-
147
Will of MAY BURTON. .. give and bequeath to my beloved wife, Sarah Burton, one third of my whole estate which I have not conveyed by deed either to my son, Benjamin Burton, or my son in law, Alesander Bradford .. I have given to each of my married daughters, except Fanny Buckner, a young negro woman at the time of their marriage .. I have furnished my said daughter, Fanny Buckner, a plantation to live on .. land to be managed by executors for the benefit and maintenance of Baldwin M. Buckner, his wife and children .. father of Baldwin M. Buckner, Mordecai Buckner, dec'd .. daughters, Judith Webb, Sarah Payne and Mary Maria Eddins .. Benjamin B. Blakey in consequence of his infirmity shall have an equal proportion with his brothers and sisters .. and their descendants of the estate of the said Judith to be divided at her death .. and besides there shall be taken out of the part coming to his mother, Judith Webb .. I give to my daughter, Lucy Collins .. all my interest in a tract of land lying in Madison County, whereon James Collins, deceased, formerly lived and of which he died seized .. and one other tract in Madison County whereon Allen Raines lived and of which he died seized .. remainder in what shall be allotted my wife, Sarah Burton, shall be equally divided between my daughters, Fanny Buckner, Judith Webb, Sarah Payne, Margarette Burton, Martha Craig and Mary Maria Eddins .. Hannah Bradford (is listed among another group of children of whom Benjamin is the only

son) .. appoint my son, Benjamin Burton, and my son in law,
Alexander Bradford, and my son in law, James Craig, my executors
.. this first day of November 1827 ..
In the presence of   (signed)
   Thomas S. Thornton   May Burton
   Alexander O. Bradford, John M. Blakey,
   John White, William Walker.
   In a codicil he gives household furniture to wife. Codicil
made 8th July 1828 with same witnesses.
   At a court held .. 24th August 1829 .. Benjamin Burton and
Alexander Bradford .. with Tandy Collins, Michael L. Eheart,
Thomas Collins and Minor Rucker, their securities .. bond in the
penalty of twenty five thousand dollars ..

p.   Estate account of REUBEN SCOTT, deceased, with George Scott
148   .. $66.00 retained in the hands of the administrator to pay off
Lucy Badger's claim .. the sum of five hundred thirty six dollars
appears to be the next estate which is to be divided between
George Scott, Alexander Hawkins in right of his wife, Ann,
Elijah Hawkins in right of his wife, Elizabeth, and Abner Bickers
in right of Henry G. Scott, dec'd, which they have this day divided and passed receipts which is one hundred and thirty four
dollars a share.

pp.   Estate account of REUBEN SCOTT with George Scott. No amount
149- totalled .. sale of estate in 1827 .. settled by Alexander Wright,
151   John Wright, Richard Richards Jr. Returned into court 22nd
June 1829.

pp.   JAMES HERNDON administrator of the estate of WILLIAM HERNDON,
150- deceased .. amount of property sold at sale the 15th October
152   1827 by consent of legatees .. $91.15 .. settlement by Philip
Mallory, William W. Hume and Edmond Row. Returned into court
22nd June 1829.

pp.   HELEN CAMPBELL who died of a sudden illness at her own house
152- in Orange County on the 26th day of February 1829 wished and de-
153   sired that all her estate which she had in possession and all
which she was entitled to of the estate of her father and also
all her interest in the estate of her brother, Archibald Campbell,
both here in Virginia, and also in the State of Kentucky, both
real and personal should be equally divided between her three
sisters and one brother namely, Jane, Ann and Elizabeth Campbell
and Dugald Campbell. The said Helen Campbell wished and desired
that in the division of the Kentucky lands they should get the
part on which her brother, Duncan Campbell's house is situated,
that her brother, Duncan, should remain in possession .. at her
death to be divided as above named .. will committed to writing
and witnessed this 2nd day of March 1829. (no signature)
Witnesses Dugald Campbell, Jane Campbell.
   May 26th 1829. This is to certify the undersigned are perfectly
willing that the noncupative will of Helen Campbell should be
proved and committed to record in the county court of Orange.
                     (signed)   John Campbell
Witness: Ann Campbell
   Weedon Sleet Senr.   Elizabeth Campbell
   At a court held .. 22nd June 1829 .. will established by the
court as that of Helen Campbell . . . .

pp. A list of the appraisement taken at the house of JOHN GOODALL,
153- deceased, July 17th 1829 .. total valuation $1088.29 .. appraisers
154 George Runkel, Samuel Ham. Returned into court 27th July 1829.

pp. Will of WILLIAM PEACHER. .. the whole of my estate .. be
154- kept together until my son, Quinton shall come at the age of twenty
155 one years or for the term of eleven years yet to come .. that my
wife enjoy all the profits arising from my said estate up to the
time of the first division if she remain widow .. after my son,
Quintin, comes of age or the term of eleven years my estate be
divided .. I leave to my wife, Frances Peacher, the land and farm
I now live on .. (division) my children James, William, Joseph,
Sarah, Quintin, Huldah, Matilda, John, Thomas and Jane ..
Frances Peacher and my daughter, Mary Ann King .. appoint my wife,
Frances Peacher, executrix, and my son, Joseph W. Peacher, execu-
tor .. this 9th day of June 1828 ..
Witnesses   (signed)
 Edmd. Row,   William Peacher
 John Wright, William Wright.
  At a court held .. 25th August 1829 .. proved by the oaths of
Edmd. Row and John Wright, witnesses .. and ordered to be recorded.
Frances Peacher, the executrix therein named came into court and
refused the executorship and Joseph W. Peacher, the executor
named .. being under the age of twenty one years .. on the motion
of Frances Peacher .. with James Coleman, Edmd. Row and Robert
Brock, her securities .. bond in the penalty of eight thousand
dollars .. certificate granted her for obtaining letter of
administration ..
  (On the margin) At a court held .. 22nd November 1830, on the
motion of James Coleman .. with Edmd. Row, his security .. bond
in the penalty of six thousand dollars .. certificate granted him
for obtaining letters of administration de bonis non on the estate
of William Peacher, deceased, during the minority of Joseph Peacher, the executor named in the will ..
  At a court held .. 28th November 1831 .. on the motion of Edmd.
Row .. with Benj. Sanders and Richard Richards, his securities ..
bond in the penalty of twelve thousand dollars .. certificate
granted him for obtaining letters of administration de bonis non
on the estate of William Peacher, deceased, with his will annexed ..

pp. An inventory and appraisement of the slaves and other personal
155- estate of JAMES FARISH, dec'd, made this 8th day of December 1828
157 .. valuation totalled $2988.10 1/3 .. made 27th October 1828 by
appraisers Jeremiah Pannill, P. Williams, John Gibson. Returned
into court 25th August 1829.

p. Estate of WILLIAM SUTTON, deceased, in account with Christian
157 F. Kinser, administrator .. settled 31st day of July 1829 by James
Shepherd, Saml. H. Stout, Edwin Nichols. Returned into court
26th August 1829.

pp. John Wright and Hugh M. Faulconer, executors of JOHN FAULCONER,
158- deceased .. account settled 30th September 1828 by Richard Richards,
160 Edmd. Row, Benj. Sanders. Returned into court 26th August 1828.

pp.   Will of GEORGE BINGHAM. .. I give and bequeath to my loving
160- wife, Priscilla, the bed and all the furniture she had when I
161   married her .. I lend to her all the land whereon I now live but
not to be cut or destroyed any more than is necessary .. to my
son, Joseph, my mill and tract of land adjoining said mill .. to
my son, John, my gray horse together with what things he has
already had .. to my daughter, Rhoda Douglass, my negro girl,
Peachy .. to my daughter, Polly Haney, one negro woman .. to my
daughter, Rebecca Bingham, one negro boy .. to my daughter, Milly
Rice, my negro lad .. I lend to my daughter, Maria Estes, one
negro boy .. I lend to my daughter in law, Mary Bingham, one negro
boy .. at her death to be equally divided among her children ..
appoint my friend, Charles Parrott, and my son, Joseph, whole and
sole executors .. this 21st day of March 1829.

Teste   (signed)
   Jonathan Haney, Bird Snow,   George Bingham
   Susan Stephens, Catherine White

   At a court held .. 28th September 1829 .. proved by oaths of
Jonathan Haney and Bird Snow, witnesses .. ordered to be recorded
.. and on the motion of Josias B. (called Joseph in will), an
executor therein named .. with Josiah Huckstep and Robert G.
Duglass, his securities .. bond in the penalty of five thousand
dollars ..

pp.   Will of SARAH OGG. .. give and bequeath unto my brother, John
161- Goodall, all my estate both real and personal consisting of one
162   hundred and twenty acres of land adjoining the lands of Capt. James
Early and others .. appoint my brother, John Goodall, sole executor .. this 12th day of February 1821.

Witnesses   (signed - her mark)
   Sanford Beasley, Joseph Davis,   Sarah Ogg
   George Runkel, Reuben Golding

   At a court held .. 27th July 1829 .. proved by the oath of
George Runkel, witness .. and on 28th September 1829 further
proved by the oath of Joseph Davis, another witness .. and ordered to be recorded.

pp.   The estate of Capt. JOHN MOORE in account with James B. Moore,
162- administrator .. settled by Thos. Coleman, John W. Sale, George
168   W. Morton 27th July 1829. Returned into court 26th October 1829.

pp.   Walter Gambrel, executor of ANTHONY PERRY, deceased, in ac-
168- count with said estate .. settled 21st July 1829 by Edmd. Row,
169   Wm. S. Fraser, Tandy Collins, J. W. Sale. Returned into court
26th October 1829.

pp.   Will of JAMES BURTON. .. my land in the state of Kentucky
169- I give to my four sons, Bezalul, James, William and John ..
172   Bezalul 312 acres .. lot No. 2 .. William 312 acres .. lot No. 4
.. James 270 acres .. having heretofore made deeds of conveyance
.. and lot No. 3 I lend to my son, John M. Burton's widow as long
as his children remain with her .. my land in the state of Ohio I give
to my three daughters .. to Frankey Goodridge 500 acres .. to
Nancy Brown 500 acres .. and to Ann Elizabeth Burton 666½ acres
.. having heretofore made them rights to the said lands .. to the
legal heirs of my son, Will Burton, $220 to pay them for their

father's part of his mother's land sold by a decree of the Orange
Court which I purchased .. I apid my daughters, Elizabeth Stone
and Polly W. Brent, dec'd, in their lifetime all that they were
entitled to from their deceased relations .. I give to my help-
less daughter, Ursula Burton, negroes .. in her mother's care ..
one half acre of the tract of land which I now live on, in my
apple orchard, inclosing the graveyard is reserved for that use
.. appoint my friends, George Stephens and George Shearman, executors .. this 26th day of November 1828.
Teste   (signed)
    Robt. Cave, James Wayt   James Burton
Codicil to dispose of land in Orange County .. after his decease
and death of wife the said tract of land to our daughter, Ann
Elizabeth Burton ..
Teste   (signed)
    Robt. Cave   James Burton
    James Wayt   Elizabeth Burton
    At a court held .. 26th October 1829 .. proved by the oaths of
Robert Cave and James Wayt, witnesses thereto, with codicil ..
ordered to be recorded .. on the motion of George Stephens, an
executor therein named .. with Joseph Stephens, Hugh Stephens,
James Wayt and James Simms, his securities .. bond in the penalty
of twenty thousand dollars ..

pp. 172- 173   An inventory and appraisement of the slaves and other perishable property belonging to the estate of MALCOLM HART, deceased
.. submitted by John Claybrooke .. appraised 30th September 1828
by appraisers John A. Porter, W. Davis, Philip Mallory. Returned
into court 26th October 1829.

pp. 174- 177   The estate of AUGUSTINE WEBB in account with John N. Webb,
administrator .. settled 1st September 1829 by Robert W. Brooking,
Richd. M. Chapman, William Smith. Returned into court 26th October 1829.

pp. 177- 181   Account of the sales of the estate of MALCOLM HART, dec'd,
made 22nd day of October 1828 .. some purchasers .. John Claybrooke, Daniel M. Smith, John Clark Jr., Robert Dedman, Reuben
Thompson, Benjamin Walker (considerable amount), John Sleet, William W. Hume, Washington Howard, James Hart, Charles Hines, Jerome
Collins, Col. Jackson Morton, Flemming Wells, Thomas Newman,
John Hart, Thomas Bronaugh .. certified by J. O. Claybrooke, administrator of the personal estate of Malcolm Hart. Returned into
court 26th October 1829.

pp. 181- 182   The following is an inventory and list of names of those who
purchased and the amount of the estate of GEORGE GRASTY, deceased,
as sold on the third, fourth, fifth and seventh days of January
1828 .. given by George Grasty, administrator de bonis non with
the will annexed of George Grasty, deceased, 24th January 1828.
George Grasty, Richmond Grady, Samuel Mason, William Cammack,
Francis B. Sulivan, Camp Faulconer, Edward Almond, John Pettis,
Henry Hume, John Mountague the younger, Frederick Aldridge, Francis Robinson, Philip Mallory, Anthony Tinder, Edmund Peacher,
Spicer Mountague. Whole amount $1538.65. Richard Richards Junr.
Acting Clerk. Returned into court 26th October 1829.

pp.   An inventory and list of names of those who purchased of the
182-   estate of ANN GRASTY, deceased, on the third, fourth, fifth,
190   seventh and ninth days of January 1828 .. submitted 24th January
1828 by George Grasty, administratory of Ann Grasty, deceased.
Andrew Grady, William Wright, George Grasty (considerable amount),
James Peacher, John H. Penny, James Stewart, Richard Rhoades,
Wyatt Brightwell, Sandford Chancellor, William Reynolds, Youel
Morris, Richard Richards Jr., Simeon Robinson, Ptolemy Brightwell,
Thomas Robinson, John Overton, John B. Johnson, William V. Chew-
ning, Francis B. Sulivan, John Pettis, John Mountague (the younger),
Edward Hobday, Jeremiah W. Graves, Benjamin Read, Richard B. Webb,
Joseph Hilman, Fielding Jones, George Perry, Jerome Collins,
Edward Almond, Jonathan Lancaster, John Southerlin, Daniel Quisen-
berry, Absolom Brightwell, Uriah Anderson, Spicer Mountague, James
Martin, William Dunaway, Newton Sulivan, Andrew Mountague, John
H. Grasty. Returned into court 26th October 1829.

p.   A list of negroes hired from the ninth day of January 1828
190   to the 31st of said month belonging to the estate of GEORGE GRASTY,
deceased .. submitted by Richard Richard Jr., acting clerk.

pp.   A list of the appraisement of the personal estate of ELLIOTT
190-   JONES, dec'd, taken the 28th October 1829 .. signed by Richd.
191   P. Winslow, D. S. for Wm. T. Burrus, SOC .. appraisers Robt. Cave,
Michael L. Eheart, Robert Chewning. Returned into court 23rd
November 1829.

pp.   On page 192 is a survey plot with legend made by commissioners
192-   appointed by the parties concerned, Lucy Henning, widow of Wil-
193   liam Henning, dec'd, Benjamin Henning and George Henning, all of
lawful age, surveyed and divided agreeable to quality and quantity
.. Lucy Henning lot No. 1; Benjamin Henning lot No. 2; George
Henning lot No. 3 .. and make return to be recorded ..5th day of
October 1829 .. by John A. Porter, George Pannill, John Mallory.
Returned into court 23rd November 1829.

pp.   Will of TABITHA SUTTON. .. earnestly request that I may be
193-   directly buried at the family burying ground by the side of my
194   deceased husband .. (grants nearly all her estate) to my son,
Wisdom Sutton, with specific request that he pay and satisfy my
friend, Benjamin Hawkins, and my housekeeper, Sarah Clarke, any
reasonable claim .. they may have .. my plantation tools .. to
my friend, Benjamin Hawkins .. appoint my friends, Benjamin Hawkins and Coleman Marshall, executors .. this 12th day of September 1829.

Witnesses   (signed - her mark)
   Paul Verdier   Tabitha Sutton
   Wm. Chapman, Charles T. Bell.

   At a court held .. 23rd November 1829 .. proved (by witnesses)
and ordered to be recorded .. on the motion of Benjamin Hawkins,
an executor therein named .. with Richard Rawlings, his security ..
bond in the penalty of one thousand dollars .. Coleman Marshall
came into court and refused ..

pp.   Appraisal of the estate of MARY DAVIS, deceased, by Isaac
194-   Davis, Edward G. Ship, James Beasley and Samuel Ham .. total
195   valuation $416.07. Returned into court 23rd November 1829.

p.   A statement of the administration accounts of William Herndon
195   on the estate of ELIZABETH RUCKER, deceased, made the 6th day of
September 1828 .. made by Edward Cason, Alexr. Bradford, Wm. H.
Mansfield. Returned into court 24th November 1829.

p.   The estate of ROBERT M. BEADLES. Account settlement of the
196   administration of James Beadles, administrator .. made by William
Robinson, John N. Sorrille. Returned into court 28th December 1829.

pp.   An inventory of the estate of WILLIAM HANCOCK, deceased, made
196-   September 18th, 1828 .. Lewis Bradley, administrator .. appraisers
199   James Marshall, Joseph Hiden, W. D. Clark. Returned into court
28th December 1829.

pp.   Estate of WILLIAM GRADY, dec'd, in account with William Grady,
198-   administrator .. settled 26th February 1829 .. Thos. Row, Thos.
199   Robinson, Edmd. Row. Returned into court 28th December 1829.

pp.   James B. Moore, administrator of ALEXANDER HOLMES .. in account
199-   with said estate .. account shows payment of $1000 each to Alexan-
201   der, Timothy, Joseph, William and Nancy Chandler .. settled 29th
January 1829 by John Terrill, Wm. Stevens, Wm. T. Burrus, John
W. Sale. Returned into court 28th December 1829.

pp.   Jesse B. Webb, executor to the estate of RICHARD C. WEBB ..
202-   settled 18th April 1829 by Thos. Row, Benj. Hume, Edmd. Row.
203   Returned into court 28th December 1829.

pp.   The estate of WILSON COLEMAN in account with James L. Coleman,
202-   administrator .. an entry September 18, 1829 .. by cash recd of
206   John Penn, exor in part of a legacy due the estate of John Penn,
dec'd, estate .. $500.00 .. settled 18th October 1829 by Wm.
Stevens, Jacob Graves, James Nelson Jr. Returned into court 28th
December 1829.

pp.   Will of NATHANIEL MIDDLEBROOK. .. I lend to my beloved wife,
206-   Mary Middlebrook, the whole of my property of every description
207   .. be under the direction and management of my sons, Garland and
Anderson Middlebrook, who are not to waste or destroy any part of
the property heretofore loaned to my wife and it is also my wish
that should either of my sons, Garland or Anderson, marry that
they shall not move their or either of their families to live in
the house with my said wife, Mary Middlebrook, though they shall
use the property at their discretion .. at the death of my wife,
I wish the property loaned to her to be equally divided between
Susan Terrill, Archibald Middlebrook, Garland Middlebrook, Patsy
Bosel and Anderson Middlebrook or their legal representatives ..
appoint my sons, Garland and Anderson, executors .. this 3rd day
of November 1829.
Witnesses   (signed - his mark)
    H. Fackler   Nathaniel Middlebrook
    Richard Faulconer, Walter Gambrel

At a court held .. 28th December 1829 .. proved (by witnesses) and ordered to be recorded .. on the motion of Garland and Anderson Middlebrook, the executors therein named, with James Terrill, their security .. bond in the penalty of one thousand dollars .. certificate granted them for obtaining a probate thereof ..

pp.
207-
208
The estate of WILLIAM PEACHER, dec'd, in account with William and Edward Peacher, executors .. settled by Thos. Row, Geo. Mason, Benj. Sanders, Edmd. Row. Returned into court 25th January 1830.

pp.
208-
209
Tartan Smith, executor of JAMES SMITH, deceased .. settled 16th January 1830 by John Terrill, James B. Moore, Geo. W. Morton. Returned into court 25th January 1830.

pp.
209-
210
Luke Thornton, administrator, in account with DANIEL THORNTON, deceased .. Agreeable to an instrument of writing presented to us by Luke Thornton, the said instrument was made and acknowledged before two justice of the peace by his mother, Sarah Thornton, the purport of said deed is giving unto her son, Luke Thornton, the profits arising from the proceeds of the estate .. the portion of the estate she had in her possession was divided between Luke Thornton and Thomas, the only two persons that were entitled to the same .. settled by Benjamin Walker, John Wiltshire, Alexr. Waugh. Returned into court 22nd February 1830.

pp.
210-
211
An inventory and appraisement of the estate of NATHANIEL MID- DLEBROOK, dec'd, taken this 5th day of January 1830 .. value to- talled $411.26 .. appraisers William I. Wiglesworth, Wm. C. Webb, Alexander Wright .. certified by executors, Garland and Anderson Middlebrook. Returned into court 22nd February 1830.

pp.
211-
214
A list of appraisement of Capt. JAMES BURTON estate taken this 27th day of November 1829 .. lots of slaves assigned to Ann Eliza- beth Burton, Bezalul Burton, Franky Goodridge, Nancy Brown .. made 27th November 1829 by Benjamin Anderson, William Wayt, George Parrott. Returned into court 22nd February 1830.

pp.
214-
216
List of the property belonging to the estate of Capt. JAMES BURTON, dec'd, sold 3rd day of December 1829 by George Stephens, executor .. amount of sale $225.80 .. Returned into court 22nd February 1830.

pp.
216-
217
Estate of GEORGE GRASTY, dec'd, in account with George Grasty, administrator .. settled 2nd January 1830 by Richard Richards, Ezekiah Richards, John W. Sale. Returned into court 22nd Febru- ary 1830.

pp.
217-
220
Inventory and appraisement of the estate of CHARLES BOSWELL, deceased, taken the 23rd day of February 1830 .. value totalled $1887.86½ .. made by appraisers John W. Sale, administrator, W. Gambrel, Ambrose Lee, John Sleet. Returned into court 22nd March 1830.

pp.
220-
224
A list of the property appraised on Saturday the 10th day of January 1824 belonging to the estate of Capt. JOHN WRIGHT, dec'd .. value not totalled .. appraisers William Herndon, Tandy Collins, Ezekiah Richard .. certified by John and Alexander Wright, the executors of John Wright, deceased. Returned into court 24th March 1830.

pp.   The estate of JOHN FAULCONER, deceased, in account with Hugh
224-   M. Faulconer and John Wright, executors .. paid Caleb Capps, at-
225   torney for Thomas Faulconer, paid Robert Wright, guardian of
Elizabeth Wright; paid John Rhoades, guardian of Lucy Rhoades,
William Rhoades and John Rhoades; Hugh M. Faulconer in right of
himself; Elizabeth Scott's part left in the hands of Hugh M.
Faulconer agreeable to the will; John Wright's part in right of
his wife; Jesse M. Grant's part left in the hands of John Wright
agreeable to the will .. settled 27th February 1830 .. Richard
Richards, Benj. Sanders, Richard Richards Junr. Returned into
court 26th April 1830.

pp.   The estate of JOHN WRIGHT, deceased in account with John and
226-   Alexander Wright, executors .. cash paid William Wright, cash paid
227   Thos. Dunaway in right of his wife, Mary Dunaway, John Wright's
part in right of himself, Alexander Wright's part in right of
himself .. settled 20th March 1830 by Richard Richards, William
I. Wiglesworth, John W. Sale. Returned into court 26th April 1830.

pp.   The estate of THOMAS ELLIS, deceased, in account with John
226-   and James H. Ellis, executors .. examined 26th February 1830 by
229   Thos. Coleman, Wm. Stevens, John W. Sale .. these commissioners
write that they completed the examination several years past and
turned their findings over to Leroy Chandler for transcribing
and believe it was never recorded and the purpose of this report
is to assure recording. Returned into court 26th April 1830.

pp.   Appraisal of the estate of CHURCHILL GEORGE, deceased .. value
230-   totals $157.49 .. made 30th September 1829 by appraisers Charles
231   T. Graves, John V. Webb, John Douglass Jr. Returned into court
26th April 1830.

pp.   Account of the sales of the estate of CHARLES BOSWELL, dec'd,
231-   made 23rd March 1830 .. some purchasers .. Harrison Somerville,
235   Edmond Terrill, Archibald Middlebrook, William Boswell, John Sleet,
William Clarke, William Cosby, Brooks Symcoe, Henry Clark, Sarah
Boswell, Reuben Lindsay, Walker Vass .. account made by John W.
Sale, administrator of Charles Boswell, dec'd. Returned into
court 24th May 1830.

pp.   William Estes administration of the estate of WILLIAM GOLDING,
235-   deceased, in North Carolina .. made by William Catterton, Geo.
236   Stephens, James Beasley. Returned into court 24th May 1830.

pp.   The estate of ANN GRASTY, deceased, with Geo. Grasty, adminis-
236-   trator .. account examined and settled 20th May 1830 by Richard
237   Richards, A. C. Wright, Ezekiah Richards. Returned into court
24th May 1830.

pp.   Estate of Dr. CHARLES TAYLOR, deceased, in account with
238-   Robert Taylor Junr., executor .. paid William T. Jenkins, ad-
239   ministrator of Elizabeth G. Jenkins, in part of her legacy left
by her father, Dr. Charles Taylor, dec'd; cash paid George W.
Morton in right of his wife, Evelina M. Morton; cash paid William
C. Moore in right of his wife, Matilda R. Moore; cash paid Catlett

Conway in right of his late wife, Hariet T. Conway; proportion to Robert Taylor in right of his wife .. account examined and settled by Richd. M. Chapman, Sam. H. Stout, Edwin Nichols. Returned into court 28th June 1830.

p.   Estate of Capt. JOHN BEADLES, deceased, in account with Wil-
240   liam Beadles, executor .. account examined and settled by Joseph Eddins, Thos. Davis, William Sims. Returned into court 28th June 1830.

pp.   Estate of Capt. JOHN BEADLES in account with William Delaney,
241-   executor .. account examined and settled by Joseph Eddins, Thos.
242   Davis and William Sims. Returned into court 28th June 1830.

pp.   Will of WILLIAM TERRILL. .. I give to Robert, George and
242-   Bookery (three boys of colour) the tract of land which I hold
244   adjoining the tract of land that I gave to my son, Edmond Terrill, dec'd, and the lands of Alexander Wright and others, which tract of land I formerly gave to my son, John Terrill, dec'd, which tract of land is by this my will to be to them the said Robert, George and Bookery .. and it is to be equally divided among them and they, the said Robert, George and Bookery, is by this my will to be free immediately .. after my decease .. I lend to my beloved wife, Nancy Terrill, all the balance of my estate during her natural life for her comfort and support .. after the death of my wife, I give to my son, James Terrill, 150 acres of land .. (description) .. I lend to my daughter, Nancy Burrus .. and at her death, or the death of her husband, Joseph Burrus .. my executors to pay my son, Reuben Terrill, one hundred pounds current money of Virginia after the death of my wife, and then the balance after paying the said legacy to my son, Reuben, is to be divided into four equal parts and one equal part of said division I give to my son, James Terrill .. one I give to be equally divided between the children of my son, Edmond Terrill, dec'd .. I leave .. one equal part of said division in the hands of my executors as trustee for my daughter, Nancy Burrus .. the fourth portion I lend to my daughter, Frances Fackler .. all my other children not mentioned above, viz. George Terrill, William Terrill and Elizabeth Chandler (which said three are now dead) and Polly Roberson of Kentucky, who is now living .. all having received their portion in their lifetimes I leave their children nothing more .. appoint my son, James Terrill, executor .. without being compelled by the court to give security .. this 5th day of September 1829.
Witnesses   (signed)
    John W. Sale, Elijah Morton,   William Terrill
    John Morton, Reuben Lindsay

    At a court held .. 23rd August 1830 .. James Terrill, an executor .. came into court and refused the executorship and Ann Terrill, the widow, having renounced the right of administration, on the motion of James Terrill and Henry Fackler .. who acknowledged bond in the penalty of ten thousand dollars each, the said James Terrill with Reuben Lindsay, his security, and the said Henry Fackler, with William Stevens his security .. certificate granted them for obtaining letters of administration .. with the will annexed ..

pp.
244-
245
A statement of the administration accounts of John W. Sale on the estate of CHARLES BOSWELL, deceased, and as settlement and division of same .. by cash paid three special legacies of fifty five dollars each that is to Brooks Simes for his infant children, Archibald Middlebrook and Sally Boswell by consent of the other legatees .. account examined and settled 22nd May 1830 by Reuben Lindsay, William Clark, Walter Gambrel. Returned into court 26th July 1830.

pp.
246-
247
Vivion Quisenberry, administrator to the estate of BENJAMIN WRIGHT, deceased .. account examined and settled 6th March 1830 by Edmd. Row, Richd. Richards, Ezekiah Richards, Richard Richards Junr. Returned into court 26th July 1830.

pp.
247-
248
The estate of JACOB WILLIAMS, deceased, to Stevens Williams, administrator .. account examined and settled 26th July 1830 by Gilbert H. Hamilton, Francis K. Cowherd, Yelverton Cowherd. Returned into court 23rd August 1830.

pp.
248-
249
Settlement of the administrationship of George Runkel and of the estate of JACOB RUNKEL, deceased .. by receipt in full from William Runkel, Emanuel Runkel, Daniel Runkel, St. Clair Runkel and Sarah Runkel for their full portion of the estate of Jacob Runkel being $15.18 each share .. made June 9, 1830 by Charles Hagish, Granville Kennedy. Returned into court 23rd August 1830.

p.
249
Inventory and appraisement of the estate of THEODOSHIA DAVIS, deceased, taken this 13th day of March 1830 .. appraisers George S. Blakey, Charles Hagish, Josiah Huckstep, T. G. Garth, administrator. Returned into court 23rd August 1830.

pp.
249-
252
The estate of JAMES DENNISON, dec'd, in account with H. (Henry) Herndon, administrator .. account examined and settled 18th August 1830 by Minor Rucker, Geo. Stephens, Alexander Whitelow. Returned into court 23rd August 1830.

pp.
252-
253
Will of MARY COOPER. .. I give and bequeath unto my seven daughters to wit, Susannah Cooper, Ann Cooper, Delilah Cooper, Mary Gooper, Frances Cooper, Rosa Cooper and Rachel Cooper all the lands which I purchased of Elijah Hawkins, William Herndon and Reuben Daniel lying in the county of Orange as long as they remain single, and should either of them marry, then the said land is to be for the joint use and benefit of the rest or for such as may remain single .. if my daughters agree to sell the land the money arising therefrom to be equally divided among all my children, viz. William Cooper, James Cooper, Benjamin Cooper, Owen Cooper, Sarah Lancaster, Susannah Cooper, Ann Cooper, Delilah Cooper, Mary Cooper, Frances Cooper, Rosa Cooper and Rachel Cooper .. appoint my son, Owen Cooper, executor .. and desire he not be compelled to give security .. this 27th day of December 1823.
In the presence of   (signed - her mark)
  Reuben Lindsay, Robert Kindell   Mary Cooper
  At a court held .. 23rd August 1830 .. proved by Reuben Lindsay and Robert Kindell .. and ordered to be recorded .. on motion of Owen Cooper, the executor therein named .. bond without security .. certificate granted him for obtaining a probate ..

pp.
254-
256
Will of WILLIS WHITE SENR. .. I give to my nephew, John White, son of Richard White .. to my two nephews, Willis and Jeremiah Pipers, the tract of land whereon I now live .. to my two nephews, George and Jonathan Graves, my tract of land whereon James White now lives .. to my nephew, John E. Roberts .. to my nephew, Fontain Roberts .. to my nephew, John Piper .. to my nephew, Richard Piper .. to my nephew, Jeremiah W. Graves .. to my nephew, Isaac W. Graves .. to my nephew, William Graves .. to my nephew, James White .. (remaining estate to be sold and divided among) my brother, Richard White, my nephew Garnett Graves, my niece, Elizabeth W. Graves, and to William Piper for the benefit of his two youngest sons, names not now recollected... one hundred dollars to my niece, Nancy Brown .. to my nephew, William White, son of Willis White .. appoint my brother in law, William Piper of Albemarle and Jacob Graves of Orange my executors .. this 7th day of April 1830.

Teste   (signed)
    Robt. Cave,   Willis White
    William Wayt, John Pittman

At a court held .. 24th May 1830 .. being offered for probate by Jacob Graves and the probate thereof being opposed by Garnett White, the same is continued until the next court on the motion of Garnett White.

At a court held .. 28th June following .. the controversy was continued for said Garnett White until the August Term next.

At a court held .. 24th August 1830 .. the said writing purporting to be the last will and testament of said Willis White, deceased, bearing date the 7th day of April 1830 and codicil thereto dated the 11th day of April 1830 having been heretofore offered for probate and recording .. the parties being fully heard .. considered writing is last will and testament of Willis White .. that Jacob Graves recover against Garrett White his costs.

At a court held 27th September 1830 .. on the motion of Jacob Graves, an executor name in the last will and testament of Willis White, deceased .. with Lewis Graves and Jonathan Graves, his securities .. bond in the penalty of ten thousand dollars .. certificate is granted him for obtaining a probate ..

pp.
256-
257
Will of JOHN OFFIELD. .. I loan to my beloved wife, Aggey Offield, during her natural life or widowhood the tract of land on which I live supposed to contain one hundred and ninety eight acres .. I also loan my wife all my negroes except the one my executors is at liberty to sell to pay my debts .. having heretofore given my daughter, Elizabeth Haws .. my will is that all my children be made equal to my daughter, Elizabeth Haws out of the property heretofore loaned to my wife .. my will is Frances Daniel receive hers this fall and Dinah Offield receive hers soon as she married .. that James Offield receive his when he marries .. my will is James Offield be sent to school to get a tolerable good english education .. appoint my friends, Francis Kirtley and Hawsey Daniel, my son in law, executors .. this 11th day of June 1830.

Witnesses   (signed)
    William Dulaney,   John Offield
    Robt. Miller, Francis Lea

At a court held .. 26th July 1830 .. will proved by the oath of
Robert Miller ..

At a court held .. 25th August 1830 .. further proved by William
Delaney ..

At a court held .. 27th September 1830 .. Francis Kirtley ..
came into court and refused to undertake the executorship .. on
the motion of Hawsey Daniel .. with Francis Kirtley, his security
.. bond in the penalty of fifteen thousand dollars .. certificate
granted him for obtaining a probate thereof in due form.

pp.   The estate of CATLETT CONWAY, deceased, with John F. Conway,
258-   executor .. Francis Conway his proportion from the sale of Haw-
261   field .. 19 November 1827, paid Hay Taliaferro $723.55; Henry
         Fitzhugh $465.66; Catlett Conway $760.60; Reuben Conway $692.82;
         John F. Conway $747.63; Reuben Conway (legatee) $147.75 .. examined
         and settled by Richd. M. Chapman, James Shepherd, Richard Cave,
         24th November 1829. Returned into court 27th September 1830.

pp.   The estate of DR. CHARLES TAYLOR, deceased, with Robert Taylor
260-   Junr. .. cash paid Robert Taylor Junr, trustee of George F. Tay-
263   lor .. to cash paid George W. Morton in right of his wife, Evelina
         M. Morton .. to cash paid Milly Taliaferro on account of Campbell
         and Atkins' land .. each received of James Shepherd, security for
         Robert W. Shepherd .. cash paid to William C. Moore in right of
         his wife, Matilda R. Moore .. cash paid Martha F. Taylor .. cash
         paid Catlett Conway in right of his late wife, Harriett T. Conway
         .. cash sent to William Milburn in right of his wife, Sarah T.
         Milburn, through the Mechanics Bank in New York by a check as
         directed by said Milburn in favor of Benjamin Taylor of Kentucky
         .. cash paid in right of my wife, Mary C. Taylor .. cash paid
         Robert Taylor Junr. as trustee of George F. Taylor .. examined and
         settled by Richd. M. Chapman, Saml. H. Stout and Richard Cave.
         Returned into court 27th September 1830.

pp.   John Terrill's executor account with the estate of G. L. GRASTY,
262-   deceased .. paid myself in part of my wife's legacy .. examined
269   and settled 18th September 1830 by William Stevens, Jacob Graves,
         Tartan Smith. Returned into court 27th September 1830.

pp.   An appraisement of the estate of WILLIAM TERRILL, deceased,
269-   the 14th day of September 1830 .. value not totalled .. appraisers
271   William Reynolds, Elijah Morton, John Morton, James Terrill, H.
         Fackler, administrator with the will annexed of William Terrill,
         deceased. Returned into court 27th September 1830.

pp.   Will of GILLISON MORRIS. (also as Gilson Morris) .. I give
271-   unto my beloved wife, Polly Morris, all my estate both real and
272   personal and after the death of my wife, my will is my estate
         should be divided between my two sons, Aden C, Morris and James
         L. Morris .. I give to my eldest son, Aden C. Morris, forty acres
         of land .. and the balance of the land where I now live to my son,
         James Lewis Morris .. I give to Mary Ann H. Bailey, the bed she
         now lies on and at my wife's death, a cow and calf .. one hundred
         dollars to be taken out of Aden C. Morris' part .. appoint my two

sons, Aden C. Morris and James L. Morris, executors .. this 28th day of February 1830.
Teste   (signed)
    Thomas A. Dempsy,   Gillison Morris
    Elijah Hawkins,   Lewis Dempsey,
    Alexander McClary.
    At a court held .. 27th September 1830 .. will proved by the oaths of Thomas A. Dempsy and Elijah Hawkins, witnesses thereto and ordered to be recorded. (In this entry is where the name "Gilson Morris" appears.)

pp.   A list of property of VALENTINE WINSLOW, deceased, appraised
272- this 24th day of September 1830 by Isaac Goodall, Joseph Eddins,
274   William Sims .. total value $3089.22½. Returned into court 25th October 1830.

pp.   An inventory taken at the house of Michael L. Eheart on the
274- 31st day of August 1830 of the property of SIMEON GRAVES, dec'd,
275   which property was delivered by Michael L. Eheart to William Dulaney as curator .. signed by William Dulaney. Returned into court 22nd November 1830.

p.   Appraisal of the estate of TANDY BOWCOCK, deceased, on the
275   1st day of October 1830 .. total value $220.44¼ .. appraisers Joseph Williams, H. Houck, William Martin. Returned into court 22nd November 1830.

pp.   Will of JOHN SHIFLETT SENR. .. I give to my beloved wife,
275- Susanner, the tract of land that I bought of Thomas Snow, the
276   tract whereon I now live, during her life and after her death .. land to be sold .. money divided .. the lower tract of land to be sold .. the land I bought of John Snow under the Rocky Mountain whereon William Knight now lives shall be sold .. the balance of my mountain land in Orange and Albemarle .. should be sold .. I desire that my son, Coward Shiflett, shall stand the executor of all my estate and my wife, Susanner .. (will dated in 1829).
Witnesses   (signed - his mark)
    Jonathan Haney   John Shiflett
    John Mallory, Robert G. Douglass
    At a court held .. 22nd November 1830 .. proved by the oaths of John Mallory and Robert G. Douglass, witnesses and ordered to be recorded .. Cowherd Shiflett, the executor therein named .. with Thomas Davis, his security .. bond in penalty of fifteen hundred dollars .. certificate granted him for obtaining a probate .. (Will mentions "my children" but names only Cowherd Shiflett.)

pp.   An inventory and appraisement of the estate of GEORGE BINGHAM,
277- deceased, 3rd day of October 1829 .. value not totalled .. apprai-
279   sers Charles Parrott, James Early, Joab Early. Returned into court 22nd November 1830.

pp.   Will of RICHARD H. TALIAFERRO. .. I appoint my friend, Wil-
279- liam Quarles, and my son, George, executors .. my will they shall
280   not be required to give security .. I give and devise to my son, Peachy Taliaferro .. all the land I own on the south side of the turnpike which I purchased partly of Thomas B. Adams and the

balance of said son, the latter being a part of a piece of land
he held in right of his wife .. all the rest of my estate not devised be held together for the term of four years from the time
of my death and the profits thereof applied to the support and
education of all my children except Peachy, unless my son, William
Taliaferro, or one of my daughters shall attain the age of twenty
one or marry before the expiration of the four years .. in which
event .. the child is to have one sixth part in value of all my
personal estate .. equally divided between my sons, George and
William Taliaferro and my daughter .. at that time I direct that
the land I bought of the executors of Doctor Charles Taylor called
Elmwood be sold .. I give and devise to be equally divided between
my son, William Taliaferro and my four daughters .. this 12th day
of August 1829.
In the presence of   (signed)
    Reynolds Chapman, Hugh S. Darby   Richd. H. Taliaferro
    At a court held .. 22nd November 1830 .. proved by the oaths of
(the witnesses) and ordered to be recorded.
    At a court held .. 27th December 1830 .. on the motion of George
G. Taliaferro, an executor therein named .. bond in penalty of
thirty thousand dollars (without security) .. certificate granted
him for obtaining a probate thereof in due form.

pp.   An inventory and appraisement of the estate of MARY COOPER,
280-   deceased, taken 13th day of November 1830 .. 100 acres of land on
282   the north side of the Fredericksburg road adjoining lands of
        Thomas Lancaster at $2 per acre .. 219 3/4 acres of land adjoining
        the lands of Jonathan Lancaster and Hezekiah Ellis at $2.50 per
        acre .. no total value shown .. appraisers Richard Richards Junr.,
        Jonathan Lancaster, Ezekiah Richards. Owen Cooper, executor, cer-
        tified inventory to be a true inventory of the estate of Mary
        Cooper. Returned into court 24th January 1831.

pp.   An inventory of the property belonging to the estate of JAMES
282-   JARRELL SENR., deceased, taken March 31st 1830 .. value not to-
284   talled .. signed (his mark) James Jarrell Junr., administrator
        of James Jarrell, deceased .. appraisers David Sholes, Joel Jar-
        rell, James Warren. Returned into court 24th January 1831.

pp.   Sale of the estate of JAMES JARRELL ..some purchasers ..
284-   James Jarrell Junr., John Jarrell Junr., Jere. Jarrell Junr.,
287   James Warren, John Jarrell Senr., James P. Sims, William Jarrell,
        Joseph Jarrell Junr., Hinkel Jarrell, David Sholes, Louisa Jarrell,
        Mary Jarrell, Pemberton Sims, Rhoda Jarrell, Fountain Jarrell,
        Jos. Taylor. Returned into court 24th January 1831.

pp.   An inventory and appraisement of the estate of WASHINGTON
287-   REYNOLDS, deceased, taken this 12th day of November 1830 .. (a
291   considerable portion of this inventory marked "dower.") ..
        value not totalled .. Philip S. Reynolds, administrator.. apprai-
        sal made 12th November 1830 by appraisers Reuben Lindsay, John W.
        Sale, George Quisenberry. Returned into court 24th January 1831.

pp.   Will of THOMAS THORNTON. .. my will that my personal estate
291-   of every description be kept together until my youngest child
292   comes of age or marries so that my wife may raise and educate my

children in the best manner she can out of my estate, but in the
event of my children quitting to live with my wife or marries, it
is my wish that my wife give each of them some of the personal
property which they are to account for at the division of my estate .. upon the division of my estate, I wish my wife to have
one third part .. I appoint my loving wife, Elizabeth, my whole
executrix .. this 26th day of January 1831.
In the presence of   (signed - his mark)
    Richard Waugh Senr.,   Thomas Thornton
    Gowry Waugh, William A. Moore,
    Reuben T. Clarke.
    At a court held .. 28th February 1831 .. proved by the oaths of
Gowry Waugh and William A. Moore, witnesses thereto and ordered
to be recorded.
    At a court held .. 28th March 1831 .. on the motion of Elizabeth
Thornton .. with Gowry Waugh and John Sleet, her securities .. bond
in the penalty of one thousand dollars .. certificate is granted
her for obtaining a probate thereof in due form.

pp.   Will of FRANCES BOSTON, wife of John Boston .. my will that
292-   the estate coming to me from my Father's estate, George Petty,
293   deceased, should be equally divided among all my children without
distinction, and should my deceased Father, George Petty, title
to the land in the state of Kentucky be good, I wish my children
to have my interest .. appoint my sons, John Boston and Alexander
Boston, executors .. this 13th day of June 1830.
Teste   (signed)
    Alex. Waugh,   Frances Boston
    James Clarke, R.T. Clarke.
    At a court held .. 28th February 1831 .. will proved by the
oaths of James Clarke and R. T. Clarke and ordered to be recorded
.. on the motion of Alexander Boston, one of the executors therein
named, with John Boston Junr., Alexander Waugh, Gowry Waugh and
Lancelot Burrus, his securities .. bond in the penalty of six hundred dollars .. certificate granted him for obtaining a probate ..

pp.   The estate of WILSON COLEMAN, deceased, in account with
294-   James L. Coleman, administrator .. examined and settled 1st of
296   February 1831 by Wm. Stevens, John Terrill, James Nelson Junr.
Returned into court 28th February 1831.

pp.   Will of ANN MINOR. .. I give and bequeath to my daughters,
296-   Sarah Elizabeth Anderson and Sarah Gilmer, my carriage and horses
298   and James H. Ellis' bond to me dated 9th of June 1817 for the sum
of six hundred dollars .. as I have purchased the interest of
said negroes of Charles M. Meriwether, who is the sole heir of my
late daughter, Ann Meriwether .. I give and bequeath to my granddaughter, Lucy Ann Gilmer, my curtain bedstead and the bed and
furniture thereto belonging .. to my granddaughter, Ann McScales,
my other bedstead .. also my mahogany tea tables .. to Sarah Elizabeth Anderson my portrait painting likeness of my brother, William,
with a request that she will leave it her son, Overton C. Anderson
.. I do not think proper and therefore I have not and do not mean
to give my grandson, Charles M. Meriwether, any part or portion of

my property or estate not because of the want of natural affection
for him or for his deceased mother but because I think he has been
suitably provided for by my husband, his late grandfather .. appoint my son in law, Dr. John Gilmer, and my grandson, Overton C.
Anderson, executors .. request they not be held to give security
.. this 15th day of October 1830.
                                   (signed) Ann Minor

   Codicil. I have never charged anything for the free use of my
plantation or the utensils belonging thereto .. enjoyed by my
son during his life and his family for which reason I have bequeathed more to my daughters .. I give and bequeath all my other
property and estate of every description not herein disposed of
to be equally divided between my daughters, Sarah Elizabeth Anderson and Sarah Gilmer, and the children of my deceased son,
Dabney Minor ..   Ann Minor, November 1st 1830.

   Codicil. I give and bequeath to the trustees of the Episcopal
Theological Society at Alexandria the sum of five hundred dollars
for the purpose of said seminary. Witness my hand and seal this
22nd day of February 1831 -- Ann Minor.

   At a court held .. 25th April 1831 .. will with codicils offered
for probate by Overton C. Anderson, an executor therein named and
there being no subscribing witnesses thereto, Fountain Meriwether
and Benjamin Coleman were sworn .. whereupon said writing was
established as the last will and testament of Ann Minor and ordered to be recorded, and on the motion of Overton C. Anderson ..
bond without security in the penalty of ten thousand dollars ..
certificate granted him for obtaining probate thereof ..

pp.   Will of JOHN SHELOR SENR. .. I give and bequeath to my daugh-
298-   ter, Catharine Jones' children, namely Evaline and the other a
299   girl unnamed .. a tract of land containing about three hundred and
twenty acres .. to my daughter, Rachel .. a tract of land lying
on turkey ridge containing one hundred twenty acres .. to my daughter, Nancy Powel .. two negroes and six hundred dollars .. to my
son, John Shelor .. tract of land on which I now live containing
three hundred twenty acres .. adjoining tract given heirs of
Catharine Jones .. all the rest .. not herein before particularly
disposed of .. equally divided among my several children, Rachel
Shelor, Nancy Powel and John Shelor and the heirs of Catharine
Jones .. I give Catharine Jones five hundred dollars as her por-
tion of my estate .. appoint my friend, George W. Price, and my
son, John Shelor, executors .. this 30th day of November 1825 ..
In the presence of   (signed - his mark)
   Daniel Miller, John N. Sorrille,   John Shelor
   James G. Blakey, James Melone.
   At a court held .. 25th April 1831 .. proved by the oaths of
Daniel Miller and John N. Sorrille, witnesses thereto and ordered
to be recorded.
   At a court held .. 23rd May 1831 .. on motion of John Shelor ..
with William Dulaney, his security .. bond in the penalty of five
thousand dollars .. certificate was granted him for obtaining
a probate thereof in due form.

pp.
299-
300

Will of DELILAH COOPER. .. I give and bequeath to my nephew, James G. Lancaster, my feather bed and furniture .. also fifty dollars to be paid him at the death of all my sisters that is now single .. I lend to my sister, Susannah Cooper, all the property I may die possessed .. equally divided among all my brothers and sisters, that is to say or their children, William Cooper, James Cooper, Benjamin Cooper, Owen Cooper, Polly Webb and Sarah Lancaster .. appoint Owen Cooper the executor .. this 21st day of January 1831 ..   (signed)
Teste   Delilah Cooper
   Richard Richards, Reuben Thompson
  At a court held .. 25th April 1831 .. proved by the oaths of (witnesses) and ordered to be recorded .. on the motion of Owen Cooper .. with Richard Richards, his security .. bond in the penalty of one thousand dollars .. certificate granted him for obtaining a probate in due form.

pp.
300-
301

Will of MARGARET DARE. .. I lend to my daughter, Elizabeth, the only child I have, one feather bed and furniture belonging thereto and sixty pounds in cash .. if she should have no children at her death, it is my will that my sister, Sally Davis and her son, John, shall have the same equally divided between them .. the above money mentioned is left in due from William Bell of Orange County as will be shown by his bond in the hands of John Goodall, my uncle, whom I appoint my executor .. if he will not act or should die before this trust shall be executed, it is my wish that my uncle, Isaac Goodall, shall act in his place .. this 20th day of April 1830 ..
Witnesses   (signed – her mark)
  Henry Bibb, D.H.,   Margaret Dare
  John Bibb, D.H., William Martin, Wm Foster.
  At a court held .. 23rd May 1831 .. proved by the oaths of Henry Bibb, D.H. and William Martin, witnesses thereto and ordered to be recorded .. and John Goodall .. being dead and Isaac Goodall by note addressed to the court refused the executorship on the motion of Jacob Spinkle (the husband of a daughter of the dec'd) who made oath .. with John Davis, who verified upon oath his sufficiency, his security .. bond in the penalty of six hundred dollars .. granted letters of administration on the estate of Margaret Dare with the will annexed ..

pp.
301-
302

An inventory and appraisement of the estate of JAMES HERNDON, deceased, as taken on the ninth day of January 1830 .. total value $635.45 .. made by appraisers John Wright, Owen Cooper, Thos. Row. Certified as a true inventory by Richard Richards, administrator of James Herndon, dec'd. Returned into court 23rd May 1831.

pp.
302-
303

List of property belonging to the estate of SAML. W. VASS, deceased, appraised by Thompson Cockerill, Ichabod Mallory, Thomas Throop May 21st 1831 .. total value $93.00 .. G. Ballard, administrator. Returned into court 23rd May 1831.

pp.   Benjamin Sanders, administrator to the estate of FRANCIS
304-   JONES, deceased .. estate value $2369.86 .. made 19th March 1830
305   by appraisers John Gibson, Jno. C. Gordon, Richd. Richards, Edmd.
         Row. Returned into court 24th May 1831.

pp.   Wm. G. Payne with the estate of WM. PAYNE, deceased .. value
304-   totalled $260.22 .. examined and settled 24th May 1831 by Richard
306   M. Chapman, James G. Blakey, J. W. Fry. Returned into court 26th
         May 1831.

pp.   A list of the appraisement of JOHN SHIFLETT, deceased, Decem-
306-   ber the 7th 1830 .. value not totalled. Returned into court 27th
308   June 1831.

pp.   Will of JOSEPH WILLIAMS. .. I give to my wife, Rozamond, during
308-   her natural life, one third part of all my estate .. and after her
309   decease to my children .. whereas I am informed that under the
         present law of this Commonwealth that it is prohibited for a widow
         from removing her property she holds for life under her write of
         dower out of this state, and having sold my land where I now reside
         and believing it will be to the interest of my wife and children
         (should I die) to remove to a new country, it is my will and desire
         that she will be at liberty to move the property she may possess
         under this will to any part she may see cause .. I give to my son,
         Francis, one dollar considering that I have heretofore given him
         more than I am able to give to my younger children .. I give to
         Michael Ansell, who married my daughter, Nancy, one dollar .. the
         residue of my estate to be equally divided among my three children,
         that is to say, my daughter Ann Williams, my son, Thomas Williams
         and my son Buford Sims Williams .. appoint my beloved wife, Roza-
         mond Williams, and my son, Thomas Williams, my executrix and execu-
         tor .. this 16th day of August 1825.
         Witnesses   (signed)
             Valentine Johnson,   Joseph Williams
           Robert Mansfield, John Williams, Wm. Martin.
             At a court held .. 27th June 1831 .. proved by the oaths of John
         Williams and William Martin, witnesses thereto, and ordered to be
         recorded.
             At a court held .. 26th September 1831 .. Thomas Williams, an
         executor therein named .. with Bluford S. Williams, his security ..
         bond in the penalty of five thousand dollars .. certificate granted
         him for obtaining a probate thereof in due form.

pp.   Appraisal of the estate of JAMES MASON, deceased .. value
309-   totalled $443.45½ .. made the 15th day of May 1822 by Benjamin
310   Sanders, William B. Webb, Philemon Richards. Returned into court
         25th July 1831.

pp.   Will of WILLIAM T. BURRUS. .. do make and publish this my
310-   last will and testament the 9th day of June 1831 .. I give to my
313   son, Joseph Burrus, the trust of land upon which he now resides
         which I purchased of Henry Clark .. I give to my son, Thomas Bur-
         rus, the tract of land which I purchased of George Quisenberry
         adjoining the lands of Richard Rawlings and others .. to my son,
         Lancelot Burrus, the tract of land called Atkins' tract adjoining

the lands of Thomas Woolfolk, Claiborne Graves and others .. I also give him at the death of Elizabeth Arnold the tract of land now held by said Elizabeth .. reserving to my wife, Martha Burrus, the right to take from the tract called Atkins timber and fine wood for the plantation .. I give to my daughter, Emily Quisenberry .. to my daughter, Harriet Moore .. to my daughter, Jane Burrus .. to my daughter, Elizabeth Burrus .. I loan to my beloved wife, Martha Burrus, all my estate which I have not heretofore disposed of upon the condition that my daughters, Jane Burrus and Elizabeth Burrus, and my sons, George Burrus, William Burrus and Robert Burrus, shall be maintained and supported .. if George shall be trouble-some, I wish an out house to be put up for him so he may not molest the family .. unto my five daughters, Nancy Frazer, Emily Quisen-berry, Harriet Moore, Jane Burrus and Elizabeth Burrus, the mill formerly owned by Nelson and Coleman .. unto my son, Robert B. Burrus, the tract of land upon which I reside containing five hundred acres .. upon trust that he shall maintain George Burrus and William Burrus so long as they live and shall maintain and support his sisters, Jane and Elizabeth, so long as they remain single .. appoint my son, Lancelot Burrus, my son in law, William S. Frazer, and my son, Robert B. Burrus, executors .. this 9th day of June 1831 ..

Witnesses   (signed)
    Thomas Coleman   Wm. T. Burrus
    John M. Goodwin, Robert Terrill Jr.

Codicil. reduces amount of money willed to daughters .. and that my son, George, shall not be furnished with any ardent spirits. Made the 16th day of June 1831. (Signed) Wm. T. Burrus in the presence of Reynolds Chapman, Thos. Coleman and Wm. Campbell.

At a court held .. 25th July 1831 .. proved by oaths of Thomas Coleman and Robert Terrill .. and ordered to be recorded.

At a court held .. 24th October 1831 .. on the motion of William S, Frazer, an executor named therein .. with Hezekiah Quisenberry, Lancelot Burrus and Thomas Burrus, his securities .. bond in the penalty of twelve thousand dollars .. certificate granted him for obtaining a probate thereof in due form.

pp. 314-315
Frances Peacher, administrator to the estate of WM PEACHER .. settled 3rd April 1831 by Thos. Row, Edmd. Row, George Mason, Benj. Sanders. Returned into court 25th July 1831.

pp. 314-317
Benjamin Sanders, Executor, to the estate of JOHN WRIGHT, deceased .. settled by Thos. Row, George Mason, Edmd. Row. Returned into court 25th July 1831.

pp. 316-317
The estate of WM. PEACHER to James Coleman, administrator .. settled by Thos. Row, Benj. Sanders, Geo. Mason, Edmd. Row. Returned into court 25th July 1831.

pp. 316-319
Henry Fackler, administrator of the estate of WILLIAM TERRILL, deceased .. settled by Wm. W. Reynolds, John T. Thornton on 6th August 1831. Returned into court 23rd August 1831.

pp.   Tandy Collins, administrator (de bonis non) on the estate of
318-   JAMES SCOTT (dec'd) with the will annexed and also on the estate
322   of MILDRED SCOTT, dec'd .. examined and settled 15th July 1831 by
          Reuben Lindsay, Benj. Hume, Edmd. Row. Returned into Court 23rd
          August 1831.

p.   Appraisement of slaves and other personal property of EDWIN
322   NICHOLS, deceased, on the premises occupied by John Nichols ..
          value totalled $680 for three slaves and a large and a small still
          .. made 20th November 1830 by appraisers Anthony Thornton, John
          Miller, Thomas S. Thornton. Returned into court 22nd August 1831.

pp.   An account of the sale made of the estate of FRANCES BURNLEY,
323-   dec'd, on the 5th day of August 1825 .. also on the 5th of Decem-
327   ber 1826. Returned into court 26th September 1831.

pp.   An account of sales of the estate of MILDRED FARISH, deceased,
327-   made by James Farish on the 22nd day of December 1826 belonging
329   to the heirs of Thomas Farish, dec'd .. James Farish, Emily T.
          Farish and John Farish among purchasers .. William W. Jones, ad-
          ministrator. Returned into court 26th September 1831.

pp.   An inventory and a list of the names of those who purchased
329-   and the amount of the estate of MARY COOPER, deceased, as sold on
333   the 23rd and 24th days of November 1830 .. some purchasers were
          Susan Cooper and sisters; Owen Cooper; James Taylor; Benjamin
          Wright .. the whole amount of Mary Cooper's estate, $655.34.
          Richard Richards Jr., clerk of the sale. Owen Cooper, executor
          of Mary Cooper. Returned into court 26th September 1831.

pp.   An inventory and a list of names of those who purchased and
334-   the amount of the estate of JAMES COOPER, deceased, as sold on the
336   24th day of November 1830 .. some purchasers were Vivion Quisen-
          berry, Reuben Thompson, Philip Reynolds, Josiah White, Hezekiah
          Ellis, Rachel Cooper, Nancy Cooper, Johnathon Johnson, Susan
          Cooper and sisters, Benjamin Cooper, Owen Cooper and others ..
          whole amount of James Cooper's estate sold $4284.42½. Richard
          Richards Jr. Clerk of the sale. Benjamin Cooper and Owen Cooper,
          administrators of James Cooper, dec'd. Returned into court 26th
          September 1831.

pp.   Amount of sale at public vendue of a part of the personal es-
336-   tate of JOHN TAYLOR, deceased, at one year's credit which came to
341   the hands of John M. Taylor to be administered. Sale on the 26th
          and 27th December 1828 .. also on the 24th January 1829 .. among
          many other entries are .. Thomas Scott, tract of land 1049½ acres
          late residence of said John Taylor, dec'd, at 12 dollars per acre;
          $4000 paid 10th Jany 1829; $4000 payable 1st Jany 1830; $2297
          payable 1st Jany 1831; $2297 payable 1st Jany 1832 amounting to
          $12594.00 .. total amount of sale, $15,174.00 .. J. M. Taylor,
          administrator with the will annexed of John Taylor, deceased.
          Returned into court 26th September 1831.

pp.   Account of John M. Taylor, administrator with the will annexed
342-   of JOHN TAYLOR, deceased, 1st January 1829 .. settled in July 1830
345   by Richd. M. Chapman, James Shepherd, Baldwin Taliaferro. Re-
          turned into court 26th September 1831.

pp.
344-
345
John Wright to the estate of JOHN FAULCONER, deceased .. settled 31st December 1830 by Edmd. Row, Benj. Sanders, Richard Richards, Richard Richards Junr. Returned into court 26th September 1831.

pp.
346-
349
The estate of WILLIAM HANDCOCK, deceased, in account with Lewis R. Bradley, administrator with the will annexed .. by sum settled by Benj. Hancock out of his portion of the estate being debt paid by testator to Barbour .. the sum of $2735.81 was received by the administrator and $2293.35 paid out .. settled by W. D. Clark, William Smith, Reuben Conway. Returned into court 26th September 1831.

pp.
348-
349
The estate of WILLIAM HERNDON, deceased, to James Herndon, administrator .. settled by John Wright, Thos. Row, Edmd. Row the 14th day of May 1830.

pp.
348-
351
The estate of WILLIAM HERNDON, deceased, with Richard Richards, administrator de bonis non .. widow's thirds or dower paid to her, $341.67 .. $683.34 to be divided into 7 parts, each legatees' part, $97.62 .. settled 14th May 1830 by John Wright, Thos. Row, Edmd. Row, who also certified each legatee had received their part. Returned into court 26th September 1831.

pp.
350-
351
The estate of JAMES HERNDON, deceased, to Richard Richards, administrator .. cash received from estate of William Herndon, dec'd, after taking out the amount of property purchased by James Herndon in his own right at the sale being his legacy and in right of George Herndon .. settled 14th May 1830 by John Wright, Thos. Row, Edmd. Row.

pp.
350-
353
The estate of WILLIAM LEE, deceased, in account with Weedon Sleet, administrator de bonis non with will annexed .. mentioned in account Patsy Lee and Abner Lee .. and $60 retained in hands of administrator for Sarah F. Berry, that being near her portion of said testator's estate .. settled 26th March 1831 by Joshua Willis, John Newman Senr., Alex. Waugh. Returned into court 26th September 1831.

pp.
352-
355
The estate of JOHN MELONE, deceased, in account with James Melone, administrator .. report that James Melone, said administrator, paid £ 44.16.7 more than came into his hands .. settled by William Dulaney, Thos. Davis, George Price. Returned into court 26th September 1831.

pp.
354-
355
Examination and settlement of John Sanders' administration of the estate of ELIZABETH SANDERS, deceased .. the whole amount of the said estate which came into the hands of the administrator appears to be $2247.93¼ .. made by Geo. Grasty, Thomas Graves, Tandy Collins, Thos. Robinson. Returned into court 26th September 1831.

pp.
356-
359
The estate of ROBERT OSBORNE, deceased, in account with Robert Cave, administrator .. examined and settled by Minor Rucker, Geo. Stephens, Pleasant Carpenter. Returned into court 26th September 1831.

pp.   An account of sales of the estate of THOMAS WHITELAW, deceased
358-   .. among purchasers .. David, Alexander, James and N. Whitelaw ..
359   total amount of the sale $3533.16. Returned into court 26th Sep-
         tember 1831.

pp.   The estate of THOMAS WHITELAW, deceased, in account with James
360-   Whitelaw, executor of said Whitelaw .. paid Willis Marshall his
361   legacy as per will, $400 .. paid eight legatees $350.42 each ..
         Henrico County, May 16, 1830 .. report to Orange Court by Syd.
         Bowles, Mosby Sheppard. Returned into court 26th September 1831.

pp.   Jesse B. Webb, executor to the estate of RICHARD B. WEBB,
360-   examined by Thos. Row, Benj. Hume, Edmd Row .. return of settle-
363   ment returned into court 26th September 1831.

pp.   The estate of JOHN WILLIS, deceased, in account with Robert
362-   Taylor, executor .. cash paid to Mrs. Milly C. Willis, 25 August
374   1811 .. to Mary E. Willis in account of her legacy .. to Mrs. N.
         C. Willis (for same) .. to Dr. Charles Taylor for attendance on
         family .. account covers period 1811-1817 .. settled by William
         Shepherd, Wm. Quarles, Reynolds Chapman. Returned into court
         26th September 1831.

pp.   Will of JOHN SANDERS. .. it is my desire that my wife, Sarah
374-   Sanders, remain upon my farm and plantation whereon I now live
375   during her natural life and have the sole control thereof .. after
         my wife has taken her six (slaves) out may be divided equally
         between my five children .. after my wife's death my whole estate
         to be divided in like manner .. my will and desire that my said
         wife shall be executing, and my son, Hansford T. Sanders, and
         Elhanon Row to be my executors .. this 24th day of March 1831.
         Witnesses   (signed)
             Thos. Row, Edmd. Row   John Sanders
           At a court held .. 24th October 1831 .. proved by the oaths of
         (witnesses) and ordered to be recorded .. on motion of Hansford
         T. Sanders and Elhanon Row, executors .. bond in the penalty of
         five thousand dollars .. Thomas Robinson and Richard Rhoades, his
         securities .. granted certificate for obatining probate ..

pp.   Settlement of Henry G. George's administration account of the
375-   estate of CHURCHILL GEORGE, deceased, made by William Douglass
377   and Charles T. Graves. Returned into court 24th October 1831.

pp.   Will of JAMES COLEMAN. .. it is my wish and desire that my
377-   son, Ambrose Coleman, should have six acres of land off to him
379   adjoining where he now lives so as to include the house he now
         lives in, the rest of his part of my estate I leave in the hands
         of my executor for him to distribute to his family as he may think
         proper and at the death of my said son, Ambrose, to be equally
         divided amongst his children .. to my grandson, Robert Morris,
         son of my daughter, Mary Morris, deceased, the sum of fifty dol-
         lars and no more .. to my grandson, James Coleman, son of Ambrose
         Coleman .. my children should be made as equally as they can and
         in as much as my son, James Coleman of Kentucky, has not received
         as much by one hundred dollars .. negroes divided amongst my
         following children, to wit, Nancy Faulconer, James Coleman and

Frances Peacher's children, that is to say they are to have their
mother's part .. (money arising from sale of estate divided) among
Nancy Faulconer, James Coleman, Ambrose Coleman's children, Frances Peacher's children and my daughter, Elizabeth Hawkins (her
husband, James Hawkins) .. in regard to the children of my deceased daughter, Mary Morris of Kentucky, as they have all except
Robert Morris, which I have given a legacy, joined a religious
society called the Shaking Quakers of that state and it being a
fixed rule of that society to make all the members give to the
head of the society all their property, I do not wish any of my
estate to them, therefore I give to my grandchildren who have
joined the society of Shaking Quakers nothing... I nominate my
son, James Coleman, and my friend, Philip Mallory, my executors
.. this 11th day of August 1831.

Attest   (signed)
    George Scott   James Coleman
    John Graves, James Graves

    At a court held .. 24th October 1831 .. proved by the oaths of
(witnesses) and ordered to be recorded .. and thereupon Philip
Mallory, one of the executors appointed .. came into court and
refused .. and James Coleman, the other executor, being absent
from the Commonwealth, the court appointed Edmund Row curator of
the estate .. who with Thomas Row and Richard Richards, his securities .. bond in the penalty of six thousand dollars ..

    At a court held 28th November 1831 .. James Coleman .. made oath
thereto according to law and together with Nancy Faulconer,
Joseph W. Peacher, Richard Richards, Anthony Tinder and Ambrose
Coleman, his securities .. bond in the penalty of six thousand
dollars .. certificate granted him for obtaining a probate thereof ..

pp.   Appraisal of the slaves and personal estate of WILLIAM PEACHER,
380-   deceased .. value totalled $4191.37½ of which $3425 was for slaves
381   .. made 14th December 1830 by Thos. Row. Geo. Mason, Benj. Sanders
        and on the same day appraised the estate of FRANCES PEACHER, de-
        ceased, total value $1830. Returned into court 28th November 1831.

pp.   An inventory of the goods and chattels of HENRY MITCHELL, de-
382-   ceased, taken this 11th day of June 1831 .. value totalled $141.12½
383   .. made 26th November 1830 by Edmund Jones, Matthew Lamb, Charles
        Parrott. Returned into court 28th November 1831.

pp.   John Claybrooke, administrator in account with the estate of
384-   MALCOLM HART .. examined and settled by James C. Dickinson, Charles
386   Y. Kimbrough. Returned into court 28th November 1831.

pp.   The estate of JOHN LEATHERS, deceased, in account with Baldwin
386-   Taliaferro, late Sheriff of Orange County to whom was committed
388   for administration with the will annexed the estate of John Lea-
        thers, deceased .. examined and settled 18th October 1831 by James
        Shepherd, Cudden Davis, Thos. A. Robinson. Returned into court
        28th November 1831.

pp.   Daniel White, executor of WILLIAM WHITE, deceased .. examined
388-   and settled by Anthony Thornton, Geo. Stephens, Minor Rucker.
391   Returned into court 28th November 1831.

pp.
391-
392

Will of MARY BEAZLEY, widow and relict of Bennett Beazley, deceased. .. I give to my sister, Sarah Long (for the good will and affection I have for her) all my stock of every kind .. appoint George Deane my lawful executor .. this 12th day of December 1831.

In the presence of   (signed – her mark)
Reuben Deane, Armistead Long   Mary Beazley

At a court held .. 26th December 1831 .. proved by the oaths of the witnesses and ordered to be recorded .. George Deane by note addressed to the court refused the executorship, and on the motion of James Long .. together with Armistead Long and Reuben Deane, his securities .. bond in the penalty of $600 .. granted letters of administration on the estate of Mary Beazley, deceased.

pp.
392-
393

The estate of RICHARD C. WEBB, deceased, to Jesse B. Webb .. executor account examined by Thomas Row, Benj. Hume, Edmd. Row and sworn 19th November 1831. Returned into court 26th December 1831.

pp.
393-
396

Appraisement of the estate of WILLIAM T. BURRUS, deceased .. value totalled $9095.06 .. made by appraisers Wm. Stevens, Jonathan Graves, Geo. W. Morton and sworn 19th day of December 1831. Returned into court 26th December 1831.

pp.
396-
397

The following is an inventory and appraisement of the property jointly owned by Susan Cooper, Rachel Cooper, Nancy Cooper, Rosey Cooper, Frances Cooper and DELILAH COOPER, deceased, as taken the 30th day of December 1831 .. Delilah Cooper, dec'd, is entitled to one sixth part of the total value of $1733.75 or $288.95 5/6, plus one bed and furniture her own property valued at $20 .. made by appraisers Jonathan Lancaster, Richard Richards Junr., Edward Hobday and sworn 30th December 1831. Returned into court 23rd January 1832.

pp.
398-
400

An inventory and appraisement of the estate of AMBROSE LEE, deceased, taken the first day of October 1831 .. total value $1235.43 .. made by appraisers Reuben Lindsay, John W. Sale, Wm. Cosby, Brooke Simco and sworn the 17th November 1831. Certified as a true inventory by Washington Hutchinson, administrator. Returned into court 23rd January 1832.

pp.
400-
404

Mr. Joseph Lee to Mr. A. LEE'S Estate .. some purchasers .. Weedon Sleet, William Webster, Jerome B. Collins, Daniel M. Smith, Miss Nancy Collins, Larkin Herndon, William Cosby, Samuel Daniel, Miss Lucy Clarke, Samuel Boswell, Mrs. Susan Lee, Dugald Campbell, Harrison Somerville, Walter Gambrill .. the amount of the perishable estate, $357.12½ .. clerk of the sale, Jerome A. Collins. Returned into court 23rd January 1832.

pp.
405-
406

A list of the personal estate of HENRY J. HERNDON, deceased, appraised at the house of Henry Herndon Senr. on Friday the 25th November 1831 .. valued at $246.87 .. by appraisers Robt. Mansfield, Robt. W. Booking, Robt. Cave and sworn 28th November 1831. Returned into court 23rd January 1832.

pp.
406-
407
Reuben Davis, administrator to the estate of JOHN DAVIS, deceased .. amount of sale, $663.29; paid by administrator, $211.14 .. balance $452.15 .. settled by Thos. Row, Richd. Richards, Ezekiah Richards and sworn the 12th day of September 1829 .. Returned into court 24th May 1831.

pp.
408-
410
Owen Cooper, Executor to the estate of MARY COOPER, deceased .. amount received by the Executor, $652.73½ to be divided by twelve legatees or $54.47½ each .. settled by Richard Richards, Vivion Quisenberry, Richard Richards Junr., Benjamin Wright and sworn 29th December 1831. The Estate of MARY COOPER, deceased, to Owen Cooper, Executor .. shows the breakdown of $352.54½, which had been deducted from monies received by the Executor. Returned into court 27th February 1832.

pp.
410-
411
Owen Cooper and Benjamin Cooper, administrators to the Estate of JAMES COOPER, deceased .. the amount in the hands of the administrators for division among twelve legatees, $3619.72½, or $301.64 1/12 each .. settled 29th December 1831 by Richard Richards, Vivion Quisenberry, R. Richards Junr., Benjamin Wright .. also an accounting of $248.70 deducted from income to the estate before the division as well as $301.64 cash paid to Jesse B. Webb in right of his wife, Mary, who was Mary Cooper. Returned into court 27th February 1832.

pp.
412-
413
The Executor to the estate of Capt. JAMES BURTON, deceased, and a list of sales, cash and bonds on hand .. totals $825.93, and is balanced by the same amount in credits .. these accounts of George Stephens, administrator of the estate of James Burton, deceased, examined by George W. Price, John Nichols, Benjamin W. White and sworn 21st December 1831. Returned into court 27th February 1832.

pp.
414-
417
List of sales of the perisahable property belonging to the estate of JOHN MOORE, dec'd, made the 18th November 1830 and sold on a credit of twelve months .. sales amount totalled $1052.57½ .. certified by James B. Moore, administrator of John Moore, dec'd. Returned into court 27th February 1832.

pp.
417-
418
A list of the property sold at the home of John Dolin belonging to the estate of JOHN LUCAS, deceased, on the 9th December 1824 .. sales amount totalled $579.95. Returned into court 26th March 1832.

pp.
418-
420
A list of the appraisement of the estate of JOHN OFFIELD, deceased, made the 6th day of November 1830 .. total value $1748.62½ .. given 6th November 1830 by appraisers William Dulaney, James Melone, William Melone, Robt. Miller. Returned into court 26th March 1832.

p.
420
A list of the Bonds that came into my hand as Executor of JAMES FARISH, deceased .. submitted by Wm. W. Jones, Executor. Returned into court 26th March 1832.

pp.
420-
421
An inventory and appraisement of JASPER HAYNES, deceased, taken at the home of John Beadles this 17th day of February 1829 .. value not totalled .. given 17th February 1829 by appraisers Catlett Conway, Isaac Goodall, James P. Sims. Returned into court 26th March 1832.

pp.   An inventory and appraisement of the estate of JAMES COOPER,
421-   deceased, taken the 13th day of November 1830 .. value not totalled
422   .. given 13th November 1830 by appraisers Richard Richards Junr.,
            Jonathan Lancaster, Ezekiah Richards .. certified a true inventory
            by Benjamin Cooper and Owen Cooper, administrators. Returned into
            court 26th March 1832.

pp.   An appraisal of the estate of BENJAMIN WINSLOW, deceased ..
422-   value not totalled .. made by appraisers Reuben Conway, A. Madison,
423   C. C. Macon. Returned into court 26th March 1832.

pp.   An appraisal of the slaves and other personal estate of HARDIN
423-   BOSTON, deceased .. shown to them for appraisement .. valued at
424         $92.47½ .. done 27th July 1831 and sworn before Edmund Henshaw ..
            made by appraisers Valentine Johnson, Robert King, Martin Baker.
            Returned into court 26th March 1832.

pp.   An inventory and appraisement of the estate of NATHANIEL TANDY
424-   taken the 24th day of February 1832 .. total value $458.82½ ..
425   given 27th February 1832 by appraisers William Reynolds, Washing-
            ton Reynolds, William W. Reynolds in accordance with an order of
            the county court of Christian in the state of Kentucky .. (the
            appraisers) made oath before John W. Sale 27th January 1825.
            Henry Tandy Senr., acting attorney in fact for Jackson Tandy, Exe-
            cutor of Nathaniel Tandy, deceased, estate. Returned into Orange
            Court 26th March 1832.

pp.   Estate of MARY DAVIS, deceased, in account with Cudden Davis,
426-   administrator .. credits and debits balance at $544.10 3/4 ..
427   settled by Richd. M. Chapman, James Shepherd, G. Ballard and
            sworn 24th March 1832. Returned into court 26th March 1832.

pp.   The estate of WM. PEACHER to James Coleman, Executor .. shows
426-   amount in the hands of E. Row as administrator de bonis non of
428   Wm. Peacher, deceased, as $237.19 .. examined and settled 9th
            January 1832 by Philip Mallory, William Hume, Benj. Sanders. Re-
            turned into court 26th March 1832.

pp.   The estate of WILLIAM LUCAS, deceased, in account with John
428-   Ezekial Lucas, administrator .. account begins 21st July 1815
429   through 24th September 1816 .. shows debits of £ 144.7.8 ..
            credits of £ 52.4.11 .. met at house of Ezekial Lucas and settled
            his administrator's account .. sworn 14th August 1821 by Robert
            Cave, T. Bowcock, William Rucker. Returned into court 26th March
            1832.

pp.   An inventory and appraisement of the real and personal estate
429-   of RICHARD H. TALIAFERRO, deceased, of the County of Orange made
434   on the 31st day of December 1830 .. shows 53 negroes valued at
            $11,200 and other personal estate valued at $3215.25, real estate
            directed to be sold, $3557.27 .. total estate value $17,972.50 ..
            made by appraisers Wm. C. Willis, Robert Taylor Jr., Tho. Scott ..
            sworn before Ambrose Madison, justice of the peace, 28th March
            1831 .. certified as correct inventory by George G. Taliaferro,
            Executor. Returned into court 26th March 1832.

pp.   A list of the property sold by Henry Tandy, attorney of Jack-
435-   son Tandy, administrator of NATHL. TANDY, deceased, the 5th of
436   September 1823 .. some purchaers .. Herndon Frazer, John Morton,
         Z. Billingsley, Mary Morton, Thos. Lancaster, Miss A. Tandy,
         Josias White, Edward Stivers, Thos. Brightwell .. amount of the
         first part of the sale, $3362.51 .. James K. Coleman acted as
         clerk to Henry Tandy .. sworn 15th February 1825 before Thos.
         Coleman, justice of the peace of Orange County. Returned into
         court 26th March 1832.

p.   An inventory and appraisement of the property belonging to
437   the estate of ACHILLES BARKSDALE, dec'd, taken the first day of
         October 1830 by Thacker V. Webb, Charles T. Graves and Buckner
         Terrill, commissioners appointed for that purpose .. total value
         of appraised items, $63.72½. Returned into court 26th March 1832.

p.   An appraisement of the negroes of NANCY BOSTON estate December
437   12th 1827 .. Amy and Nancy valued at $300 and $60 respectively ..
         made by appraisers Joshua Willis, Luke Thornton, Weedon Sleet.
         Returned into court 26th March 1832.

pp.   The estate of ROBERT T. MOORE in account with Robert Taylor,
438-   agent for Mary M. Dillard, formerly Mary M. Moore, administratrix
447   of Robert T. Moore, deceased .. James D. Dillard, husband of Mary
         M., late Mary M. Moore, administratrix of Robt. T. Moore paid
         $500 .. administration account of Mary M. Dillard .. and James D.
         Dillard, her husband, settled by Wm. Quarles, Reynolds Chapman,
         Richard M. Chapman and given by them the fifteenth day of July 1820
         .. December 31, 1827 .. William C. Moore and Robert L. Coleman,
         guardians of Edmund C. Moore and Lucy M. Moore, orphans of Robert
         T. Moore, deceased, each to have received in the settlement of
         James D. Dillard's accounts the sum of one hundred and fifty dol-
         lars. Returned into court 26th March 1832.

pp.   An inventory and appraisement of the estate of ANTHONY BERRY,
448-   deceased .. value not totalled .. no appraisers shown. Returned
449   into court 26th March 1832.

pp.   An appraisal of the estate of ANN BOSTON shown to us by the
449-   administrators .. value totalled $1480.50 .. made 14th October
450   1827 by appraisers Joshua Willis, Weedon Sleet, Luke Thornton.
         Returned into court 26th March 1832.

pp.   An inventory and appraisement of the property of JOHN WHITE
450-   SENR., deceased, left in trust to John White Junr., Augustine
451   Gaines and William Watts for the support of Ann Gillasby made
         this 2nd day of July 1831 .. shown by John White Junr., Executor
         total value, $2321.19 .. made by appraisers Michael L. Ehart,
         S. S.Porter, Wm. Porter. Returned into court 26th March 1832.

pp.   Will of EDWARD ANCELL. .. I lend the whole of my estate
451-   both real and personal to my loving wife, Sarah, during her natural
452   life and at her death I lend the land whereon I now live to my
         daughter, Mary, and my son, John Ancell, to be enjoyed by them
         during each of their single state .. the balance of my estate not
         already given or loaned to be sold .. money arising from such sale
         to be equally divided in ten parts .. one part to my daughter, Ann
         Marshall .. to my son, Henry Ancell's children .. to my son, Robert

Ancell .. to my son, Edward Ancell .. to my son, William Ancell's
children .. to my son, Michael Ancell .. to my son, James Ancell
.. to my daughter, Elizabeth Lacy .. to my daughter, Mary Ancell
.. to my son, John Ancell .. my will and desire is after the marriage of my daughter, Mary, and my son, John, the land that I lent
them be sold and divided as hereafter directed .. appoint my sons,
Michael Ancell and John Ancell, whole and sole Executors .. this
25th day of December 1831 ..
Teste   (signed - his mark)
    John Mallory   Edward Ancell
    Charles Parrott, William Catterton
    At a court held .. 26th March 1832 .. proved .. and ordered to
be recorded .. on the motion of Michael and John Ancell .. with
Robert Ancell and William Catterton, their securities .. bond in
the penalty of $2000 .. certificate granted them for obtaining a
probate thereof ..

pp.   Will of JAMES THOMPSON. .. I give and bequeath all my property
452-   of every description soever to my four sisters, Frances, Martha,
453   Jane and Sarah, to be fairly and equally divided between them ..
        I request my friend, Thacker V. Webb, to be my sole executor ..
Teste   (signed)
    Hord Watts   James Thompson
    Codicil. 18th March 1832 .. my father owes me $85.00 and $40 for
the hire of boy, Bill, for the present year. Philip P. Barbour
owes me $150.00 for services to the 20th November 1831 and from
that date to the present date at the same rate.
    At a court held .. 26th March 1832 .. proved .. and ordered to
be recorded .. on the motion of Thacker V. Webb .. with John V.
Webb, his security .. bond in the penalty of $1400 ..

pp.   Will of ABRAHAM EDDINS. .. I give unto my beloved wife (negroes)
453-   during her natural life and at her death I desire them to be sold
455   and the money equally divided among my children, except my son,
        Smith .. (choice of various property to wife) .. after my decease
all my estate not heretofore mentioned shall be sold at public
sale .. balance divided among all my children except James Fontain
and Alfred, who have each had a negro each .. I desire my grandson,
Abraham May Burton Eddins, and my granddaughter, Margaret Eddins,
children of my son, Smith Eddins, shall jointly have an equal share
of my estate with the rest of my children (except the said Smith
Eddins) .. I give to my son, Smith, the sum of one dollars as his
full portion of my estate .. appoint my friends, William Collins
and John N. Sorrille, executors .. this 18th day of February 1832 ..
In the presence of   (signed)
    St. Clair Taylor   Abraham Eddins
    William B. Goodwin, Joseph Eddins
    At a court held .. 26th March 1832 .. proved .. further proved
27th March 1832 .. and ordered to be recorded .. William Collins
and John N. Sorrille, appointed executors, refused .. and Mary
Eddins, the widow .. waived her right of administration .. on the
motion of Alfred Eddins .. with James P. Sims, Richard P. Winslow
and Benjamin W. Beadles, his securities .. bond in the penalty of

ten thousand dollars..

In the margin: At August Court 1848 administration granted to
Alfred Eddins revoked and administration granted to Alfred D.
Almond with will annexed.

pp.   In obedience to three orders of Orange County Court, one to
455-   refer a suit of Ira B. Brown, administrator of William Estes,
456   deceased, against William Estis Jr., one for a distribution of the
bonds arising from the sales of the negroes belonging to the estate of Wm. Estis, dec'd, and one to settle the accounts of Ira
B. Brown, administrator of Wm. Estis, dec'd .. We Thomas Durrett,
James Beazley and Isaac Davis Junr .. find Estis indebted to the
estate for the amount for which he was sued .. the whole amount
of the estate including the bonds for the negroes, $4965.48 ..
charges and claims against the estate, $890.32 .. for distribution
among 12 legatees making the sum for each one, $39.59 2/3, which
sum they have received .. given by commissioners 22nd March 1832.
Returned into court 26th March 1832.

p.   .. we Thomas Durrett, James Early and George Stevens proceeded
456   to sell the negroes of WM. ESTIS, deceased, and report as follows ..
Returned into court 28th March 1832.

pp.   A map of the division of the estate of JOHN MOORE is on page
457-   457 with explanations also following on page 458 .. the plan re-
459   presents the outlines and division of 602 acres and 38 poles of
land lying in the County of Orange of which Capt. John Moore died
seized .. William C. Moore, surveyor .. division made by John W.
Sale, Geo. W. Morton, Thos. Coleman .. names appearing on the plat
.. Lot No. 1, 81 acres, 22 poles, John T. Moore; Lot No. 2, 202
acres, Dower; Lot No. 3, 81 acres, Richard B. Moore; Lot No. 4,
81 acres, Frances T. Moore; Lot No. 5, 78 acres, 2 rood, 8 poles,
Gabriel B. Moore; Lot No. 6, 78 acres, 2 roods, 8 poles, James B.
Moore .. Returned into court 29th March 1832.

pp.   Division of the personal estate of Capt. JOHN MOORE, deceased,
459-   of Orange County .. shows a division of the slaves into 5 lots ..
461   in consequence of the resignation of William C. Moore, one of the
legatees to any part of the slaves belonging to the said estate
.. given the 4th December 1830 by John W. Sale, Wm. W. Reynolds,
Thos. Coleman. Returned into Court 29th March 1832.

pp.   The estate of FRANCIS JONES, deceased .. paid Mary Jones,
462-   Milly Jones, Reubin Gaines, C. Payne and Ruddy Hawkins thirteen
463   dollars each in the house at the death of Fr. Jones .. in the hands
of Benjamin Sanders, administrator of the estate of Fr. Jones,
$1537.92 .. settlement made by John Gibson, Richard Richards,
Edmd Row and given 29th March 1832. Court 23rd April 1832.

pp.   James Coleman, executor to the estate of JAMES COLEMAN, deceased,
462-   .. property sold 12th Decr 1831 .. settled by Philip Mallory, George
465   Pannill, William W. Hume, showing $1471.60 in the hands of the exe-
cutor 11th January 1832. Returned into court 23rd April 1832.

pp.   The estate of JOHN MOORE, deceased, in account with James B.
464-   Moore, administrator .. balance in the hands of the administrator,
471    $345.77½ .. settled by James Shepherd, Sam H. Stout, W. M. Chapman.
Returned into court 23rd April 1832.

pp.   The appraisement of the estate of JOHN CLARKE, deceased, De-
472-   cember 14, 1831 .. value not totalled .. made by appraisers Joshua
474   Willis, Luke Thornton, John Newman Senr., Weedon Sleet. Returned
           into court 23rd April 1832.

pp.   Appraisal of all the personal estate of JAMES THOMPSON, de-
474-   ceased .. 14th day of April 1832 .. total value $460.08 .. made by
475   appraisers Robt. W. Brooking, Wm. Smith, T. Cockerill. Returned
           into court 28th May 1832.

pp.   The following is an inventory and list of the names of those
475-   who purchased and the amount of the estate of GOODRICH L. GRASTY,
481   deceased, as sold the 6th, 7th and 8th days of December 1831 ..
           some purchasers .. Elizabeth Grasty purchased numerous articles
           valued at $980.62½, John Terrill, Peter Johnson, Richard Wood,
           Capt. Jacob Graves, James B. Moore, John Ellis, Charles Quisenberry,
           Vivion Quisenberry, Jonathan Johnson, John P. Coons, John H. Gordon,
           George W. Morton, guardian for Mary Ann Grasty (sorrel mare, bed
           and furniture, Bureau and cover, $91.00), John Terrill, guardian
           for John Grasty (shotgun, $3; clock, $5; bed and furniture, $30) ..
           whole amount of sale, $1954.70½ .. R. Richards Jr., clerk of the
           sale. Returned into court 28th May 1832.

pp.   Estate of DR. WILLIAM SHEPHERD, deceased, in account with James
482-   Shepherd, Executor .. an entry: to the estate of Andrew Shepherd
485   of Georgia for a Dft (draft) in favour of Thompson Shepherd negoi-
           ated thro' Anthony Buck .. October 18, 1829 .. Reynolds Chapman
           for this sum ($100.00) gotten for Thompson Shepherd to send to
           Garnett Andrews of Georgia to pay a Dft of Testator's executors
           on the estate of the late Andrew Shepherd of Georgia which Dft.
           was protested by Mrs. Mary Shepherd, Executrix of said estate ..
           balance due estate 17th October 1831, $1019.16 .. submitted by
           Tho. Scott, Jos. Hiden, Richard Cave. Returned into court 28th
           May 1832.

pp.   A schedule of property appraised belonging to the estate of
486-   JOSEPH WILLIAMS, deceased, December 17th 1831 .. value totalled
487        $3549.90 .. sworn 25th May 1832 by appraisers John V. Webb, Charles
           T. Graves, W. Porter. Returned into court 28th May 1832.

pp.   A list of property appraised .. of the estate of EDWARD ANCEL,
488-   deceased, this 20th of April 1832 .. total value $569.50 .. made
489   by appraisers Benjamin W. White, William Melone, John Mallory.
           Returned into court 28th May 1832.

pp.   Appraisal of the estate of JAMES COLEMAN, deceased, this ninth
488-   day of December 1831 .. value totalled $4857.80 .. made by apprai-
489   sers Jeremiah Pannill, George Pannill, William W. Hume. Returned
           into court 28th May 1832.

pp.   Appraisement of the property of Mrs. POLLY BEESLY, dec'd, Jany
492-   3d 1832 .. value totalled $187.29 .. sworn 3rd January 1832 by ap-
494   praisers Gasper Smith, George Deane, Jacob Fleck. Returned into
           court 28th May 1832.

pp.   A bill of sale of the property of MARY BEAZLEY, deceased, sold
495-   the fourth day of January 1832 .. James Long, administrator ..
496   total amount not shown. Returned into court 28th May 1832.

pp.   We do render to the said Court the following list and apprai-
497-   sement of the estate of JOHN SHELOR, deceased .. value totalled
500      $1658.90 .. made by appraisers T. G. Garth, Abram Eddins, Michael
         Mayers, John Shelor .. additional entries bring total value of the
         estate to $2105.53. Returned into court 28th May 1832.

pp.   Amount of sale of the estate of JOHN SHELOR, deceased, made
500-   the 3rd day of June 1831 .. purchasers .. John Shelor, John Shelor
503   for the children of Catharine Jones, Catharine Jones, Benjamin
         Powell, Rachel Shelor, James R. Sims .. total amount of the sale,
         $446.44. Second sale made December 8th 1831 .. (in addition to
         above purchasers) .. William Deane, Augustine Smith, William
         Powell .. sale amount totalled $946.08½. Returned into court 29th
         May 1832.

pp.   Estate of ANN GRASTY to George Grasty, administrator .. account
504-   begins 29 Oct 1827 .. settled by Ezekiah Richards, Alexander Wright,
505   Richard Richards .. estate indebted to administrator in the sum of
         $444.70½. Returned into court 28th May 1832.

pp.   Appraisal of all the personal and real estate of ABRAHAM EDDINS,
506-   deceased .. made by appraisers T. G. Garth, William H. Moyers,
510   George Runkel. The full amount of property, $6485.03. Returned
         into court 25th June 1832.

pp.   The estate of MRS. ANN MINOR, deceased, in account with Over-
510-   ton C. Anderson, Executor .. account debits and credits, $3220.67 ..
511   given 15th June 1832 by Jno. Graves, Jacob Graves, Benj. Coleman.
         Returned into court 23rd July 1832.

pp.   The estate of JAMES FARISH, dec'd, in account with William W.
512-   Jones, executor .. account totals $3232.49 and a deduction of
515      $161.62, 5 per centum commission .. credits $3283.55 with $110.56
         deducted for balance due executor .. settled by Jeremiah Pannill,
         George Pannill, P. Williams, who made oath 13th day July 1830.
         Returned into court 23rd July 1832.

pp.   Will of SALLY GRYMES. .. It is my wish and I hereby require
516-   of my son, Peyton Grymes, that he become my Executor (relieving
517   him from security therefor) .. I direct that all my estate be kept
         together in the hands of my executor for the purposes hereinafter
         mentioned, to wit, I give to my son, Peyton Grymes, in trust for
         the sole use and benefit of my eldest daughter, Mary S. Bayly ..
         residue .. for my three unmarried daughters, Lucy, Hannah F. and
         Sarah Berkeley Grymes .. I give and bequeath to my son, Peyton
         Grymes, all that tract or parcel of land on which I now reside ..
         provided nevertheless he suffer his three unmarried sisters to
         occupy .. during their natural lives or until they respectively
         marry .. as to my sons John Randolph and Thomas Nelson Grymes,
         I have nothing worthy of their acceptance after providing for my
         helpless daughters. And as for my daughter, Elizabeth Pope Braxton,
         she has already been amply provided for by her aunt, Judith Robin-
         son .. this 7th day of February 1827 ..
         In presence of   (signed)
            Elizabeth Gordon, Lucy M. H. Burney,   Sally Grymes
            George B. Bayley, Lewis B. Williams

Codicil provides for board and lodging costs from estate if her unmarried daughters decide to change residence .. made 13th May 1831.

At a court held .. 23rd July 1832 .. proved .. and ordered to be recorded.

At a court held .. 27th August 1832 .. on motion of Peyton Grymes .. bond in penalty of $8000 (without security) .. certificate granted him for obtaining a probate thereof.

pp. 518-519
Estate of GEORGE GRASTY, deceased, to George Grasty, administrator .. settled and submitted 24th day May 1832 by Richard Richards, Ezekiah Richards, Alexander Wright. Sum for the perishable part of the estate, $105.34½ to be divided into four equal parts. Returned into court 27th August 1832.

pp. 519-520
Will of LUCY MINOR of Woodlawn Farm in Orange County. .. I desire that the sum of six hundred dollars be raised from the sale of such of the slaves lately received from my Uncle Lewis's Estate as my Excors shall think proper to part with and divide among my children as follows to Dabney and Francis Minor, my youngest sons .. to Cordelia S. Dabney .. to make her interest in the land sold to her Brother, Henry .. to my daughter, Mary Ann .. the land whereon I live to be sold .. my Exors will charge my three daughters with the advances made them at the time of their marriage, that is with the sum of fifteen hundred dollars a piece without interest .. I devise my three sons, Henry S. Minor, Dabney Minor and Francis .. equivalent to each of my three daughters, Mary Ann, Ann M. and Cordelia .. I appoint my son, Henry S. Minor, and Peter Scales, Executors .. not be called to give security .. this 31st day of May 1832 ..

In the presence of   (signed)
    Jacob W. Herndon   Lucy Minor
    Benj. Coleman, Overton C. Anderson

At a court .. held 27th August 1832 .. proved .. and ordered to be recorded .. on the motion of Peter Scales, an executor therein named .. bond in the penalty of $4400 (without security) .. certificate granted him for obtaining a probate ..

pp. 521-528
Account of the sales of the estate of THOMAS ELLIS, deceased, made the 14th day of December 1831 .. some purchasers .. William Atkins, Lewis Andrews, Oswald Brockman, Brockman Bell, Richard Biggers, Richard Bibb, William Campbell, Charles Y. Crawford, James B. Daniel, Thomas J. Ellis (a considerable portion), John Ellis, William Ellis, James H. Ellis, Rowland Gooch, Lewis Harris, Colby Graves, Richard Pinkard, David Thompson, Reuben Thompson, Albert G. Shepherd .. total $4635.24¼ .. Garrard Atkins clerk for the Executors .. sworn before George Morris, 23rd May 1832. Returned into court 24th September 1832.

pp. 528-535
The estate of VALENTINE WINSLOW, deceased, in account current with Richard P. Winslow, administrator .. amount due Ann Winslow as her thirds of the estate after the payment of the debts, $152.71 2/3 .. and $61.04 4/5 each to A. Eddins, Richard P. Winslow, Henry B. Winslow, Robert B. Winslow, Martha Ann Winslow .. settled by John N. Sorrille, Newton Hume, George W. Price. Returned into court 24th September 1832.

pp.   Settlement of the estate of JOHN WRIGHT, deceased, in account
534-   with Benjamin   .. sworn and settled 29th March 1832 by
535   Robert Roach, Thos. Row, Richd. Richards. Returned into court
        24th September 1832.

pp.   Executor account of Josias Bingham on the estate of GEORGE
536-   BINGHAM, deceased .. amount of sales, $121.42 .. examined and sworn
537   18th September 1832 by James Early, Joab Early, Charles Parrott ..
        sum of money in hands of the executor, $4.42½. Returned into
        court 22nd October 1832.

pp.   Will of HENRY S. MINOR. .. Wishing not to travail my wife by
538-   exacting from her promises or vows not to intermarry after my death,
539   but on the contrary I wish her to return to society as free to do
        and to act in all things that may promote her comfort and happiness
        as she was before I married her and therefore I desire that she
        retain in her possession all the property belonging to me real and
        personal during her widowhood but in the event of her marriage
        again I devise that all that portion of my estate and the value of
        such as may have converted which I received by my wife shall be
        returned to her and that the balance of my estate I give and be-
        queath to my son, James Lewis Minor for his support and education
        .. I constitute my wife, Margaret, my executrix, with her friends
        Edward Hull and Jacob W. Herndon, co-executors .. this 30th day
        of August 1832.
        In the presence of   (signed)
            Fontaine Meriwether   Henry S. Minor
            P. Scales, Benj. Coleman.
        I desire my gun and knife be given to my brother, Frank.
            At a court held .. 22nd October 1832 .. proved .. and ordered
        to be recorded .. on the motion of Jacob W. Herndon, an executor
        .. bond in the penalty of $1200 .. without security .. certificate
        is granted him for obtaining a probate thereof ..
        (Compiler's note: This name may be Henry L. Minor.)

pp.   Copy of book of sales of part of the estate of JOHN BROCKMAN,
540-   deceased .. some purchasers .. Brockman Bell, John Henderson,
541   Capt. Wm. Campbell, Os. Brockman, Asa Brockman, Jacob Brockman ..
        total amount of the sales, $2047.36½. Returned into court 27th
        November 1832.

pp.   Division of the negroes belonging to the estate of GOODRICH
541   L. GRASTY, deceased .. dower lot No. 1, amount $1900 .. Lot No. 2,
544   John Grasty; lot No. 3, Mary Ann S. Grasty, lot No. 4, Thomas
        Grasty, lot No. 5, John Terrill's son, Goodrich; lot No. 6, John
        H. Gordon to cash by the will as a special legacy .. sworn 2nd day
        December 1831 by commissioners William Stevens, Jacob Graves,
        James B. Moore, Reuben Lindsay. Returned into court 27th Novem-
        ber 1832.

pp.   Division of the negroes belonging to the estate of MOSES BURGIS,
544-   deceased, by James Nelson, administrator, with the will annexed
546   of said deceased at the request of the legatees April 27th 1816 ..
        first wife's negroes .. Samuel Faulconer in right of Edward Bur-
        gis, a legatee .. Samuel Faulconer, guardian for Burgis Faulconer
        and Sarah Faulconer, orphans of Sarah Faulconer, deceased, formerly
        Sarah Burgis, Nancy Burgis, John P. Burgis, second wife's negroes
        .. William Almond in right of his wife, and Catherine E. Burgis
        .. 11th September 1832 .. division examined by Thos. Row, Richd.

Richards, Edmd. Row, and certified each legatee have received the said negroes. Returned into court 27th November 1832.

p.
546
The following disposition of her property was made during the last illness of MISS MARSHA GORDON, late of Orange County, in our presence and by us reduced to writing .. to wit, I leave all my effects to my Sisters to be equally divided between them. Gordonsville, July 12th 1832. Chas. Beale, Susan Campbell jr.

At a court held .. 26th November 1832 .. noncupative will established and ordered to be recorded .. and on motion of Lucy Gordon .. with Charles Beale, her security .. bond in the penalty of three thousand dollars .. certificate granted her for obtaining letters of administration upon the estate of the said Marsha Gordon.

pp.
546-
547
Will of WILLIAM H. MARTIN. .. all my estate of land, negroes and monies together with every other part and parsel of my estate of every kind to be sold at auction .. money equally divided among all my children, to wit, Mallory Martin, Jane Arnall, Joanah Bickers, the two sons of Lucinda Martin, to wit, William P. Mallory and Philip M. Mallory, William Martin and Thomas Martin .. but if Ichabod Mallory, father of the said William and Philip shall harass me in my life time or my Executors with a land law suit, all the expence that he, the said Ichabod, may run me or my estate to shall come out of the part of said William P. and Philip M. Mallory .. I appoint Mr. John Woolfolk and Mallory Martin to be my executors .. this 17th day of November 1832 ..
No witnesses   (signed) William H. Martin

At a court held .. 24th December 1832 .. This writing purporting to be the last will and testament of William H. Martin, deceased, being presented in court for probate by Mallory Martin .. there being no subscribing witnesses .. Ichabod Mallory, Joseph Jackson, and Proctor Bickers were sworn .. said writing established as the last will and testament of William H. Martin and ordered to be recorded .. and on the motion of Mallory Martin .. with Benjamin C. Bickers, William Martin, Thomas Martin and Ichabod Mallory, his securities .. bond in the penalty of ten thousand dollars .. certificate granted him for obtaining a probate ..

pp.
548-
549
Richard Richards Senr., administrator to the estate of JAMES HERNDON, deceased .. paid Elizabeth Herndon, her part of dower .. and guardian of all the legatees .. account settled by Edmund Row, Thomas Row, John Wright. At a court held .. 27th November 1832 .. report ordered to lie. At a court held .. 24th December 1832 .. report not being excepted was approved.

pp.
548-
551
James Nelson, administrator with the will annexed of the estate of Moses Burgess, deceased .. legatees received $117.09, except John Burgess, who received $105.67 .. account examined and settled by Thomas Row, Richard Richards, Edmund Row .. sworn 11th September 1832. At a court held .. 27th November 1832 .. report returned and ordered to lie. At a court held .. 24th December 1832 .. report not being excepted, same approved and ordered to be recorded.

pp.   An appraisal of the estate of RICHARD B. WEBB, deceased, as
550-   shown to us by William S. Frazer, Deputy Sheriff of Orange County,
552   this 15th December 1832 .. made by appraisers Edmund Row, Geo.
Mason, Ezekiah Richards. Returned into court 24th December 1832.

p.   A list of the appraisement and inventory of the estate of
552   William H. Martin, deceased, 29th December 1832 .. value not totalled
.. appraisers L. Burrus, Wm. Stevens, Tartan Smith, Robert Terrill
Junr. Returned into court 28th January 1833.

pp.   State of Georgia, County of Chatham. I JOHN T. SCOTT of Vir-
554-   ginia but at present of Savannah in the County of Chatham and state
556   of Georgia do make and publish this my last will and testament.
I give, devise, bequeath and relinquish to my wife, Huldah Scott,
all my estate .. and property real and personal of Dr. Richmond
Lewis, deceased .. to her my rights under my Father's will .. appoint my wife, Huldah Scott, executrix, and Lewis Rawlings, executor .. at Savanah this 12th day of October 1832.
Witnesses   (signed)
  W. C. Daniel   Jno. T. Scott
  W. Williams, Richard R. Cuglar (or Cuylor)
Certificates from officials of Georgia inserted in the book.
  At a court held for the County of Orange .. 26th November 1832
.. last will and testament of John T. Scott presented .. commissioners appointed to take and certify to the court the attestation
of said witnesses (residents of Georgia).
  At a court held for the County of Orange .. 28th January 1833 ..
ordered said writing be established as the last will and testament
of John T. Scott and that the said attestations and certificate
also be recorded.

pp.   An inventory and appraisement of the estate of MRS. SALLY GRYMES,
556-   deceased .. made the 7th September 1832 .. value $2418.12½ .. made
558   by appraisers Wm. Jones, James Sommerville, Armistead Gordon, Benj.
Sanders, Jno. R. Spotswood. Returned into court 25th March 1833.

pp.   An account of sales of the property of MRS. SALLY GRYMES, dec'd,
558-   made on the 1st day of November 1832 by her executor. Returned into
559   court 25th March 1833.

pp.   Will of JOEL RUCKER. .. I give and bequeath unto my son, Minor
559-   Rucker, one small tract of land supposed to contain about forty five
560   acres adjoining the lands of Thomas Eddins, Richard White and Blyfil
Rucker, one other small parcel of land adjoining the land of Blyfil
Rucker .. (two other small tracts) .. purchased by my son, Minor,
but the title is in me all which right and title I give unto the
said Minor Rucker .. bequeath unto Minor Rucker all my slaves ..
bequeath unto Minor Rucker all my stock of every description .. except I give to my son, Blyfil Rucker, ten dollars and unto my three
grandchildren, heirs of Elzy Rucker, deceased, namely Kitty, Joseph
and Edmond, thirty dollars to be equally divided amongst them by my
executor .. appoint my son, Minor Rucker, my only executor .. this
21st day of July 1831 ..
In the presence of   (signed)
  D. C. Garth,   Joel Rucker
  Benjamin Burton, J. B. Bradford.

At a court held .. 25th March 1833 .. proved .. ordered to be recorded .. and on the motion of Minor Rucker, the Executor .. with
Benjamin Burton, his security .. bond in the penalty of three thousand dollars .. certificate was granted him for obtaining a probate ..

pp.   Will of WILLIAM WRIGHT SENR. .. I give to my first wife's child-
560-   ren, that is to George B. Wright, John Wright, Larkin Wright, Fran-
561   ces Sleet, wife of John Sleet, Nancy Rhodes, deceased, who was the
wife of George Rhodes, and Lucy Rhodes, deceased, who was the wife
of Richard Rhodes .. I lend unto my wife, Rachel Wright, one feather
bed and furniture and one third part of my real and personal estate
for and during the term of her widowhood .. I give to William A.
Moore, who married my daughter, Mary, by deed, about fifty acres ..
I give to my daughter, Elizabeth Thornton, some personal estate ..
and I leave her thirty dollars .. I give to my daughter, Jane Herndon, wife of Larkin Herndon, sixty dollars .. I give to my daughter,
Elender Newman, wife of Andrew Newman, thirty dollars .. I give to
the children of Susannah Waugh, wife of Gorah Waugh, forty dollars
.. in trust for her children .. I have given to my daughter, Leancy
Bledsoe, wife of Moses Bledsoe, some personal estate .. I give her
one negro boy .. to my son, William M. Wright by him paying to my
two sons, Alexander Wright and Samuel Wright, one hundred dollars,
that is fifty dollars each one, all the land I may die possessed of
(including the part lent to my wife at the expiration of her widowhood) .. I give to my daughter, Melinda Thornton, wife of Daniel
Thornton, one negro girl .. (money arising from the balance of the
estate) to be equally divided between Elizabeth Thornton, Jane Herndon, wife of Larkin Herndon, and the children of Susannah Waugh, wife
of Gorah Waugh .. it is my wish that my son, William M. Wright and
my wife to live together .. I appoint Richard Richards Jr. and my son,
William M. Wright .. executors .. this 21st day of July 1832 ..
In the presence of   (signed)
    Elhanon Row   William Wright Sr.
    Jesse M. Webb, Alexan. Despecker.
    At a court held .. 25th March 1833 .. proved .. and ordered to
be recorded .. and on the motion of (executors) .. separate bonds
.. Richard Richards Jr. with Edmund Row and Richard Richards, his
securities, and the said William M. Wright with John Payne, his
security .. each in penalty of fifteen hundred dollars .. certificate
was granted them for obtaining a probate thereof in due form.

pp.   The will of CHARLES PARROTT. .. I hereby certify that we were
561-   personally present at the last sickness of Charles Parrott, deceased,
563   at his residence in the County of Orange and on being asked whether
he wished to make a will, he stated that he did, and further stated
for fear of accidents he wished us to take notice that he wished his
will to run in the following manner as near as we can now recollect ..
First, he wished his wife, Sarah Parrott, to keep together all his
estate .. until his youngest child should become of age .. giving
to each child as they became of age or might marry such property or
part as she could best share .. at the division of his estate .. his
wife to have her thirds .. he was asked whether he had hopes of his
recovery, he answered he had strong hopes that he was permitted to
see the light of another day. He was taken with a bleeding from his

lungs in a few hours after this conversation which soon ended his
natural existence and that he wished his wife, Sarah Parrott, to act
as executor of such his will.

                                        George Shearman
                                        Frances Shearman

   At a court held .. 25th March 1833 .. it being stated to the court
that Charles Parrott, late of this county, deceased, made and published a noncupative will and that he left several infant children,
to wit, Lucy E., Sarah A., Charles H., Evelina S., Nathaniel B.,
and Columbia M. Parrott. On the motion of Sarah Parrott, widow of
the said Charles Parrott, Reynolds Chapman, clerk of this court, was
appointed guardian to the said infants to defend their rights ..
   At a court held .. 26th March 1833 .. George Shearman and Frances
Shearman examined in open court .. on their depositions the will
was established .. and ordered to be recorded .. Sarah Parrott came
into court and refused the executorship .. on the motion of Sarah
Parrott with Bagalleel Brown and William T. Brown, her securities ..
bond in the penalty of fifteen thousand dollars .. certificate was
granted her for obtaining letters of administration .. with the noncupative will annexed in due form.

pp.   The estate of MRS. SALLY GRYMES, deceased, in account with Pey-
563-   ton Grymes .. account begins 10 July 1832 and goes through 31 Decem-
564   ber 1832 .. an entry shows $38.75 paid Doctor James Somerville ..
        $1337.72 paid to Lucy Grymes .. $50 for enclosing the burial ground
        .. balance due estate $1190.37½ .. given the 21st day of March
        1833 by Mann A. Page, Reynolds Chapman, James Shepherd. At a court
        held .. 25th March 1833 .. report returned and ordered to lie ..
        At a court held .. 22nd April 1833 .. report not being excepted,
        same approved and ordered to be recorded.

pp.   The Estate of HENRY MITCHELL, deceased, in account with Benja-
564-   min L. Mitchell, administrator .. balance in hands of administrator,
565     $73.97 .. given 16th March 1833 by Robt. Cave, W. Porter, Joseph
        Williams. At a court held .. 26th March 1833 .. report returned
        and ordered to lie. At a court held 22nd April 1833 .. report not
        being excepted, same approved and ordered to be recorded.

p.   Will of FRANCIS COWHERD. .. I give to my son, Francis K. Cowherd,
565   (slave) and his choice of my stills .. to my son, John S. Cowherd,
        and his sister, Harriet Scott, the whole of my tract of land lying
        in Louisa County commonly called Cain's Tract .. to my daughter,
        Sarah Henshaw (slave) .. I lend to my wife for the term of her natural
        life only one third part of the residue of my estate .. upon condi-
        tion my unfortunate son, Garrett, be supported by her but he is not
        to have any power by law or equity to transfer or alienate any
        property hereby disposed of .. to my three daughters, Mary S. Cow-
        herd, Lucy Cowherd and Elizabeth Cowherd, the residue of my estate
        of every description .. for the preservation of their Brother, Gar-
        rett .. appoint my two sons, Francis K. Cowherd and John S. Cowherd,
        executors .. this 8th day of January 1833 ..
In the presence of   (signed)
     Asa Williams, James Robertson,   Francis Cowherd
     Lawrence D. Robertson, Coleby Cowherd,
     Garrett Scott, Yelverton Cowherd
   At a court held .. 22nd April 1833 .. proved and ordered to be re-
corded.

No page 566.

pp.   The estate of THOMAS JENKINS in account with Charles Taylor,
567-   administrator .. account begins in 1828 and shows debits and credits
568   of $79.61 3/4 .. made 15th March 1833 by Thos. A. Robinson, Joseph
            Stephens, Saml. H. Stout. At a court held .. 25th March 1833 ..
            report returned and ordered to lie. At a court held .. 22nd April
            1833 .. report not being excepted, same approved and ordered to be
            recorded.

pp.   Owen Cooper and Benjamin Cooper, administrators to the estate
567-   of JAMES COOPER, deceased .. a further settlement .. one entry shows
570   payment of $215.39½ to Susan Cooper, Ann Cooper, Frances Cooper,
            Rosey Cooper and Rachel Cooper in their own right and in right of
            Delilah Cooper, deceased .. cash paid Jesse B. Webb in right of his
            wife, $35.89 11/12 .. this amount also retained by Owen Cooper and
            Benjamin Cooper .. settled 9th February 1833 by Richard Richards,
            Richard Richards Jr., and Benjamin Wright. At a court held .. 26th
            March 1833 .. report returned and ordered to lie. At a court held
            .. 22nd April 1833 .. report not being excepted, same approved and
            ordered to be recorded.

pp.   The estate of ROGER SLAUGHTER in account with Gabriel Long, one
569-   of the executors .. account begins 9th November 1828 through 12th
572   February 1833 .. an entry, $752.18, 12th Feby 1833, Martin Slaughter's
            legacy left him by his grandmother, Mourning Slaughter, deceased,
            and received by Roger Slaughter, his guardian, from the administra-
            tor of Henry T. Slaughter, deceased .. account settled 25th February
            1833 by John W. Sale, Geo. W. Morton, Jacob Graves. At a court held
            .. 25th February 1833 .. report returned and ordered to lie. At a
            court held .. 22nd April 1833 .. report not being excepted, same
            approved and ordered to be recorded.

pp.   A list of the sale of the personal estate of WILLIAM WHITE, de-
571-   ceased, it being the widow's dower, taken on the 25th day of April
572   1833 .. whole amount of $484.79 .. certified 25th April 1833 by Jona-
            than Twyman. Returned into court 27th May 1833 and ordered to be
            recorded.

pp.   An inventory and appraisement of the personal estate of WILLIAM
573-   WHITE, dec'd, it being the widow's dower taken on the 24th day of
574   April 1833 .. appraisers Robt. Cave, Geo. Stephens, Blyfil Rucker,
            Alexander Whitelaw. Returned into court 27th May 1833.

pp.   Inventory and appraisement of the real and personal estate of
574-   MRS. LUCY MINOR, deceased .. account shows among other entries 1145
585   acres of land @ $12 per acre, $13,740 .. 39 slaves by name with
            total value, $8,341 .. total appraisal of the estate $25,541.39 ..
            appraisers Fontaine Meriwether, William Carpenter, Benj. Coleman,
            Waller Holliday, Thos. J. Ellis .. this inventory does not show the
            debits due from the estate .. under the belief such was not called
            for or required .. the inventory was certified by P. Scales, executor
            of Mrs. Lucy Minor. Returned into court 27th May 1833.

pp.   Will of BRAXTON OSBORNE. .. I give and bequeath to my beloved
585-   wife, Nancy Osborne, all my property which I now possess or may have
586   in my possession at my decease .. I give to my Brother, Holland Os-
            borne, the sum of one shilling, also to my Brother, Fielding Osborne,

the sum of one shilling .. I do hereby assent my friend, Henry Houck, my executor confidentially hoping that he will discharge the trust imposed on him ..

In the presence of   Signed the 6th day of May 1825
   John T. Rennolds   Braxton Osborn
   William Walters, George Walters.

At a court held .. 27th May 1833 .. proved .. and ordered to be recorded .. whereupon Henry Houck came into court and refused the executorship.

pp. 586-588

Inventory and appraisement of the estate of JOHN SAMUEL, deceased, taken this 9th day of April 1833 by Curtis L. Brockman, Uriel Terrill, Daniel M. Smith .. shows 32 slaves by name with appraised value of $6080 .. total appraised value of the estate, $6339.05 3/4 .. Andrew B. Samuel, administrator with the will annexed of John Samuel, deceased. Returned into court 27th May 1833.

pp. 588-589

Inventory and appraisement of the estate of CATHARINE SAMUEL, deceased, taken the 9th day of April 1833 by Curtis Brockman, Uriel Terrill and Daniel M. Smith .. value totalled $168.87½ .. certified by Andrew B. Samuel, administrator of Catharine Samuel with the will annexed. Returned into court 27th May 1833.

pp. 589-590

Examination of the bonds and promissory notes due the estate of JOHN DOLING, dec'd .. shows bonds against James Doling, George McCay, William Tullock .. given the 20th April 1833 by H. Houck, B. L. Mitchell, Braxton Osborne. Returned into court 24th June 1833.

pp. 590-591

Washington Hutcherson, administrator of the estate of AMBROSE LEE, deceased .. settled by Thos. Coleman, John W. Sale, Richard Richards Jr. At a court held .. 27th May 1833 .. report returned and ordered to lie. At a court ..26th June 1833 .. report not being excepted, same approved and ordered to be recorded.

pp. 592-593

The estate of DR. CHARLES TAYLOR, deceased, in account with Robert Taylor Junr., Executor .. account is in regards to a suit in the superior court of chancery for the Staunton District by the successors of the loyal company against the securities of George G. Taliaferro, one of whom was Doct. Charles Taylor .. account settled by Richd. M. Chapman, Reynolds Chapman, Sam H. Stout. At a court held .. 27th May 1833 .. report returned and ordered to lie. At a court held .. 24th June 1833 .. report not being excepted, same approved and ordered to be recorded.

pp. 592-594

The estate of JULIUS OLIVER in account with Blyfil Rucker, Executor .. settled 17th May 1833 by Geo. Stephens, Jonathan Twyman, Robert Cave. At a court held .. 27th May 1833 .. report returned and ordered to lie. At a court held .. 24th June 1833 .. report not being excepted, same approved and ordered to be recorded.

pp. 594-596

An inventory and appraisement of the estate of JOEL RUCKER, deceased, made the 16th April 1833 .. shows among other entries 14 slaves appraised value of $4367.25 .. total estate value $4667.25 .. given the 16th April 1833 by appraisers Robt. Cave, Geo. Stephens, Edward Cason. Returned into court 22nd July 1833.

pp.   Edmund Row, executor to the estate of WILLIAM ADAMS .. further
596-   settlement .. settled 21st September 1832 by Philip Mallory, Richd.
597   Richards, Benj. Sanders .. some entries .. paid Robert Adams in
           part, paid John Herndon in right of his wife, paid Catherine Adams,
           paid John White in right of his wife, paid Polly Adams .. (each
           #2,000) .. paid William Adams' share to John Herndon, Robert Adams,
           Washington Heard in right of his wife, William Jones in right of
           his wife, John White, Polly Adams. At a court held .. 24th June 1833
           .. report returned and ordered to lie. At a court held .. 22nd
           July 1833 .. report not being excepted, same approved and ordered
           to be recorded.

pp.   The estate of TANDY BOWCOCK with Moses T. Harris, administrator
598-   .. balance due estate, $301.23 .. settled 25th May 1833 by James Mil-
600   ler, B. L. Mitchell, Joseph Williams. At a court held .. 24th June
           1833 .. report returned and ordered to lie. At a court held .. 22nd
           July 1833 .. report not being excepted, same approved and ordered
           to be recorded.

p.   An inventory of the estate and appraisement of WILLIAM WRIGHT,
598   deceased, as taken the 8th day of April 1833 .. total value $1231.62½
           .. made by appraisers Robert Dedman, Thos. Row, Benj. Sanders ..
           certitied by Richard Richards Jr., executor of William Wright Senr.
           Returned into court 22nd July 1833.

pp.   Will of JOHN JONES. .. as soon as convenient my executor to
600-   sell all my estate and monies arising from the said sale to be
601   placed in trust to go to maintain my wife, Margaret Jones, during
           her natural life .. if not sufficient .. so much of the principal
           money as he thinks proper to support her but not exceed twenty dol-
           lars a year .. after the death of my wife, Margaret Jones, the money
           arising from the sale to be equally divided between my four sons,
           Asia, Micajah, Thomas and John Jones and that my two daughters,
           Frances and Sally Jones, have no more of my estate than they have
           already received .. appoint my friend, Anthony Tinder, my sole execu-
           tor .. this 27th day of October 1829 ..
           Attest   (signed)
                Fielding Jones   John Jones
                Richard Johnson, Henry (X) Jones
             At a court held .. 23rd September 1833 .. proved .. ordered to be
           recorded .. and on the motion of Anthony Tinder, executor .. with
           Richard Richards and Fielding Jones, his securities .. bond in the
           penalty of one thousand dollars .. certificate was granted him for
           obtaining a probate thereof in due form.

pp.   Will of ELIZABETH COLEMAN. .. I give to my granddaughter, Eliza
601-   F. Coleman .. I give to my grandson, George W. Coleman .. to my grand-
602   daughter, Elizabeth Coleman .. these legacies to be paid by my execu-
           tor as soon as practicable after my death .. I give the remainder of
           my estate of whatever description to my son, Thomas Coleman, my
           daughter, Elizabeth Grasty, and to the children of my deceased son,
           Wilson, the same to be equally divided among them (one third to each)
           .. appoint my two grandsons, John P. Coleman and Thomas Grasty,
           executors .. this 10th day of June 1833 ..
           In the presence of   (signed)
                James Nelson Jr.   Elizabeth Coleman
                Lewis Andrews, Tandy H. Lane.

At a court held .. 22nd September 1833 .. proved .. ordered to be
recorded .. and on the motion of John P. Coleman, one of the executors .. with James L. Coleman, his security .. bond in the penalty
of $300 .. certificate was granted him for obtaining a probate ..

pp.   An inventory of the personal estate of BRAXTON OSBORNE, deceased,
602-   taken the 13th day of September 1833 .. value totalled $1447.67 ..
603   made by appraisers H. Houck, George Walters, John Rennolds. Returned
into court 23rd September 1833.

pp.   Sale book of property belonging to the estate of JOHN SAMUEL,
603-   deceased, this 23rd day of May 1833 .. shows purchasers Andrew B.
605   Samuel, Joshua Willis, Robert Willis, Daniel M. Smith, Uriah Terrill,
Thomas Brown, Isaac W. Graves .. Andrew B. Samuel administrator.
Returned into court 28th October 1833.

pp.   Sale book of the property belonging to the estate of CATHARINE
605-   SAMUEL, deceased, this 23rd day of May 1833 .. some purchasers ..
606   Daniel M. Smith, Edmond Terrill, Andrew B. Samuel .. total amount
of both sales .. $312.51¼. Returned into court 28th October 1833.

pp.   Will of ROBERT MANSFIELD. .. wish my wife, Mourning Mansfield,
607-   to enjoy the tract of land whereon I live, also four of the choice
608   of the slaves .. the balance of my estate of every kind I wish to
be equally divided among my children and my three young grandchildren, namely, James W. Mansfield, William H. Mansfield, Thomas
M. Mansfield, Robert C. Mansfield, Joseph A. Mansfield, Mildred M.
Taliaferro, Nancy H. Graves, Mary Clarke, Sarah H. Eddins, Susanna W.
Austin, my three grandchildren, Amanda M. F. Snell, Lucy Ann M.
Snell and Rawcer Spicer Snell .. at the death of my wife, Mourning
Mansfield, I direct that the tract of land whereon I now live be sold
and the negroes and all the other property .. money arising therefrom to be equally divided amongst my children and grandchildren ..
appoint my sons, William H. and Joseph A. Mansfield, executors ..
this 9th day of June 1830 ..
Teste   (signed)
    B. Thomas Jr., Robt. Cave,   Robt. Mansfield
    W. Martin, John Williams
At a court held .. 28th October 1833 .. proved .. ordered to be
recorded .. and on the motion of Joseph A. Mansfield, an executor
.. with Isaac Graves, John Taliaferro and William Eddins, his securities .. bond in the penalty of twenty thousand dollars .. certificate was granted him for obtaining a probate thereof in due form.

pp.   An account of the sales made of the estate of FRANCES BURNLEY,
608-   deceased, on Friday, 5th August 1825, on a credit of twelve months
611   .. an additional sale made 30th September 1826 .. an additional sale
made the 5th December 1826 .. amount of the sales, $2010.16½ ..
Returned into court 25th November 1833.

pp.   The estate of WILLIAM T. BURRUS, dec'd, in account with William
612-   S. Frazer, Executor .. amount due the estate, $119.10, making total
615   account of $1464.64 .. settled 23rd July 1833 by Robert Terrill Jr.,
Reynolds Chapman, Wm. Stevens. At a court held .. 26th August 1834
(sic) report returned and ordered to lie. At a court held .. 25th

November 1833 .. report not being excepted, same approved and ordered
to be recorded.

pp.   Estate of JOHN PLUNKETT, deceased, in account with William Way-
616-   land, the administrator .. amount of $487.55½ settled 15th August
617   1833 by Alexander Bradford, Joseph Cave, Blyfil Rucker. At a court
        held .. 26th August 1833 .. report returned and ordered to lie. At
        a court held .. 25th November 1833 .. report not being excepted,
        same approved and ordered to be recorded.

pp.   The estate of JOSEPH REYNOLDS, deceased, in account with Philip
617-   ·S. Reynolds, administrator of Washington Reynolds, deceased, who was
618   the administrator of Joseph Reynolds .. in 1822 paid $5.00 to William
        G. Wigglesworth, one of the legatees .. to William W. Reynolds, one
        of the legatees .. settled by Elijah Morton, James Nelson Jr., Wil-
        liam C. Webb. At a court held .. 27th August 1833 .. report returned
        and ordered to lie. At a court held .. 25th November 1833 .. report
        not being excepted, same approved and ordered to be recorded.

pp.   The estate of THOMAS DURRETT, deceased, to William Wood, adminis-
618-   trator .. settled 18th July 1833 by Edward G. Ship, James Beazley,
619   Thos. Sorrille. At a court held .. 26th August 1833 .. report re-
        turned and ordered to lie. At a court held .. 25th November 1833
        .. report not being excepted, same approved and ordered to be recorded.

pp.   The estate of JOHN SHIFLET, deceased, to Howard Shiflet, adminis-
620-   trator .. account consists of sale and cash received by the executor
621   August 21, 1833 .. settled 21st August 1833 by George S. Blakey,
        James Beazley, James Simms. At a court held .. 27th August 1833 ..
        report returned and ordered to lie. At a court held .. 25th November
        1833 .. report not being excepted, same approved and ordered to be
        recorded.

pp.   The estate of HENRY HERNDON, deceased, in account with Henry
620-   Herndon, administrator .. settled by Robert Cave, William Eddins,
622   Blyfil Rucker. At a court held .. 24th December 1832 .. report re-
        turned and ordered to lie. At a court held .. 25th August 1833 ..
        report not being excepted, same approved and ordered to be recorded.

pp.   Will of ROBERT G. DOUGLASS. .. I give my beloved wife after my
622-   just debts is paid .. and after her death to be equally divided
623   amongst all my children .. I appoint Josias Bingham, executor ..
        this 30th day of August 1833.
        Attest   (signed)
          Nathan T. Mallory   Robert G. Douglass
          Howard (X) Shiflet, John Roberts.
          At a court held .. 25th November 1833 .. offered for probate ..
        proved .. said writing established as last will and testament of
        said Robert G. Douglass, deceased .. on the motion of Josias Bingham,
        the executor appointed by the said will .. with James Simms, his
        security ..bond in the penalty of two thousand dollars .. certificate
        was granted him for obtaining a probate thereof in due form.

pp.   A list of the appraisement of the real and personal estate of
623-   the late ROBERT MANSFIELD, deceased, taken at the house of the said
627   deceased on 21st November 1833 .. value totalled $10,308.26 ..
        given by appraisers Robert Cave, Robt. W. Brooking, William Martin,
        Henry Herndon. Returned into court 23rd November 1833.

pp.   A list of the sale of the property belonging to the estate of
627-   ROBERT MANSFIELD, deceased, sold on the second, third and fourth days
635   of December 1833 .. total amount of the sale, $4028.26 3/4 .. certi-
        fied correct by Robert Cave, clerk. Returned into court 23rd Decem-
        ber 1833.

p.   The will of DANIEL THORNTON. The deposition of D. Gatewood and
635   Benjamin Wiltshire purporting the noncupative will of Daniel Thorn-
        ton, deceased, is established by the court as the will of the said
        Thornton and ordered to be recorded as follows. The last request
        of Daniel Thornton a short time before his death he, the said Thorn-
        ton, after directing where to be buried and requested that his father,
        Luke T. Thornton, should take his children and to act and to do a
        father's part by them and to enable him further to do so should have
        the whole and sole management of his affairs and to settle up all
        his business of every description as he might think proper. Given
        under our hands and seals the 11th day of October 1833.

                                        D. Gatewood
                                        Benjamin Wiltshire

End of Will Book 7.

p.
1

Appraisal of the personal property of DANIEL THORNTON, deceased .. value totalled $125.12½ .. made 22nd February 1834 by appraisers Wm. Mallory, Joshua Willis, Reuben T. Clark. Returned into court 24th February 1834.

pp.
1-
4

An inventory and apprasement of the estate of REUBEN LINDSAY, deceased, made 24th day December 1833 .. 52 slaves shown by name and appraised value .. whole amount of appraisement, $16,545.42½ .. appraisers William C. Moore, Jacob Graves, George W. Morton .. James G. Lindsay, administrator. Returned into court 24th February 1834.

Compiler's note. Reuben Lindsay died intestate. His wife was Frances (Fanny) Mills. He was the son of Adam and Elizabeth Garnett Lindsay; Frances was the daughter of Nathaniel and Frances Thompson Mills. They had six children; James Garnett Lindsay, Sarah Frances Lindsay, Julia V. Lindsay, Susan Ann Lindsay, George C. Lindsay and Evelina A. Lindsay. Reuben Lindsay and his family appear frequently in the compiler's book, Pamunkey Neighbor of Orange County, Virginia.

pp.
4-
6

Will of FRANCES BRUCE. .. I release my grandson, Philip Williams, from all obligations to pay one thousand dollars loaned him .. no account shall be taken of the same in the division of my estate .. I give and bequeath to Doctor George Morton all my household furniture, except my bed and bedding, and release to him the hire of William which has or may have accrued up to the time of my death on consideration of my maintenance .. I confirm to Doctor George Morton the title of thirty three acres of land more or less purchased of Adam Goodlett and divide with the lands of the late General James Williams, deceased, among his legatees under the supposition that I had conveyed it to him, the said Genl. James Williams in his lifetime and which is now in the possession of the said George Morton .. I give and bequeath to my grandson, William B. Williams, my bed and bedding .. I give and bequeath to Frances Jael Williams, my negro girl .. I give to Lucy Ann Pendleton (slaves) .. I give and bequeath to Elizabeth S. Morton (slaves) .. as soon as my executor shall have taken probate of this my last will and testament proceed to collect all monies due me .. divide among my five grandchildren, Charles B. Williams, William W. Williams, Philip Williams, Lucy Ann Pendleton and Elizabeth S. Morton .. appoint Doctor George Morton sole executor .. this 17th day of March 1829 ..

In the presence of   (signed)
   Sally Johnson   Frances Bruce
   Wesley Hill, John Bridwell.

At a court held .. 24th February 1834 .. proved .. ordered to be recorded .. and on the motion of George Morton, the executor .. with Jeremiah Morton, his security .. bond in the penalty of ten thousand dollars .. certificate granted him for obtaining a probate thereof ..

pp.
6-
8

An inventory and appraisement of the estate of FRANCIS DADE, deceased, taken on the 29th of November 1819 by John Taylor, Chas. Taylor, Wm. Quarles and Richard H. Taliaferro .. lists 28 slaves by name with appraised value of $9,450 .. total estate valued at $11003.82 .. Peyton Grymes and Harriett, his wife, administrators with the will annexed of Francis Dade, deceasded. Returned into court 24th March 1834.

pp.   An account of the sales of the estate of FRANCIS DADE, deceased,
8-   made on Wednesday 1st of December 1819 .. Peyton Grymes principle
13   purchaser .. total amount of the sale, $1583.85 .. "Life of Washing-
         ton" sold at $13.00 not belonging to the estate .. amount of sales
         of five shares turnpike stock belonging to the estate of Francis
         Dade, deceased, sold at Buck's auction room, Fredericksburg, for
         cash, $175 .. slaves also sold at Buck's auction room and at Orange
         Court House .. memo of negro hires on 1st January 1821 at Orange
         Court House by Peyton Grymes .. also on 23rd January 1823. Returned
         into court 24th March 1834.

p.   Will of ROBERT TERRILL. .. my will and desire is that if for the
14   payment of my debts it would be better that my half of the tanyard
         in Spotsylvania County should be sold instead of other property, it
         must be done to be judged of by my executor .. I will all my estate
         both real and personal to my beloved wife, Elizabeth .. I wish the
         court to require no security of my executrix .. appoint my beloved
         wife, Elizabeth, executrix .. this 23rd day of January 1833.
         In the presence of   (signed)
             John Terrill   Robert Terrill
             James Terrill, Uriel Terrill
           At a court held .. 24th March 1834 .. proved .. ordered to be re-
         corded .. on motion of Elizabeth L. Terrill, executrix .. bond in
         the penalty of five thousand dollars without security .. certificate
         granted her for obtaining a probate thereof in due form.

pp.   Will of FRANCIS CATTERTON. .. I give unto my beloved wife all
14-   my real and personal property during her single life and after that
15   to be equally divided amongst all my children. I appoint Josias
         Bingham and Michael Catterton, executors .. this 5th day of January
         1834 ..
         Attest   (signed)
             John Mallory   Francis Catterton
             Garret Morris, Francis (X) Mallory
           At a court held .. 24th March 1834 .. proved .. ordered to be re-
         corded .. and on the motion of Michael Catterton, one of the execu-
         tors .. with Josias Bingham, his security .. bond in the penalty of
         three hundred dollars .. certificate is granted him for obtaining a
         probate thereof in due form.

pp.   The estate of JAMES EARLY, deceased, to Wm. Early .. amount totals
15- $1144.52, 26th September 1826 by George W. Price, James Melone,
18   Isaac Davis Jr. .. and on 14th December 1833 in the amount of $1143.52
         .. settled 14th December 1833 by Isaac Davis Jr., George W. Price,
         W. Dulaney .. a third report (undated) in amount of $459.45 .. examined
         and settled 18th April 1833 by John Booten, William Dulaney, James
         Beazley .. another account examined and settled 13th December 1833
         by William Dulaney, George W. Price, James Beazley. At a court held
         .. 23rd December 1833 returned and ordered to lie for exceptions.
         At a court held .. 24th March 1834 .. James Simms and George Stephens,
         who had filed exceptions .. and the administration of his estate ..
         having withdrawn their exceptions .. the court with (their) assent
         .. doth order the same to be recorded.

pp.
19-
20

Appraisal of the estate of CHARLES PARROTT, deceased, as shown us by his administratrix .. this 30th December 1833 .. and make report as follows .. total value $12,104.75 .. includes forty slaves .. given by Sarah Parrott, administratrix with the will annexed of Charles Parrott, dec'd, 3rd April 1834 .. appraisers T. G. Garth, James Beazley, Isaac Davis Jr. Returned into court 28th April 1834.

pp.
20-
21

Appraisement of the estate of LUCY M. WILLIS made this 18th day of April by Thomas Scott, George G. Taliaferro, Peyton Grymes .. shows four negroes valued at $1000.00. Returned into court 28th April 1834.

pp.
21-
22

On the 22nd day of February 1834, the undersigned as administrator of DANIEL THORNTON, deceased, made a sale of the personal estate which is the amount and is as follows .. amount totals $162.72 .. signed by Luke Thornton, administrator of Daniel Thornton, dec'd .. certified a true inventory by George M. Mallory, the clerk. Returned into court 28th April 1834.

pp.
22-
24

Appraisal of the estate of CHARLES PARROTT, deceased, as shown to us by the agents of the administratrix and by leave to make the following report .. given under our hands the 1st April 1834 .. value not totalled .. appraisers T. H. Brown, Ira Harris, Benj. S. Brown. Sarah Parrott's report made 3rd April 1834. Returned into court 26th April 1834.

pp.
23-
24

The estate of WM. TERRILL in account with James Terrill, administrator .. amount $285.15 .. examined and settled by James Nelson Jr., Thomas Coleman, John W. Sale. At a court held .. 23rd December 1833 .. report returned and ordered to lie. At a court held .. 26th May 1834 .. report not being excepted, same approved and ordered to be recorded.

pp.
25-
32

John Terrill's executorship account against the estate of G. L. GRASTY, deceased .. entries among many other include .. to the widow, Elizabeth Grasty, this sum ($580.62½) as her third part of the perishable estate .. to G. W. Morton, guardian for Mary Ann Grasty, legatee ($125.00) .. John H. Gordon in right of his wife .. to Thomas Grasty, a legatee .. to myself as guardian for John Grasty and Goodrich Terrill, legatees .. to P. Mallory, a legacy .. amount $3164.83 .. Eliza F. Gordon, wife of John H. Gordon .. to myself in right of my wife, Susan A. Grasty .. account of John Terrill, executor of the estate of Goodrich L. Grasty .. examined and settled 24th February 1834 .. by Jacob Graves, James Coleman, William C. Moore. At a court held .. 24th February 1834 .. report returned and ordered to lie for exceptions. At a court held .. 26th May 1834 .. report not having been excepted to, same approved and ordered to be recorded.

pp.
33-
41

The estate of FRANCIS DADE, deceased, in account with Harriett Dade, administratrix .. covers period 1816-1832 .. amount expended $12615.50 .. another account 1817-1818 .. amount $11651.39 ..another account 1819-1828 .. amount $11626.08 .. from the information which they could obtain it appears by the account of Harriett Grymes, late Harriett Dade, that before her intermarriage with the said Peyton

Grymes, there came into her hands $11,651.39 to be administered, a
large portion of which arose from the sale of the tract of land belonging to the said Harriett before her intermarriage with Francis
Dade, deceased .. examined and settled by James Shepherd, Richd. M.
Chapman, Thomas Scott. At a court held .. 24th March 1834 .. report
returned and ordered to lie for exceptions. At a court held .. 26th
May 1834 .. report not having been excepted to, same approved and
ordered to be recorded.

pp.   Account of the sales of the estate of REUBEN LINDSAY, deceased,
41-   made 26th December 1833 .. Frances Lindsay, widow, purchased
45       $919.57 of the total amount of $1282.81. Returned into court 28th
         June 1834.

pp.   Appraisal of the personal estate of HAY TALIAFERRO, deceased,
45-   shown us by the administrator, G. G. Taliaferro .. and report the
47   following appraisement this 19th day of June 1834 .. total value
         $17,510 .. made by appraisers Law. T. Dade, Richd. H. Willis, Robert
         T. Willis. Returned into court 23rd June 1834.

p.   Appraisal of the personal estate of JAMES HANEY together Michael
47   Moyers .. value totalled $38.43½ .. appraisers George Dean, Henry
         Moyers, John Shelor. Returned into court 23rd June 1833.

pp.   Inventory and appraisement of the estate of ROBERT TERRILL JR.,
48-   dec'd .. balance due from Joseph Reynolds ($60) for the rent of half
49   the tanyard the present year payable 1st of January 1835 .. value
         not totalled .. certified a correct inventory 16th June 1834 by
         Elizabeth L. Terrill, executrix .. given the 16th June 1834 by
         appraisers Wm. Stevens, William C. Moore, James G. Lindsay. Re-
         turned into court 23rd June 1834.

pp.   John Claybrook, administrator in account with the estate of
49-   MALCOLM HART, deceased .. value totalled $38.03 2/3 .. given the 1st
50   day of December 1833 by Charles Y. Kimbrough, Jno. N. Moss. At a
         court held .. 26th May returned and ordered to lie for exceptions.
         At a court held 28th July 1834 .. report not having been excepted to,
         same approved and ordered to be recorded.

pp.   The estate of JAMES FAULCONER, deceased, to Thos. Faulconer,
50-   administrator .. balance on hand after expenditure of $14.14, $4.14 ..
51   examiners found James Faulconer was possessed of no personal estate
         but by proper vouchers to us produced by the administrator that there
         was left to James Faulconer, dec'd, by his grandfather of Kentucky
         a legacy which has since come in his hand (the admor) amounting to
         ten dollars .. settled 28th November 1833 by Benja. Sanders, Robert
         Roach, Thos. Row. At a court held .. 25th March 1834 .. returned
         and ordered to lie for exceptions. At a court held .. 28th July
         1834 .. report not having been excepted to, same approved and or-
         dered to be recorded.

pp.   The estate of LEWIS G. POWELL, deceased, to William Dulaney,
51-   executor .. settled 19th April 1834 by George W. Price, Tho. Sorrille,
52   John N. Sorrille. At a court held .. 26th May 1834 .. returned and
         ordered to lie for exceptions. At a court held .. 28th July 1834 ..
         report not having been excepted to, same approved and ordered to be
         recorded.

pp.   The estate of JOHN ATKINS, deceased, in account with Thomas
53-   Ellis and Hezekiah Atkins, executors .. John and James H. Ellis, the
55   executors of Thomas Ellis, dec'd .. make account after decease of
Thomas Ellis with Hezekiah Atkins .. amount in estate, $5706.50 ..
settled 17th October 1833 by John W. Sale, Wm. Stevens, Peter Johnson. At a court held .. 28th November 1833 .. returned and ordered
to lie for exceptions. At a court held .. 28th July 1834 .. report
not having been excepted to, same approved and ordered to be recorded.

pp.   Appraisal of the estate of JAMES NEWMAN in current money .. the
55-   following property shown us by George Newman Senr. .. 5 negroes, a
56   horse, a bed and a trunk .. appraised value $771.50. Returned into
court 28th July 1834.

pp.   An inventory and appraisement of the property belonging to the
55-   estate of SUSAN PATTERSON, deceased, made this 5th day of September
56   1833 .. appraised value, $18.70 .. made by appraisers Blyfil Rucker,
Jonathan Twyman, Ezekiel Lucas. Returned into court 28th July 1834.

pp.   An inventory and appraisement of the estate of WILLIAM TERRILL,
56-   deceased, taken the 18th day of July 1834 .. value totalled $6560.15 ..
57   made by appraisers William C. Moore, Wm. Stevens, John W. Sale.
Returned into court 28th July 1834.

p.   An account of sale of the estate of SUSAN PATTERSON, deceased,
58   made 5th September 1833 .. total amount of sale, $19.26, signed by
Hiram G. Edwards, Clerk. Returned into court 28th July 1834.

pp.   An inventory and appraisement of the estate of ROBERT CAMPBELL,
58-   deceased, appraised this 26th July 1834 .. value totalled $1548.07½ ..
59   made by appraisers Thos. Row, Edmd. Row, James Nelson Jr. Returned
into court 25th August 1834.

pp.   Will of GEORGE PARROTT. .. I wish the land on which my father
59-   now lives to be sold for the purpose of paying my debts supposed to
60   contain 200 acres and should that not be sufficient, and if my executors can spare any of my personal estate toward discharging my debts
(but if they think none can be spared without an injury to my family),
it is my wish and desire that they shall sell a certain negro girl
.. I wish my wife to keep all my estate together until my youngest
child becomes of age or during her widowhood provided she marries
then for her to have the third part of my estate after the payment
of my just debts .. I will the balance of my estate to my children
.. I appoint my wife, Elizabeth Parrott, and William Catterton my
executors .. this 2nd day of July 1834 ..
Attest   (signed)
  Daniel White, Geo. Stephens,   George Parrott
  Geo. Shearman, James Archer.
   At a court held .. 25th August 1834 .. proved .. ordered to be recorded .. and on motion of William Catterton, an executor .. with
Michael Catterton, his security .. bond in the penalty of five thousand dollars .. certificate is granted him for obtaining a probate ..

pp.
60-
62

An inventory and appraisement of the estate of JOHN BOSTON, deceased .. nine negroes appraised value of $2320 .. total appraisal
not totalled .. made 16th August 1834 by appraisers Alex. Waugh,
James Willis, Curtis Brockman .. certified by Alexander A. Boston,
administrator of John Boston, deceased. Returned into court 25th
August 1834.

pp.
62-
63

Will of MAJOR OAKS SENR. .. I give unto my beloved wife, Welthy
Oaks, one negro girl .. and one bed and furniture .. I loan unto my
beloved wife, Welthy Oaks, all my estate both real and personal as
long as she remains a widow .. my daughter, Elizabeth Oaks, should
live with her mother in law as one of her family and be supported so
long as she remains single or that my wife should hold my estate in
possession .. at the expiration of my wife's widowhood or death ..
my estate to be sold .. money arising .. to be divided into eight
equal parts one of which I give to Lucy Terry, one other to Elizabeth
Oaks, one other to Mary Wright, one other to Thomas Oaks, one other
to Miniard Oaks and one other part to my son, Major Oaks .. I lend
unto my daughter, Nancy Mason, one other equal part .. and at her
death, I give it unto all her children except Charles Mason to be
equally divided among them .. I leave in the hands of my executor ..
one other part for the benefit of my daughter, Mourning Wallace, to
be paid to her as he may think she stands in need of it .. I lent
my son, John Oaks, one hundred and thirty dollars which is due I now
give to him as his full part of my estate .. my desire that an inventory of my estate be taken but no appraisement until my property
is taken into the hands of my executor .. I appoint Richard Richards
.. my executor .. this 6th day of August 1831 ..
In the presence of   (signed)
    Alexander Grady   Major Oaks
    William Wiltshire, Mourning Mason.
  At a court held .. 23rd December 1833 .. proved. At a court held
.. 25th August 1834 .. proved .. ordered to be recorded .. and on
the motion of Richard Richards, the executor .. with Richard Richards
Jr., and Ezekiah Richards, his securities .. bond in the penalty of
two thousand dollars .. certificate is granted him for obtaining a
probate thereof in due form.

p.
64

An inventory and appraisement of the perishable property belonging
to the estate of FRANCES BRUCE, deceased .. consists of eight negroes
with an appraised value of $2550 .. made by appraisers Jeremiah
Pannille, Thomas W. Gray, Edwin E. Gibson, George Pannill. Returned
into court 25th August 1834.

pp.
64-
65

An appraisement of the personal estate of DAVID SHOLES, deceased,
July 8th 1834 .. value totalled $391.35, including one negro girl
with an appraised value of $325.00 .. given 15th August 1834 by
appraisers James Finks, Oliver Finks, James P. Sims. Returned into
court 22nd September 1834.

pp.
65-
66

A list of an appraisement of the estate of MILDRED EDDINS taken
September 16th 1834 .. no totalled valuation .. includes four negroes
with appraised value of $980.00 .. made by appraisers Isaac Goodall,
Joseph Eddins, William Collins. Returned into court 22nd September
1834.

pp.   A sale of the estate of MILDRED EDDINS, deceased, taken September
66-   the 16th 1834 .. value of sale not totalled .. returned into court
68   22nd September 1834.

pp.   The following is an inventory and a list of the names of those
69-   who purchased and the amount of the Estate of ROBERT TERRILL, de-
71   ceased, as sold on Monday the 11th day of August and Thursday the
4th day of September 1834 on a credit of twelve months .. some purchasers .. John Terrill, Elizabeth L. Terrill (largest portion),
George W. Morton, James M. Jenkins, Lancelot Burrus, William Graves,
Joshua Kendall .. total amount of sale, $745.06. Returned into court
22nd September 1834.

pp.   We .. do proceed to value the personal estate of JOHN DURRETT
71-   and find the value to be as follows .. $163.74½ .. made 10th day of
72   October 1830 by Armistead Gordon, Lawson Barnett, Samuel T. Skinker.
Returned into court 27th October 1834.

p.   Account of sales of the estate of JOHN DURRETT .. amount not
72   totalled .. purchasers Page P. Finney, Enoch Cable, Jacob Stout,
James McNeal and Jacob Hilander. Returned into court 27th October
1834.

pp.   The estate of THOMAS CHILES, deceased, to James Chiles Jr., ad-
73-   ministrator .. 9th August 1833, $35.13, paid Elizabeth Chiles in
74   part of her portion of the estate .. sum paid Elizabeth Groom, late
Elizabeth Chiles .. settled 9th August 1833 by Lancelot Burrus, Geo.
W. Morton, William Stevens. At a court held 28th July 1834 .. report
returned and ordered to lie for exceptions. At a court held .. 27th
October 1834 .. report not having been excepted to, same approved
and ordered to be recorded.

pp.   The estate of WILLIAM H. MARTIN in account with Mallory Martin,
73-   Executor .. settled 14th May 1834 by L. Burrus, James G. Lindsay,
76   Wm. Stevens. At a court held .. 28th July 1834 .. report returned
and ordered to lie for exceptions. At a court held .. 27th October
1834 .. report not having been excepted to, same is approved and
ordered to be recorded.

pp.   A list of the appraisement and inventory of the estate of WILLIS
75-   WHITE, dec'd, this 12th day of October 1830 .. shows 28 negroes by
77   name with appraised value of $4615 .. total appraised value $5566.70
.. made 12th October 1830 by appraisers Geo. Stephens, Alex. Bradford,
Jno. Webb, Wm. Wayt. Returned into court 27th October 1834.

pp.   Edmd. Row, administrator de bonis non upon the estates of WILLIAM
78-   and FRANCES PEACHER, dec'd .. $100 part of a legacy due William
79   Peacher Jr. .. estate sold by James Coleman Sr., dec'd .. paid Martha
Pettis in part on a bond .. same for Edmund Peacher .. paid account
of Uriah Peacher and Joseph W. Peacher .. settled 19th August 1834
by Philip Mallory, Benja. Sanders, Richard Richards. At a court held
.. 25th August 1834 .. report returned and ordered to lie for exceptions. At a court held 24th November 1834 .. report not having been
excepted to, same approved and ordered to be recorded.

pp.   The appraisement of the estate of ISAAC DAVIS JR., dec'd .. value
79-   not totalled .. includes twenty three negroes with appraised value
80   of $7150 .. made 1st November 1834 by appraisers William Davis, James
        Beazley, Washington White. Returned into court 24th November 1834.

pp.   A list of the property appraised at the house of Mary Whitelaw
80-   on the 11th November 1834 belonging to the estate of DOCTOR DANL.
82   WHITELAW .. included 34 negroes with appraised value of $9065 ..
        total appraised value of the estate, $11,647 .. made by appraisers
        Edward Cason, Wm. Eddins, Robt. Cave. Returned into court 24th
        November 1834.

pp.   An inventory and appraisement of the perishable estate of SAMUEL
82-   BOSWELL, dec'd, taken the 30th day of September 1834 .. value totalled
83      $668.00 .. made by appraisers James Terrill, Wm. Boswell, Brooks
        (X) Simco. Returned into court 24th November 1834.

pp.   Estate of MARY PORTER, dec'd, in account with Benjamin F. Porter,
83-   administrator .. account shows expenditures for year 1824 and credits
84   .. a balance of $470.78 due the administrator .. settled 28th August
        1830 by Robert Taylor Jr., Smith Stubblefield, Joseph Atkins. Re-
        turned into court 25th November 1834.

pp.   An inventory and appraisement of the estate of GEORGE PARROTT,
84-   dec'd, taken the 4th day of October 1834 by Geo. Shearman, Daniel
85   White, Geo. Stephens .. total appraised value, $3503.12½ .. inclu-
        ding eight negroes with an appraised value, $1930.00. Returned
        into court 22nd December 1834.

pp.   Edmund Peacher, executor of WILLIAM PEACHER, deceased .. the
85-   amount charged to Alexander Peacher for a negro woman .. which he
87   had some years ago & was by the will of the deceased to be accounted
        for at the division, $375 .. the amount of $1909.52 to be divided
        among ten legatees .. to receive $69.62 each to make them equal to
        Alexander Peacher then the remainder is to be divided into ten parts
        .. nine legatees portions each $197.91 .. Alexander Peacher's por-
        tion of present division, $128.29 .. in a separate accounting ..
        there is an entry of $175 paid Alexander Wright for boarding Frances
        Peacher, deceased, 1832 and 1833 .. settled 16th day of August 1834
        by Edmund Row, Richard Richards, Richard Richard Jr. At a court held
        27th October 1834 .. report returned and ordered to lie for exceptions.
        At a court held .. 22nd December 1834 .. report not having been ex-
        cepted to, same approved and ordered to be recorded.

pp.   The estate of HENRY J. HERNDON, dec'd, to Henry Herndon, adminis-
87-   trator .. settled 20th September 1834 by Robt. Cave, Blyfil Rucker,
88   John Taliaferro. At a court held .. 27th October 1834 .. report re-
        turned and ordered to lie for exceptions. At a court held .. 22nd
        December 1834 .. report not having been excepted to, same is approved
        and ordered to be recorded.

pp.   The following is an inventory and appraisement of the estate of
88-   ELIZABETH COLEMAN, deceased .. value totalled $1508.62½ .. given the
89   29th October 1832 by appraisers William C. Moore, Wm. Stevens,
        James Nelson Jr. Returned into court 26th January 1835.

pp.   Will of AGNES BICKERS. .. I give to my son, Abner Bickers, my
89-   household and kitchen furniture, also one negro boy .. my wish that
90   all my land in the county of Orange be sold and equally divided
            amongst my four children, Joseph Bickers, Matilda Smith, Aley Brown
            and Susan Jones .. appoint my son, Joseph Bickers, Philip Smith, as
            executors to sell the said land and divide the money equally ..
            my executor shall pay to my son, Alexander Bickers, ten dollars,
            to Joshua Bickers, ten dollars, to Elizabeth Long, ten dollars, to
            Caleb Bickers, five dollars, to Brumfield Bickers, five dollars
            should they ever apply .. appoint my son, Abner Bicker, as executor
            to pay the last five heirs named forty dollars .. this 1st day of
            October 1831 ..
            Test   (signed her mark)
              Henry Newman, Obed Gregory,   Agnes Bickers
            Wilson Coleman, George Sims, Philip Mallory
              At a court held .. 23rd February 1835 .. proved .. ordered to be
            recorded .. on motion of Abner Bickers, the Executor .. with Henry
            Newman, his security .. bond in the penalty of one thousand dollars
            .. certificate is granted him for obtaining a probate thereof ..

pp.   A list of the property sold at the sale of MAJOR OAKS, deceased,
90-   on Friday the 5th day of December 1834, and the names of those who
93   purchased and the amount of the Estate of the said deceased ..
            some purchasers .. Miniard Oaks, Thomas Oaks, Major Oaks, Nancy
            Mason, Michael Wallice, Mourning Wallice, Thomas M. Horn, William
            B. Webb, Edmund Peacher, Hugh M. Faulconer, Willis Southerlin, James
            Jacobs, James Taylor, Col. Thomas Row, Thomas Martin, Richard Johnson,
            Samuel Mason, William Cammack, Sandy Campbell, Capt. Benjamin Sanders,
            Robert Dedman, Thomas Brightwell, Thomas Robinson, James Canaday,
            William Martin, John Almond, William Cammack Jr., Jerome B. Collins,
            Elizabeth Oaks, Weedon Richards, Wealthy Oaks, John Oaks .. amount
            of sales, $1740.19½ .. Richard Richards Jr., Clerk. Returned into
            court 23rd February 1835.

pp.   Commissioners appointed to allot to Mrs. Susan Taliaferro, widow
93-   of HAY TALIAFERRO, dec'd, one third part in value of slaves belonging
95   to the estate of her deceased husband as her dower therein and also
            to divide the remaining two thirds of the slaves of the said deceased
            between the children of the said deceased, do make the following
            report that they first allotted to the said widow the following named
            slaves and at the annexed prices and values to wit .. (14 slaves
            with the appraised value of $4225) .. remaining .. into 8 lots of
            two or three each lot .. they then allotted to Doctor Alfred Talia-
            ferro, who held a power of attorney to act for Hay and Edwin, his
            brothers, lots no. 1, 4, 7; to Daniel M. F. Thornton lot no. 3;
            to Robert A. Mayo, lot no. 2; to Lawrence H. Taliaferro, lot no. 5;
            to Horace D. Taliaferro, lot no. 6; to Catlett C. Taliaferro, lot no.
            8 .. (report shows reconciliation to assure each received value of
            $712.50) .. submitted 27th January 1835 by Richard Cave, John F.
            Taliaferro, Mann A. Page. Returned into court 23rd February 1835.

p.   Appraisal of the personal estate of THOMAS JOHNSON, dec'd, in
95   words and figures, to wit .. total value $36.00 .. made 10th October
            1834 by appraisers Thos. Robinson, James Jones, George Mason. Re-
            turned into court 23rd March 1835.

p.   An appraisal of the personal and real estate of JOHN JONES, de-
96   ceased .. value not totalled .. given 9th October 1833 by appraisers
        Benja. Sanders, Thos. Robinson, Thos. Row .. certified a true inven-
        tory by Anthony Tinder, executor. Returned into court 23rd March
        1835.

pp.   An appraisal of the personal estate of PETER APPERSON, dec'd ..
96-   total value $267.75 .. given 14th day of November 1834 by appraisers
97   Benja. Sanders, Thos. Robinson, Thos. Row. Returned into court 23rd
        March 1835.

p.   An inventory and appraisement of the estate of IKEY RICHARDS
97   and taken the 26th day of December 1834 .. total value, $29.25 ..
        made by appraisers Thos. Row, Thos. Robinson, Benja. Sanders. Cer-
        tified a true inventory by Weedon Richards. Returned into court
        22nd March 1835.

pp.   An inventory and appraisement of the estate of MAJOR OAKS, de-
98-   ceased, as taken the 18th day of November 1834 .. value totalled
99      $1833.31 3/4 of which $1300 was the appraised value of five slaves
        and $205 the value of 205 acres of land @ $1 per acre .. made by
        appraisers Benja. Sanders, Thos. Robinson, Thos. Row. Certified a
        true inventory by Richard Richards, executor. Returned into court
        23rd March 1835.

pp.   An inventory and appraisement of the perishable estate of WILLIAM
99-   CLARK, dec'd, taken the 31st day of January 1834 .. value totalled
100     $750.18 .. made by appraisers Benja. Hume, Joshua Willis, Gowry
        Waugh, Willis Overton. Returned into court 23rd March 1835.

pp.   Account of the sales of the estate of WILLIAM CLARK, deceased,
101-   made the 18th day of February 1834 .. some purchasers .. Lucretia
103   Clark (largest purchaser), Benja. Walker, Willis Overton, John Clark,
        Albert Palmer .. total value of sale not shown. Returned into court
        23rd March 1835.

pp.   A list and appraisement of the personal estate of SAMUEL HAM,
103-   dec'd, made the 26th December 1834 .. total valuation not shown but
104   includes eleven slaves with an appraised value of $3441.67 .. made
        by appraisers Granville Kennedy, William Moyers, Jacob Haines ..
        certified a true inventory by Th. G. Garth, administrator. Returned
        into court 23rd March 1835.

pp.   An appraisement of the personal estate of THOMAS WALKER, deceased,
104-   February 4th 1835 .. value totalled $711.36, including four slaves
106   with an appraised value of $620 .. made by appraisers James P. Sims,
        John Sims, Joel Smith. Returned into court 24th March 1835.

pp.   An inventory and appraisement of the personal estate of AUGUS-
106-   TINE GAINES, dec'd, taken 8th October 1834 .. by Michael L. Eheart,
107   William Wayland, L. S. Porter, W. Porter .. total value $1990.84 of
        which $1625 is the appraised value of eight slaves. Returned into
        court 24th March 1835.

pp.   An appraisement of the estate of WILLIAM T. BARNES, deceased,
107-   taken the 12th day of December 1834 .. one tract of land called Bell's
110   Tract containing 144 acres @ $4 per acre .. one half of mill and 4
        acres of land .. twenty-two slaves with an appraised value of $4165

.. total value of estate appraisal $6115.00 .. made by appraisers William Collins, Jacob Graves, Jonathan Graves. Returned into court 24th March 1835.

pp.
110-
111

The estate of JAMES SMITH, deceased, in account with Tartan Smith, executor .. examiners found executor indebted to the estate in the amount of $930.13 3/4 .. made on 27th September 1834 by Lancelot Burrus, Geo. W. Morton, John W. Sale. At a court held 25th November 1834 .. report returned and ordered to lie for exceptions. At a court held .. 27th April 1835 .. report not having been excepted to, same is approved and ordered to be recorded.

pp.
110-
112

Will of REUBEN OAKS. .. my will and desire that my son, John Oaks, take possession of my estate after my decease and keep it to-gether, manage it as he thinks proper and keep possession of it during the natural life of my wife, Susannah Oaks, on the following terms .. he must take care of and maintain his mother, Susannah Oaks, during her life and maintain my two daughters, to wit Sally Oaks and Eliza Oaks, during his mother's life unless they should marry .. then they should have no part of my estate unless my son, John, should think proper to lend a negro to the one that marrys .. I give my daughter, Sally Oaks, one third of my negroes with one third of the balance of my estate .. I give to my daughter, Eliza Oaks (same) .. I wish the Orange County court to appoint three men as soon as it can be done after my wife's death to divide my negroes into three lots .. I appoint my son, John Oaks, Executor .. this 17th day of January 1835.

In the presence of   (signed his mark)
    Thos. Woolfolk, Claibourne Graves,   Reuben Oaks
    Welthy (X) Oaks, John M. Goodwin

At a court held .. 27th April 1835 .. proved .. ordered to be re-corded .. and on the motion of John Oaks, the Executor .. bond with-out security .. penalty of two thousand dollars .. certificate granted him for obtaining a probate thereof in due form.

In the margin. At a court held .. 28th February 1842 .. John Oaks, the executor of Reuben Oaks, deceased, being dead .. on the motion of Claibourne G. Graves .. with Richard Richards his security .. bond in the penalty of three thousand dollars .. certificate granted him for obtaining letters of administration on the estate of Reuben Oaks, unadministered by the said John Oaks, with his will annexed in due form.

p.
113

The estate of SUSAN PATTERSON in account with A. G. Edwards, ad-ministrator .. amount of the sales of her estate, $19.25 .. settled 17th January 1835 by Alfred J. Twyman, Minor Rucker, Robt. Cave. At a court held .. 26th January 1835 .. report returned and ordered to lie for exceptions. At a court held .. 27th April 1835 .. report not having been excepted, same is approved and ordered to be recorded.

pp.
113-
116

An inventory and appraisement of the estate of WALTER KEY, de-ceased, in the County of Orange, made June 25th 1834 .. value totalled $2144.66 .. given in September 1834 by appraisers Robert King, Martin Baker. Returned into court 25th May 1835.

pp.   An inventory and appraisement of the estate of WALTER KEY, deceased,
116-   made July 23d 1834 .. value not totalled .. made by appraisers John
118   H. Craven, N. H. Lewis, Hugh Minor. Returned into court 25th May
            1835.

pp.   An inventory and appraisement of the estate of WILLIAM TERRILL,
118-   dec'd, taken the 1st day of April 1835 .. total valuation, $6865.50
120   .. including twenty five slaves appraised value of $3430 (3 had no
            appraised value) .. made by appraisers Elijah Morton, Philip L. Rey-
            nolds, William Reynolds, William W. Reynolds .. James Terrill and
            John Terrill, administrators. Returned into court 25th May 1835.

pp.   An appraisement of the estate of ELIZABETH ESTES, deceased ..
120-   value not totalled .. includes ten slaves with an appraised value
121   of $2425 .. made by appraisers Edwd. G. Ship, William Melone, Benja-
            min W. White. I adopt the above inventory as my own (signed) James
            Beasley, administrator. Returned into court 25th May 1835.

pp.   Sale book of the estate of ELIZABETH ESTES, deceased, January
121-   14th 1835 .. some purchasers .. John Estes, Joab Early, Ezekiel
122   Wilhoit, James Ancell, William Morris, Chapman Collier, Washington
            Shiflett, Madison Shiflett, Howard Shiflett, George Gentry, Isaac
            Lamb, Edward Ancell .. value of sale not totalled. Returned into
            court 25th May 1835.

pp.   Estate of THOMAS C. GORDON, dec'd, to Armistead C. Gordon ..
123-   settled 20th December 1834 by John H. Gordon, Lawson Barnett, Samuel
124   T. Skinker. At a court held .. 22nd December 1834 .. report returned
            and ordered to lie for exceptions. At a court held .. 25th May 1835
            .. report not being excepted to, same is approved and ordered to be
            recorded.

pp.   A list of the appraisement of the estate of AGNES BICKERS, dec'd,
124-   taken the 21st day of May 1835 .. value totalled $720.75 of which
125         $625 was the appraised value of a seventeen year old lad .. made by
            Jeremiah Pannille, William W. Hume, George Pannille. Returned into
            court 25th May 1835.

pp.   Will of ANN FAULCONER. .. it is my wish that my estate both real
125-   and personal to be sold by my executor .. and the money to be divided
126   into twelve equal parts .. I give unto my children, Camp Faulconer,
            William Faulconer, Richard Faulconer, John C. Faulconer, Ambrose
            Faulconer, George Faulconer, Spencer Faulconer, Mary Ann Wright and
            Lucy Highlander each one an equal part .. with the exception that
            Forty dollars is to be taken from Lucy Highlander's share .. I lend
            my daughter, Nancy Faulconer, during her life, one other part .. I
            give unto my granddaughters, Martha Ann Faulconer, Margaret Elizabeth
            Faulconer and Nancy Jane Faulconer, children of my daughter, Elizabeth
            Faulconer, deceased, one other part .. my son, Camp Faulconer, pur-
            chased some property at the sale of his father's estate for which he
            is yet due me, he is to be accountable for it in the division of my
            estate but he is not to be charged with the interest .. appoint my
            son, Richard Faulconer, and Richard Richards, executors .. this 10th
            day of February 1835.
            In the presence of   (signed her mark)
                Ezekiah Richards, Samuel Mason,   Ann Faulconer
                Wyatt Brightwell.

At a court held .. 25th May 1835 .. proved .. ordered to be recorded .. and on the motion of the (executors), with Thomas Robinson,
John Wright Senr., Richard Richards Jr., and Ezekiah Richards, their
securities .. bond in the penalty of two thousand dollars .. certificate is granted them for obtaining a probate thereof ..
(Compiler counts only eleven parts distributed.)

pp.   Will of NANCY MASON. .. my will and desire that the whole of
126-   my property that I leave after my debts are paid to be equally divi-
127   ded between my three daughters, Rebecca, Sarah and Mary, nevertheless
        it is my wish and desire that the portion that may fall to my daugh-
        ters, Rebecca Cammack and Mary Richards, be kept in the hands of my
        exor and dealt out to my daughters, Rebecca and Mary, for their bene-
        fit so that neither of their husbands shall have the control of it
        .. and I am justly indebted to my daughter, Sarah Mason, in the sum
        of seventy dollars with interest thereon from January 1833 up to the
        present time and as I do not expect to pay her during my life ..
        (executor to pay her before dividing the estate) .. residue of my es-
        tate as well as what is coming from my father, Major Oaks', estate ..
        (disinherits sons) they, my sons, having never shown that respect
        and feeling to me that was due from sons to a mother, I therefore
        give them no part of my property whatever .. appoint my friend,
        Benjamin Sanders, my executor .. this 27th day of August 1824.
        Witnesses   (signed her mark)
            Edmd. Row, Richard Johnson   Nancy Mason
        At a court held .. 25th May 1835 .. duly proved by the oath of
        Richard Johnson and the said Richard Johnson further deposing that
        Edmund Row .. hath removed from this Commonwealth .. it was con-
        sidered by the court that the said writing be established as the last
        will and testament of Nancy Mason and recorded.
            In the margin. At a court held .. 28th September 1835 .. on the
        motion of Benjamin Sanders, the executor named .. with Richard
        Richards, his security .. bond in the penalty of $600 .. certificate
        granted him for obtaining probate thereof in due form.

pp.   Will of MILLEY WOOD. .. I give to my daughter, Elender Mitchell,
127-   all the rents that are due me for my dower land and also all other
128   estate which I may die possessed except the legacies hereafter men-
        tioned. I give and bequeath to my daughters, Nancy Dickinson, Polly
        Henderson and Alley Harvey, each of them the sum of one shilling to
        be paid by my executor .. I give and bequeath to my sons, Richard,
        Hezekiah, William and James Wood, each of them the sum of one shil-
        ling .. the above mentioned estate to be given by my executors to my
        daughter, Elender Mitchell, to do as she may think proper to do with
        and to give the same to whom she may think proper to give it to ..
        appoint John Mitchell and William T. Wood, my executors .. this
        20th day of March 1833 ..
        Teste   (signed her mark)
            Joseph Pendleton   Milley Wood
            Griffin Mitchell, William P. Wood.
        At a court held .. 25th August 1835 .. proved .. ordered to be
        recorded .. and on the motion of John Mitchell, the executor .. bond
        without security .. penalty of five hundred dollars .. certificate
        was granted him for obtaining a probate thereof in due form.

pp.   1835 May 20th. Appraisement of REUBEN OAKS' estate .. total
128-   valuation $1516 of which $1400 is for seven slaves .. made by apprai-
129   sers Claibourne Graves, Benj. Cooper, John Henderson. Certified a
        true inventory by John Oaks, executor. Returned into court 22nd
        June 1835.

pp.   Will of ELIJAH JONES. .. I give to my son, Geo. Jones, Sarah
129-   Jones and Joseph Jones all the slaves I may die possessed of to be
130   equally divided between them .. I give my son, James Jones, a feather
        bed and furniture if he has not one, if he has it is not my purpose
        to give him another .. I give Frances Lennans (?) one hundred fifty
        dollars .. the residue of my estate to be equally divided between my
        six children, viz. Geo. Jones, Sarah Jones, James Jones, John Jones,
        Wm. Jones and Joseph Jones .. before division my son, John Jones,
        to account for a sow and pigs and a cow and calf .. appoint my son,
        Joseph Jones, to be my only executor .. this 18th day of October 1832 ..
        In the presence of   (signed his mark)
            Jno. Payne,   Elijah Jones
          John H. Grasty, Geo. Grasty.
          Codicil .. crops coming in present year to remain with possession
        of present family the year 1835 .. 7th January 1835.
          At a court held .. 25th May 1835 .. proved ..
          At a court held .. 22nd June 1835 .. further proved in open court
        .. and ordered to be recorded .. and on the motion of Joseph Jones,
        the executor .. with Benjamin Hume, his security .. bond in the
        penalty of six thousand dollars .. certificate granted him for ob-
        taining a probate thereof in due form.

pp.   Amount of the sale of the personal estate of BRAXTON OSBORN sold
130-   this 20th day of November 1833 .. amount of sales not totalled ..
133   some purchasers .. Jacob Bell, J. T. Reynolds, H. Houck, P. A. Hans-
        brough, Benj. Scott, John Taliaferro, Waller Scribner, Thomas White,
        W. Houseworth, Edwin C. Taliaferro, A. M. Barksdale. Returned into
        court 22nd June 1835.

pp.   A list of the appraisement of the property of CAPT. JAMES BURTON,
133-   dec'd, left in the hands of the widow .. appraised amount of fourteen
135   slaves, $2332.50 .. no totalled amount for other property .. made by
        appraisers George Parrott, Benjamin Anderson, John Graves, William
        Wayt .. on the 28th February 1834, appraisers John Graves, William
        Wayt and Benjamin Anderson met at the residence of the late Capt.
        James Burton to appraise the corn that was due the estate. Returned
        into court 27th July 1835.

pp.   A list of the sales made on Friday 2nd day of May 1834 of the
135-   property belonging to the estate of JAMES BURTON, dec'd .. total
140   amount for sales not shown .. Returned into court 27th July 1835.

pp.   James G. Lindsay, administrator on the estate of REUBEN LINDSAY,
140-   deceased .. examined and settled 19th March 1835 by Thos. Coleman,
142   Lewis Andrews, John W. Sale, Richard Richards Jr., who find the
        balance in the hands of the administrator to be $595.77 1/3. At a
        court held .. 27th April 1835 .. returned and ordered to lie for
        exceptions. At a court held .. 27th July 1835 .. report not being
        excepted to, same is approved and ordered to be recorded.

pp. 142-143

A list of the negroes given up by the widow of SAMUEL THOMPSON, dec'd, to be divided amongst said Thompsons 27th May 1835 .. divided into five lots .. Reuben Thompson first lot; Eliza Graves, formerly Eliza Thompson, second lot; Susan Austin, formerly Susan Thompson, third lot; Sarah Thompson fourth lot; and William Thompson, fifth lot .. made by Lancelot Burrus, Lewis Andrews, John Terrill, Daniel M. Smith. Returned into court 27th July 1835.

pp. 143-144

Basil Haney to the estate of JAMES HANEY, dec'd .. to this paid Granville Kennedy, John Shelor and John N. Sorrille for settling the administration $1 each .. settled 24th January 1835. At a court held .. 23rd March 1835 .. report returned and ordered to lie for exceptions. At a court held .. 27th July 1835 .. report not being excepted to, same is approved and ordered to be recorded.

pp. 145-146

An inventory and appraisement of the estate of ELIZABETH BURTON, deceased, taken on the 12th June 1834 by George Shearman, George Stephens, William Wayt (appraisers) .. total value $1850.60 3/4 .. on 24th October 1834 appraised crops belonging to estate of Mrs. E. Burton .. value totalled $92.73. Returned into court 27th July 1835.

pp. 146-147

James Jarrell admor of JAMES JARRELL, dec'd, in account with said estate .. land sold in April 1830 .. amount $354.00 .. legacies of $34.07½ paid each, Theodoshia Eddins, Roda Breeding, Mary Jarrell, William Jarrell, Jeremiah Jarrell, John Jarrell, Pemberton Jarrell, Joseph Jarrell, Hinkle Jarrell, Fountain Jarrell, Louisa Jarrell, and a portion in the hands of the administrator .. examined and settled 3d day March 1835 by James Clark, Reuben Booton. At a court held .. 27th April 1835 .. report returned and ordered to lie for exceptions. At a court held .. 27th July 1835 .. report not being excepted to, same is approved and ordered to be recorded.

pp. 148-154

The Estate of JOHN DOUGLASS, dec'd, in account with John Douglass, Executor of the said deceased .. account begins 24th October 1828 .. through 16th January 1830 .. settled by T. V. Webb, Charles T. Graves, Buckner Terrill. At a court held .. 22nd December 1834 .. report returned and ordered to lie for exceptions. At a court held .. 27th July 1835 .. report not being excepted to, same is approved and ordered to be recorded.

pp. 154-156

Commissioner's Office, Orange Court House, January 1, 1835. Order to examine, state and settle John C. Wells' account of administration of the estate of JOHN CLARK, dec'd, proceeded .. administrator presented a memorandum of debts due by bonds in the total amount of $1632.63 .. submitted by Commissioner Richard Chapman. At a court held .. 23rd March 1835 .. returned and ordered to lie for exceptions. At a court held .. 27th July 1835 .. report not being excepted to, same is approved and ordered to be recorded.

pp. 156-157

An inventory and appraisement of the estate of HUDSON COLYER, dec'd, made 22nd August 1835 .. value totalled $44.41½ .. E. C. Colyer, administrator .. made by appraisers William H. Moyers, John N. Sorrille, Granville Kennedy. Returned into court 24th August 1835.

pp.   Appraisal of the estate of ELIJAH JONES, dec'd .. value totalled
157- $3886.87½, including $3450 for the appraisal of eight slaves .. ap-
158   praisement taken 8th day of August 1835 by Thos. Row, Thomas Robin-
           son, Elhanon Row, Joseph Jones. Returned into court 24th August 1835.

p.   Appraisal of the personal estate of REUBEN NEWMAN, deceased ..
159   consists of fifteen slaves with an appraised value of $5725 .. (also)
           one negro girl .. which Mr. Henry Newman says he sold for $325 ..
           made by appraisers George Pannill, Jeremiah Pannille, Philip Mallory.
           Returned into court 28th August 1835.

pp.   Will of ISAAC DAVIS. .. I give to my sons, Thomas and Isaac
159-   Davis, the tract of land I purchased of Reuben Conway .. to each of
161   them one third of my tract of land lying in the state of Kentucky on
           the fork of Cumberland River .. to my son, Elijah K. Davis, the tract
           of land whereon I now live containing about six hundred acres .. I
           give to the grandchildren of my deceased daughter, Sarah Twyman, one
           hundred dollars each, that is to say, Robert Davis Twyman, William
           Horace Twyman, Isaac Smith Twyman, James Winston Twyman and Sarah
           Twyman .. monies due me from Major David Trimble, Roger Clemans and
           James Young, when collected, shall be divided between my daughters,
           Frances Durrett, Mary Whitelaw and Susannah Winston Blakey, among
           the grandchildren of my daughter, Sarah Twyman, and my grandchildren
           of my daughter, Elizabeth Durrett, one fifty part to my daughter,
           Frances Durrett, one fifth part to my daughter, Mary Whitelaw, one
           fifth part to my daughter, Susanna W. Blakey, and one fifth part to
           be divided between the children of my daughter, Sarah Twyman, and
           one fifth part to be divided between the children of my daughter,
           Elizabeth Durrett .. all my negroes shall be sold among my children
           .. one eighth part each to Thomas Davis, Isaac Davis, Elijah K.
           Davis, Frances Durrett, daughter, Mary Whitelaw, to my daughter,
           Susanna W. Blakey .. among my grandchildren of my daughter, Sarah
           Twyman .. children of my daughter, Elizabeth Durrett .. appoint my
           sons, Thomas and Isaac Davis, and Elijah Davis, executors .. this
           18th day of March 1829 ..
           Test   (signed)
               John C. Harrison, Clifton Rhodes,   Isaac Davis
               Benjamin W. White, Edward G. Ship,
               James Beasley, Bezaleel B. Parrott
           At a court held .. 28th August 1835 .. proved .. ordered to be re-
           corded .. Elijah Davis, who is appointed an executor .. refused the
           executorship .. Thomas Davis, the other surviving executor, made
           oath .. with Elijah K. Davis, his security .. bond in the penalty of
           thirty thousand dollars..

pp.   Will of JEREMIAH WHITE. .. I leave to my wife, Milley White, a
161-   negro woman .. I give to my granddaughter, Judah Pratt .. which her
163   mother left at her death .. I give to my daughter, Fanny Cox ..also
           fifty acres of land adjoining the land of my son, William White ..
           to my son, William White, one hundred acres of land .. to my son,
           Winston White (same) ..lend to my daughter, Judah White, fifty acres
           of land .. to my wife, Milley White, the tract of land whereon I now
           live .. after her death to be equally divided among my grandchildren
           lawfully begotten of the body of my daughter, Sally Wood .. the bond

outstanding against James Wood due my son, John White, deceased, to the amount of twenty dollars is to come out of the legacies of my daughter, Sally Wood .. to my son in law, William Pratt, one dollar .. appoint my friends, Daniel White, son to William, and John White, son to Richard White, executors .. this 17th day of December 1834 ..

Teste   (signed)

    Joseph Cave   Jeremiah White

    R. Thomas, William Williams.

    At a court held .. 28th September 1835 .. proved .. ordered to be recorded .. and on the motion of Daniel White .. with William White, Blyfil Rucker and William D. Wilson, his securities .. bond in the penalty of ten thousand dollars .. certificate was granted him for obtaining a probate thereof in due form.

pp. 163-164
An appraisement of the personal estate of SIMEON GRAVES, dec'd .. made at May Term 1835 .. value totalled $21.50 .. made by appraisers Oliver Finks, Catlett Conway, William Collins. Returned into court 26th October 1835.

pp. 164-166
An account of the sales of the personal estate of SIMEON GRAVES, dec'd, made by Benjamin Hume, administrator, June 19th 1835 .. Layton Graves only Graves' purchaser .. sale amount $91.81½. Returned into court 26th October 1835.

pp. 166-168
A list of the property rendered on the premises of Mr. Jeremiah White, deceased, and appraised by William Herndon, John Taliaferro, William Eddins and Jos. Mansfield, the 1st day of Octr 1835 .. value totalled $2864.00. Returned into court 26th October 1835.

pp. 168-169
Anthony Tinder, executor to the estate of JOHN JAMES, deceased .. the amount of property sold per the sales book, $120.16 3/4 .. amount of land sold, $286.50 .. amount expended and commission, $148.63½, which amount is enumerated .. settled by Thomas Row, Richard Richards, Richard Richards Jr. At a court held .. 24th August 1835 .. returned and ordered to lie for exceptions. At a court held .. 23rd September 1835 .. report not being excepted to, same is approved and ordered to be recorded.

pp. 169-174
The estate of LUCY MINOR, deceased, in account with P. Scales, executor thereof .. sale of perishable property on 9th November 1832 .. value of library appraised @ $100 .. paid Miss Fanny Chandler for services rendered as housekeeper .. paid Coakley 17th July 1832 for 2 family bibles $20, one bequeathed to each of her three daughters, and $10 subsequently left with Overton Anderson for a third .. the interest in the slaves was $1500 each .. in the residue of the estate to H. L. Minor, Garrett Meriwether and wife, Samuel H. Dabney and wife, P. Scales and wife, Dabney Minor, Francis Minor in amount of $540.16 2/3 each paid January 1834 .. settled by Coalby Graves, Fontaine Meriwether, Thomas J. Ellis.. At a court held .. 24th August 1835 .. returned and ordered to lie. At a court held .. 23rd November 1835 .. report not being excepted to, same approved and ordered to be recorded.

pp. 174-175
The estate of BRAXTON OSBORNE, dec'd, in account with William L. Mitchell, administrator of Ben L. Mitchell, who was administrator of Braxton Osborne, dec'd .. amount of $436.74½ settled by Robert

Cave, Joseph Williams, William Martin, H. Houck. At a court held ..
27th July 1835 .. returned and ordered to lie for exceptions. At a
court held .. 23rd November 1835 .. report not being excepted to,
same approved and ordered to be recorded.

pp.   The estate of WILLIS WHITE, deceased, in account with Jacob Graves,
176-   executor .. the subscribers found account supported except "56 cents
179   charged for toll paid on turnpike road" .. a commission of eight per
cent was allowed .. "we will give the reasons for that opinion. The
court will see from the number of claims against the estate how many
persons the executor has had transactions with and therefore the
number of debts he has had to settle and paid .. the executor has
also had the execution of the most troublesome and important law
suit against him as executor in the Circuit Court of Orange .. two
laborious and tedious trials .. numerous witnesses .. settled by
James Shepherd, Cudden Davis, Richd. Rawlings. At a court held ..
27th July 1835 .. returned and ordered to lie. At a court held ..
23rd November 1835 .. approved and ordered to be recorded.

pp.   The estate of JOHN OFFIELD to Hawsey Daniel, administrator ..
178-   amount shown, $227.26¼ .. settled 12th September 1835 by William
179   Melone, Robert Miller. At a court held .. 28th September 1835 ..
returned and ordered to lie. At a court held .. 23rd November 1835
.. approved and ordered to be recorded.

pp.   Richard Richards Jr., executor to the estate of WILLIAM WRIGHT
180-   SENR. deceased .. William M. Wright, one of the acting administrators
183   .. 1834 paid $30 to Robert Wright in right of Larkin Herndon's wife,
Jane Herndon, in part of legacy .. paid Elizabeth Thornton in part
of her legacy .. paid Andrew Newman in right of his wife in part of
legacy .. paid Robert Wright in part of legacy .. paid $30.87½ to
William M. Wright, one of the executors of the said deceased, this
amount for Gorah Waugh's children that being their proportionate
part of the money in the hands of Richard Richards Jr. .. settled
27th August 1835 by Vivion Quisenberry, Benja. Sanders, Richard
Richards. At a court held .. 28th September 1835 .. returned and
ordered to lie. At a court held .. 23rd November 1835 .. approved
and ordered to be recorded.

pp.   The estate of JAMES WHITE, dec'd, in account with Anderson White
182-   .. report mentions assets of $62.22 in hands of Anderson White 12th
183   December 1829 .. disbursement of $76.51, 23rd March 1833 .. given
23rd March 1833 by James Simms, James Beazley, Isaac Davis Jr.
At a court held .. 28th September 1835 .. returned and ordered to
lie. At a court held ..23rd November 1835 .. approved and ordered
to be recorded.

pp.   The estate of WILLIAM H. MARTIN in account with Mallory Martin,
182-   administrator .. 10th January 1834 paid Thomas Martin $500 on account
185   of his legacy .. paid Benjamin C. Bickers $500 on account of his
legacy .. paid Ichabod Mallory, guardian of his children, William P.
Mallory and Philip M. Mallory, $254.92 .. paid Jane Arnold on ac-
count of her legacy, $500 .. paid myself as one of the legatees,
$500 .. paid William Martin $500 on account of his legacy .. settled
6th day of September 1834 by Lancelot Burrus, Wm. Stevens, Hezekiah

Quisenberry. At a court held .. 27th May 1735 .. returned and ordered
to lie. At a court held .. 23rd November 1835 .. approved and ordered to be recorded.

pp.   The estate of ELIZABETH BURTON, deceased, in account with Wil-
184-   liam B. Watts, her administrator .. paid George Stevens, executor of
187   James Burton proportion of hire of negroes .. same for Bazalia Bur-
         ton .. settled 19th August 1835 by Johathan Twyman, George Shearman,
         Wm. Walker. At a court held .. 25th August 1835 .. returned and
         ordered to lie. At a court held .. 23rd November 1835 .. approved
         and ordered to be recorded.

pp.   An inventory and appraisement of the personal estate of NANCY
186-   TERRILL, deceased .. value not totalled .. given 18th day of November
187   1835 by appraisers William C. Moore Senr., Geo. W. Morton, John
         Morton. Returned into court 24th November 1835.

pp.   An account of sales of the property belonging to the estate of
188-   JEREMIAH WHITE, dec'd, made by Daniel White, his executor, the 9th
192   day of November 1835 .. some purchasers .. William White, Richard
         Simms, Capt. Michael L. Eheart, Paschal Vaughn, Capt. Edward Cason,
         William Pratt, William T. Jenkins, Capt. Henry Houck, Samuel Scrib-
         ner, Curtis Wilhoite, Mildred White, Bluford Brockman, Winston White,
         Juda White .. whole amount of sale, $3205.80½ .. Returned into court
         28th December 1835.

pp.   Subscribers this 22nd day of December 1830 appraised the following
192-   property of THOMAS C. GORDON, dec'd, produced to us by Armistead
193   Gordon, his administrator .. one silver watch, $10 .. one pocket
         pistol, $1.50 .. one plaid cloak, $5.00 .. appraisers Charles W.
         Levell, Lawson Barnett, Samuel T. Skinker. Returned into court
         22nd February 1836. In another inventory with the total value of
         $85.10 made 8th day of July 1831, appraisers were Jno. R. Jones,
         Wm. A. Bibb, James R. Watson. Returned into court 22nd February 1836.

pp.   Amount of sales of the property belonging to THOMAS C. GORDON,
193-   deceased, made at Charlottesville the 8th day of July 1831 .. amount
194   totalled $50.86½. Returned into court 22nd February 1836.

pp.   Hugh M. Faulconer, executor to the estate of JOHN FAULCONER,
194-   dec'd .. settled 4th December 1835 by Thos. Row, Benja. Sanders,
195   James O. Massey. At a court held 29th March 1836 .. returned and
         ordered to lie. At a court held .. 23rd May 1836 .. approved and
         ordered to be recorded.

pp.   The estate of JOHN SHELOR, dec'd, in account with John Shelor,
196-   executor .. settled 10th March 1835 by William Dulaney, Michael
197   Moyers, T. G. Garth. At a court held 28th December 1835 .. returned
         and ordered to lie. At a court held .. 23rd May 1836 .. approved
         and ordered to be recorded.

pp.   The estate of JOHN BROCKMAN, dec'd, in account with Oswald Brock-
196-   man, executor .. 5th February 1833, paid $70 each to Brockman Bell
199   in right of his wife for horse, and to Js. Mallory in right of his
         wife for a horse .. settled 5th February 1833 by John W. Sale, Thos.
         Coleman, Jacob Graves, Jonathan Graves. At a court held .. 24th
         November .. returned and ordered to lie. At a court held .. 23rd
         May 1836 .. approved and ordered to be recorded.

pp.
198-
199
The estate of JOHN BROCKMAN, dec'd, in account with Oswald Brockman, the executor .."we have made an estimate of the portion to which each devisee is entitled and we find that if the funds were now divided the portion of Samuel, Elijah, John and Thomas Brockman and Elinor Ireland would be $258.76, and of Molly Mallory, $158.76. The funds that is above mentioned came into the executor's hands by virtue of a deed from Elizabeth Brockman to said executor to be divided according to the will of John Brockman, dec'd, by reference to said deed it will be found that the said Elizabeth relinquished her portion of the property willed her for life to be divided as aforesaid." .. settlement made 20th November 1835 by Jacob Graves, Thos. Coleman, Jonathan Graves. At a court held 24th November 1835 .. returned and ordered to lie. At a court held .. 23rd May 1836 .. approved and ordered to be recorded.

pp.
200-
201
Oswald Brockman, administrator of THOMAS BROCKMAN, deceased, in account with said estate .. settled 20th November 1835 by Thomas Coleman, Jacob Graves, Jonathan Graves. At a court held .. 24th November 1835 .. returned and ordered to lie. At a court held .. 23rd May 1836 .. approved and ordered to be recorded.

pp.
200-
203
The estate of JAMES THOMPSON, dec'd, in account with Thacker V. Webb, executor of said deceased .. account begins 14 April 1832 .. settled 28th December 1835 by Charles T. Graves, George Bradley, T. Cockerill .. sworn before Garland Ballard 28th December 1835. At a court held .. 26th January 1836 .. returned and ordered to lie .. At a court held .. 23rd May 1836 .. approved and ordered to be recorded.

pp.
202-
205
The estate of WILLIAM T. BURRUS, dec'd, in account with William S. Frazer, executor .. submitted 28th December 1835 by Wm. Stevens, George W. Morton, Reynolds Chapman. At a court held .. 26th January 1836 .. returned and ordered to lie. At a court held .. 23rd May 1836 .. approved and ordered to be recorded.

pp.
206-
207
The estate of ROBERT MANSFIELD, deceased, in account with Joseph A. Mansfield, executor .. amount remaining in hands of the executor, $3484.41 .. settled 7th day of October 1835 by Joseph Snell, Daniel White, Robert W. Brooking. At a court held .. 23rd November 1835 .. returned and ordered to lie. At a court held .. 23rd May 1836 .. approved and ordered to be recorded.

pp.
207-
210
A list of the sale of the perishable property belonging to the estate of Capt. JAMES BURTON, dec'd, sold on 2nd May 1834 .. there was a second sale 22nd October 1834 .. report of sale followed by an estate account .. subscribers met at house of Robert Cave .. settled George Stephens' executorship account 9th September 1835. Robert Cave, Jonathan Twyman, Blyfil Rucker. At a court held .. 23rd November 1835 .. returned and ordered to lie. At a court held .. 23rd May 1836 .. approved and ordered to be recorded.

pp.
210-
211
Settlement of Luke Thornton's administratorship of the estate of DANIEL THORNTON, dec'd .. a fee of $200 for boarding and clothing two children for two years .. settled 26th September 1835 by Joshua Willis, Thomas Brown, Benja. Hume. At a court held .. 23rd November 1835 .. returned and ordered to lie. At a court held 23rd May 1836 .. approved and ordered to be recorded.

pp.   The estate of WILLIAM WHITE, dec'd, in account with Daniel White,
211-   executor .. on 25th September 1835 subscribers George Stephens,
212   Paschal Twyman, Blyfil Rucker, met at house of Daniel White to settle his account. At a court held .. 26th October 1835 .. returned
and ordered to lie. At a court held .. 23rd May 1836 .. approved
and ordered to be recorded.

pp.   Will of NICHOLAS BICKERS. .. having already given to my son
212-   (some wrote in margin in blue ink, "Joel") his full share of my es-
214   tate, I give and devise to him the sum of twenty five cents only ..
to my beloved wife, Jane .. all the estate of which I may die possessed except two feather beds and their furniture and two cows and
calves .. to my sons, Moses and William, each a feather bed and furniture and a cow and a calf .. to my son, Benjamin C., at the death
of my wife, the land on which he resides, containing by survey made
by Reuben Lindsay, seventy acres .. I lend to my daughter, Joanna
Marshall .. my daughter, Polly Hawkins, being well off and having
no children and my other children being all poor .. one dollar only
.. I give to my son, Joel .. appoint my friends, John Taylor and
William Quarles, executors .. this 17th day of March 1825 ..
Witnesses   (signed)
      James Shepherd   Nicholas Bickers
      W. M. Chapman, Reynolds Chapman
   At a court held .. 27th June 1836 .. proved .. ordered to be recorded .. and John Taylor and William Quarles, the executors being
appointed .. being dead .. on motion of Coleman Marshall (who married
a daughter of the testator) .. with Benjamin Hawkins and John Payne,
his securities .. bond in the penalty of five thousand dollars ..
certificate was granted him for obtaining letters of administration ..

pp.   28th May 1836. John Lancaster, Andrew Samuel and John W. Evans
214-   .. did appraise the personal estate of NICHOLAS BICKERS, deceased,
215   and found it amounted in value to the sum of two thousand eight
hundred and fifteen dollars and eighty seven cents. Returned into
court 27th June 1836.

pp.   Inventory of the cash, bonds and accounts in the possession of
215-   WILLIAM T. BURRUS at the time of his death June 20th 1831 .. total
216   amount $850.67 with $21.38 doubtful .. made by William S. Frazer,
executor of William T. Burrus, dec'd. Returned into court 27th June
1836.

pp.   An appraisal of the estate of PHILIP SLEET, deceased .. consists
216-   of a negro man, woman and four girls with appraised value of $2750
217   .. made by Joshua Willis, Andrew B. Samuel, Alexander A. Boston.
Returned into court 27th June 1836.

pp.   Will of JAMES MADISON. .. I devise to my dear wife during her
217-   life the tract of land wherein I now live .. and if she shall pay the
220   sum of nine thousand dollars within three years to be distributed
as hereinafter directed, then I devise same to her in fee simple ..
if she does not pay, property to be sold .. if wife does pay, I bequeath the said money to be equally divided among all my nephews and
nieces which shall at that time be living, their such issue shall
take the place of its or their deceased parent .. I devise my grist
mill with the land attached thereto to my wife .. to my niece, Nelly
C. Willis, the lot of land lying in Orange County purchased of Bos-

well Thornton .. I devise my house and lot or lots in the city of
Washington to my wife .. it is my desire that the report as made by
me (Constitutional Convention) be published under her authority ..
(makes several bequests of money arising from sale thereof) .. to my
brother in law, John C. Payne .. two hundred and forty acres of land
in which he lives .. appoint my dear wife to be sole executrix ..
this 15th day of April 1835 ..

In the presence of   (signed)
    Robert Taylor, Reuben Newman Senr.   James Madison
    Reuben Newman Junr., Sims Brockman
  Codicil. Additional discussion of nine thousand dollars.
  At a court held .. 25th July 1836 .. offered for probate by Dolly
P. Madison .. proved ..codicil proved .. ordered to be recorded ..
on motion of Dolly P. Madison, the executrix .. bond without security
.. penalty of one hundred thousand dollars .. certificate was granted
her for obtaining a probate thereof in due form.

(The complete will of James Madison is included in the compilers'
book, Pamunkey Neighbors of Orange County, Virginia, pp. 386-390.
For the distribution of the $9,000 see the appendix.)

pp.   Will of MARTIN BAKER of Gordonsville, Orange County, Va. .. I lend
221-   to my wife, my Gordonsville estate, land, slaves, crops, stock,
222   furniture, plantation utensils, etc. .. I wish the tract of land I
        own in the county of Giles, a track on Chickohimony swamp in the
        county of Hanover and a small lot adjoining Woodson Pleasants in
        Solomon Mark's plan in county of Henrico sold .. my interest or claim
        in my Father's estate, I wish disposed of in same manner .. I lend
        to my wife, Maria .. I give my son, John M. Baker, my gold watch I
        imported and now wear .. to each of the rest of my children one hund-
        red and fifty dollars to them equal to him .. I wish my daughter,
        Marion, to have a likely negro girl .. if my daughter, Marion, should
        recover from her lameness .. appoint my nephew, William M. Baker,
        and Thomas Swift Jr., executors .. this 15th day of June 1835 ..
        Teste   (signed)
            Leroy Chandler   Martin Baker
            George Parrott, James Quarles
          At a court held .. 23rd May 1836 .. proved in open court by Leroy
        Chandler. At a court held .. 25th July 1836 .. further proved in
        open court .. and ordered to be recorded .. on motion of William M.
        Baker, an executor .. with Cleavers Baker, John R. Quarles and Richard
        S. Boulware, his securities .. bond in the penalty of twenty thousand
        dollars .. certificate was granted him for obtaining a probate ..

pp.   Will of MARY KENNEDY, wife of Reuben Kennedy. .. in conformity
222-   with the power reserved to me in a marriage contract with my said
224   husband, Reuben Kennedy, make and appoint this to be my last will
        and testament .. I give .. the lot of land whereon I live containing
        twenty acres as being the same lot of land which I got in the divi-
        sion of my Father, William Handcock's, estate and laying near Orange
        Court House to my son, Edwin Spencer Gartin and my daughter, Mary
        June Gartin to be divided between them .. (her part) to include the
        dwelling house, kitchen and orchard .. to my son, William Handcock
        Gartin, fifty dollars, and to my daughter, Patsy Sharrack, thirty
        dollars .. appoint my husband, Reuben Kennedy, and my son, Charles

S. Gartin, executors .. this 10th day of April 1836.
In the presence of   (signed her mark)
   Gilbert H. Hamilton   Mary Kennedy
   William Brown, William Roach
    At a court held .. 25th July 1836 .. proved in open court .. ordered
to be recorded. At a court held .. 24th October 1836 .. Charles S.
Gartin and Reuben Kennedy, who were appointed executors, refused ..
on the motion of Col. C. Digges (who married a daughter of the tes-
tatrix) it is ordered George Morris, Sheriff of the County of Orange,
take the estate .. and administer the same.

pp.   Will of WEDEN SLEET. .. my sons, George, Weden and John J.
224-   Sleet .. have received one hundred and twenty five dollars hereto-
225   fore of me, I wish my son, William C. Sleet, to receive the same
amount when he arrives to the age of twenty one years .. unto my
daughter, Louisa Sleet .. unto my daughter, Sarah Ann Sleet .. to my
beloved wife, Patsy Sleet .. after her death to be equally divided
among my six children .. my desire Mr. Benjamin Walker and my son,
George Sleet, or either of them, shall execute this will .. this
30th day of October 1835 ..
In the presence of   (signed)
   Richard Waugh, Charles Deane,   Weedon Sleet
   Alexander A. Boston, George P. Boston
    At a court held .. 25th July 1836 .. proved in open court .. or-
dered to be recorded .. Benjamin Walker, one of the executors, came
into court and refused .. and George Sleet, the other executor, not
being a resident of this Commonwealth .. on the motion of Richard
Richards Jr. .. with Benjamin Hume and Richard Richards his securities .. bond in the penalty of seven thousand dollars .. certificate
granted him for obtaining letters of administration with the will
annexed ..

pp.   A list of the personal estate of the late JOHN PENCE, dec'd ..
225-   by Benjamin White, administrator .. with the value of each article
226   .. total valued at $10,652.00 with most of the appraised value in
19 slaves .. made 19th August 1836 by appraisers Blyfil Rucker,
Paschal Twyman, John Pittman. Returned into court 26th August 1836.

pp.   An inventory and appraisement of the estate of JOSHUA KENDALL,
226-   dec'd, taken the 5th August 1836 .. total value $3354.93 .. made
228   5th day August 1836 by appraisers Jacob Graves, John W. Sale, Jno.
P. Coleman. Returned into court 22nd August 1836.

pp.   Inventory and appraisement of the estate of ANN FAULCONER, dec'd,
228-   as taken the 25th day of June 1835 .. value totals $3681.56½ .. in-
229   cluding 9 slaves with appraised value of $2275 .. made 23rd June 1835
by Benja. Sanders, Thos. Row, James O. Massey .. certified a true
inventory by Richard Richards and Richard Faulconer. Returned into
court 22nd August 1836.

pp.   Will of MATHIAS MORRISS. .. I give and bequeath all my real and
229-   personal estate to Lucy Ham for waiting on me in my illness .. I
230   leave to my brother, James Morriss, executor of my will .. this
13th day of November 1835.
Test   (signed his mark)
   Nathan Mallory, Slaton (X) Shifflette   Mathias Morriss

At a court held .. 22nd August 1836 .. proved in open court and ordered to be recorded.

pp. 230-231

Will of WILLIAM COX. .. I loan to my beloved wife all my estate during her natural life .. and that each of those children that have not rec'd anything, one bed, furniture and such other things as I gave to those that are married .. after her death, I wish three disinterested persons be appointed to lay it off into six lots, making two of the land whereon I now live and one of the land over the river and three of the negro property .. it is also my will that Frankey and Elizabeth to have the lotts of land whereon my house stands .. I desire for the above lotts made of the negro property to be drawn for by Sarah Estes, Joab Cox and (blank) Cox unless they can agree to division among themselves .. appoint my wife and Warrin Cox, executors .. this 23rd day of July 1835 ..
In the presence of   (signed)
    Joab Cox, Thomas Durrett, Sarah Cox   William Cox
    At a court held .. 22nd August 1836 .. proved in open court .. and ordered to be recorded .. on motion of Warrin Cox, an executor .. with Thomas Durrett and Joab Cox, her securities .. bond in the penalty of two thousand dollars .. certificate was granted him for obtaining letters of administration of the estate ..

pp. 231-232

An appraisal of the slaves belonging to the estate of ELIZA BOXLEY, deceased .. 11 slaves with appraised value of $5100 .. made by appraisers Richd. M. Chapman, Mann A. Page, Richd. Rawlings. Returned into court 23rd August 1836.

pp. 232-233

An appraisement of the estate of EDWARD ANCELL, dec'd .. value not totalled .. appraisers William Melone, Joel Herndon, Washington White. Returned into court 23rd August 1836.

pp. 232-235

The estate of WALTER KEY in account with Joseph Hiden, administrator . At a court held .. 23rd May 1836 .. returned and ordered to lie. At a court held .. 26th September 1836 .. approved and ordered to be recorded. Account settled 19th May 1836 by Philip S. Fry, W. M. Chapman, Tho. A. Robinson.

pp. 234-237

The estate of NANCY TERRILL, dec'd, in account with James Terrill, administrator .. $50 paid Lancelot Burrus as trustee for Nancy Burrus being for rent of houses, gardens and orchard .. settled 31st December 1835 by William C. Moore, Jacob Graves, Wm. Stevens. At a court held .. 23rd May 1836 .. returned and ordered to lie. At a court held .. 26th September 1836 .. approved and ordered to be recorded.

pp. 236-238

Richard Richards, administrator to the estate of BOB (called Bob or Robert Terrill), a man of colour .. April 1, 1834 amount received by administrator, $184.10 .. settled 14th May 1836 by Thos. Row, Benja. Sanders, James Nelson Jr. At a court held .. 23rd May 1836 .. returned and ordered to lie. At a court held .. 26th September 1836 .. approved and ordered to be recorded.

pp. 238-240

An inventory and appraisement of the estate of WEEDON SLEET, dec'd, taken the 24th September 1836 .. four slaves with an appraised value of $2200 .. "one old man Lewis worth nothing" .. total valuation $4272.37½ .. made by appraisers Joshua Willis, Andrew B. Samuel, Alexander A. Boston. Certified a true inventory by Richard Richards Jr. Returned into court 26th September 1836.

pp.   A list of the appraisement of the estate of WILLIAM H. STANARD,
240-   dec'd, 17th August 1836 .. total value $3145.92 .. of which $1900 is
242   for four slaves .. made by appraisers George W. Price, Ro. Pritchett,
        Wm M. Bailey. Returned into court 26th September 1836.

pp.   The estate of EDWARD ANCELL in account with Michael and John
242-   Ancell, executors .. settled 18th August 1836 by William Melone,
243   Joel Herndon, James Beazley. At a court held .. 23rd August 1836 ..
        returned and ordered to lie. At a court held 28th November 1836 ..
        approved and ordered to be recorded.

pp.   John Wright, executor to the estate of JOHN FAULCONER, deceased
244-   .. in the amount to be divided into ten parts .. cash paid John
245   Rhoades full legacy; Robert Wright, guardian, full legacy; John M.
        Faulconer in part of legacy; paid Jesse M. Grant in part of legacy;
        paid Spencer Faulconer in full of legacy; paid William Faulconcer
        in part of legacy; paid William Roach, trustee of Elizabeth Scott;
        paid J. C. Gibson, attorney in behalf of Elizabeth Scott .. settled
        5th August 1836 by Richard Richards, Benjamin Wright, Richard Richards
        Jr. At a court held .. 23rd August 1836 .. returned and ordered to
        lie. At a court held .. 28th November 1836 .. approved and ordered
        to be recorded.

pp.   Richard Richards executor to the estate of MAJOR OAKS, deceased
244-   .. cash paid Thomas Oaks in part of his legacy; cash paid Elizabeth
247   Oaks .. cash paid Nancy Mason; cash paid Major Oaks; cash paid Wil-
        liam Knight in right of his wife; cash paid William Cammock in right
        of his wife; cash paid Sarah Mason; cash paid Miniard Oaks; cash
        paid Mourning Wallace; cash paid Weedon Richards in right of his
        wife; cash paid Samuel Mason Jr.; cash paid Wealthy Oaks .. cash paid
        John Terry in right of his wife, Lucy Terry (who was Lucy Oaks) ..
        settled 14th May 1836 by Thos. Row, Thos. Robinson, Benja. Sanders,
        James Nelson Jr. At a court held .. 22nd August 1836 .. returned and
        ordered to lie. At a court held .. 28th November 1836 .. approved and
        ordered to be recorded.

pp.   The estate of AUGUSTINE GAINES, dec'd, to John White, administra-
248-   tor .. settled 26th July 1836 by Wm. Walker, Benjamin Burton, Wm.
249   Simms. At a court held .. 22nd May 1836 .. returned and ordered to
        lie. At a court held .. 28th November 1836 .. approved and ordered
        to be recorded.

pp.   Appraisal of the personal estate of NANCY MASON, dec'd .. total
250-   value, $225.97½ .. made by appraisers Robert Roach, Richard Richards,
251   Thos. Row .. certified a true statement by Benjamin Sanders, execu-
        tor of Nancy Mason, dec'd. Returned into court 28th November 1836.

pp.   An inventory and appraisement of the estate of THOMAS BURRUS,
251-   dec'd, taken the 15th day of November 1836 .. total value, $253.84
252   of which $125 was appraised value of "old negro man Daniel" .. made
        by appraisers Richard Richards Jr., Richard Richards, Owen Cooper.
        Certified a true inventory by Lancelot Burrus, administrator. Re-
        turned into court 28th November 1836.

pp.   The appraisement and inventory of the goods and chattels of
252-   MARY KENNEDY, deceased .. total value, $474.35 .. made by appraisers
253   W. D. Clark, A. Madison, Robert Taylor Jr. Returned into court 26th
        December 1836.

pp.   Sale of the property belonging to the estate of THOMAS BROWN,
253-   dec'd, December 1st 1836 .. amount of sales $274.74 3/4 .. certified
255   correct by Charles Scott .. the half of these belonging to Edward
           Brown. Returned into court 23rd January 1837.

pp.   December 1st 1836. Inventory and appraisement of the estate of
255-   THOMAS BROWN, dec'd .. total value, $250.23½ .. made by appraisers
257   Charles Scott, Benj. Hawkins, Coleman Marshall. The remaining half
           to Mr. Edward Brown. Returned into court 23rd January 1837.

pp.   List of the appraisement of the estate of MOSES BLEDSOE, dec'd,
256-   taken the 27th day of January 1837 .. total value $6721.50 of which
257        $6550.00 was appraised value of nineteen slaves .. made by appraisers
           Philip Mallory, Thomas Robinson, Elhanon Row, Wm. S. Frazer. Re-
           turned into court 27th February 1837.

pp.   Appraisal of the personal estate of ISAAC GRAVES, deceased, as
257-   shown to us by the executors of the sd Graves, dec'd .. value not
259   totalled .. includes eight slaves with appraised value of $2950 of
           which two have no appraised value .. given 19th March 1836 by apprai-
           sers Brockman Bell, John Terrill, Peter R. Johnson, Oswald Brockman.
           Returned into court 27th February 1837.

pp.   Will of JAMES DANIEL. .. my estate both real and personal to be
259-   kept together .. and I do lend the same to my beloved wife .. she
261   shall give with the advice and consent of my executor .. to my three
           youngest children (Beverly, Mary and Sarah) as they may marry or
           come of age .. it is my will and desire that the lot of negroes and
           other property deeded from my sister, Frances Henderson, to my son,
           William Travis Daniel .. appoint my friend, Jacob Graves, and my son,
           William Travis Daniel, so soon as he may arrive to the age of twenty
           one, my executors .. this 9th day of April 1836 ..
           In the presence of   (signed his mark)
               William F. Graves, Garrit Graves,   James Daniel
               Isaac M. Graves, William Graves
               At a court held .. 27th February 1837 .. proved .. ordered to be
           recorded .. Jacob Graves refused .. William Travis Daniel being
           under age of twenty one .. on motion Sarah Daniel, widow of the
           testator .. with Brockman Bell and Richard S. Boulware, her securi-
           ties .. bond in the penalty of twelve thousand dollars .. she is
           appointed to collect and preserve the goods, chattels and credits
           of the said James Daniel, dec'd, until the executors named in the
           will shall appear and qualify or until the further order of the court.

pp.   An inventory and appraisement of the estate of MARTIN BAKER,
261-   deceased, made 29th July 1836 .. value not totalled .. made by apprai-
265   sers Leroy Chandler, John M. Herndon, William T. Davis. Returned
           into court 27th February 1837.

pp.   An inventory of the personal estate of BENJAMIN L. MITCHELL,
265-   dec'd, made by me as administrator this ninth day of April 1835 ..
266   William L. Mitchell. Total value $223.57 3/4 .. sworn by appraisers
           Samuel Scrivener, Davis Bowler, William Douglas 3rd September 1836.
           Returned into court 27th February 1837.

pp.   Sale of NICHOLAS BICKERS by the administrator, C. Marshall ..
266-   amount of sale, $117.30. Returned into court 27th March 1837.
267

pp.   The estate of ELIZABETH ESTES, dec'd, to James Beazley, adminis-
268-   trator .. total value, $1415.68 3/4 .. made 16th January 1837 by
269   appraisers Ro. Pritchett, Benjamin White, Elijah K. Davis. Returned
       into court 23rd January 1837 .. and ordered to lie. At a court held
       .. 27th March 1837 .. approved and ordered to be recorded.

pp.   The estate of WILLIAM GRADY, dec'd, to William Grady, administrator
270-   .. July 5th 1830 paid Lewis Rawlings, admor of John Grady, dec'd
271   .. $328.05 William Grady's portion of the estate .. settled 16th
       November 1831 by Thomas Row, Benj. Sanders, Richard Richards, Edmd.
       Row. At a court held .. 24th October 1836 .. returned and ordered
       to lie. At a court held .. 27th March 1837 .. approved and ordered
       to be recorded.

pp.   Account of Howard Shifflet to the estate of LEWIS DAVIS, dec'd ..
270-   sale of two tracts of land, $386.14, and $19.20 to James Nelson for
273   surveying said land .. settled 18th November 1836 by George S. Blakey,
       Jacob Raines, James Beazley. At a court held .. 28th November 1836 ..
       returned and ordered to lie. At a court held 27th March 1837 .. ap-
       proved and ordered to be recorded.

pp.   Estate of ELIZA J. BOXLEY, dec'd, in account with Albert Boxley,
272-   administrator .. Alexander Holladay, attorney .. A. Boxley received
275    $2.30 as guardian .. commissioners found $5722.81 for assigning to
       the distributees, Albert Boxley, William Boxley, John Graves and
       John Kimbrough to each $812, likewise to Martha Boxley and Virginia
       Boxley, children of Joseph Boxley, deceased, to each of the said
       children, $406 .. also to Mary Boxley and Elizabeth Boxley, children
       of John C. Boxley, $406 each .. likewise to John W. Boxley, Lucy Ann
       Boxley and Mary Boxley, children of John C. Boxley, dec'd, $220.66
       each .. settled 8th September 1836 by Lewis Johnson, James Gardner,
       Jonathan Johnson. At a court held .. 26th September 1836 .. returned
       and ordered to lie. At a court held .. 27th March 1837 .. approved
       and ordered to be recorded.

pp.   Richard Richards, administrator to the estate of ROBERT CAMPBELL,
274-   dec'd .. property sold 26th July 1834 .. settled 17th September 1836
276   by Thos. Row, Benj. Sanders, James Nelson Jr. At a court held ..
       24th October 1836 .. returned and ordered to lie. At a court held ..
       27th March 1837 .. approved and ordered to be recorded.

pp.   We, Blyfil Rucker, John Pittman and Paschal Twyman, commissioners
276-   .. have on 25th day August 1836 proceeded to value and allot the
277   slaves belonging to the estate of JOHN PENCE, dec'd .. lot no. 1,
       to William Pence; lot no. 2, to John Herndon in right of his wife;
       lot no. 3, widow's lot. Returned into court 27th March 1837.

pp.   Will of GEORGE STUBBLEFIELD. .. bequeath to my wife, Mary, one
277-   third of my estate both real and personal during her natural life
278   (in case she should live longer than I do) to her death the said
       property shall be placed in the hands of Philip Williams and George
       Morton for the benefit of my son, Thomas L. Stubblefield and his
       wife, Polly .. (wills items each dealing with segements of his estate

for trust to Thomas L. Stubblefield and wife, Polly) .. to my daughter, Frances Smith, a negro .. appoint Philip Williams and George Morton, my executors .. this 15th day of May 1832 ..

Witnesses   (signed)
    Edwin E. Gibson   Thomas Stubblefield
    Henry Newman, William W. Hume

      At a court held .. 27th March 1837 .. proved .. ordered to be recorded .. George Morton refused ..

pp.   A list of the appraisement of the personal estate of JOHN FEARNEY-
279-   HOUGH, deceased, March the 8th 1837 .. value $299.95 .. made by ap-
280   praisers John Taliaferro, W. Porter, William Wayland. Returned into
       court 27th March 1837.

pp.   January 10, 1833. An account of the sale of WILLIAM H. MARTIN'S
280-   property sold by the executor, Mallory Martin, agreeable to the last
286   will and testament of William H. Martin .. some purchasers .. Colo.
       C. Digges, William Mallory, William Bickers, Newman Kennedy, William
       Bullock, Benjamin Bickers, Lancelot Burrus, William Brockman, James
       Frazier, Nicholas Bickers, Joseph Burrus, Mrs. John Payne, Robert
       Burrus, William Martin, Thomas Martin, Fontain Rogers, Willis Over-
       ton, Mallory Martin, Tartan Smith, William P. Southerland .. total
       amount of sale, $4072.58 .. "There was found a small account against
       Jane Arnall with the other papers belonging to the estate of William
       H. Martin which has been lost or mislaid. The amount I do not re-
       collect. Capt. Stevens, who examined the papers, may. M. Martin."
       There also is a list of bonds. Returned into court 24th April 1837.

pp.   Will of FORTUNATUS WINSLOW. .. all the perishable property of
287-   my estate .. sold .. pay debts .. if insufficient .. executrix may
288   sell any property I now possess .. pay remainder .. I lend to my wife,
       Mary Winslow, all my estate both real and personal during the term
       of her natural life .. after her decease, I give the same to my grand-
       children, Mary Elliot Bell Smith, Robert Smith, Martha Smith, Eva-
       lina Smith and William Washington Smith, all children of my only child,
       a daughter, Frances Mary Miller Bell Smith .. except Mary Elliot Bell
       Smith is to have five hundred dollars more than others .. appoint
       my wife, Mary Winslow, executrix .. this 10th day of May 1824.

In the presence of   (signed)
    Thos. Sorrille,   Fortunatus Winslow
    Wm. Beadles, Moses Winslow.

      At a court held .. 24th April 1837 .. William Beadles testified
the other witnesses signed the same in his presence but were now dead
.. ordered to be recorded .. Mary Winslow, appointed executrix, refuses .. motion James Beadles .. with Newton Hume and Noah Smith,
his securities .. bond in penalty of three thousand dollars .. certificate was granted him for obtaining letters of administration...

pp.   The estate of JOHN SHELOR, dec'd, to John Shelor, executor ..
288-   paid $204.54 to Jeremiah Walker who married Rachel Shelor as part
290   of her legacy .. bond against William S. Powell .. settled 23rd May
       1833 by Th. G. Garth, William Dulaney, John N. Sorrille, Michael
       Moyers. At a court held .. 22nd July 1833 .. returned and ordered to
       lie. At a court held .. 22nd May 1837 .. approved and ordered to be
       recorded.

pp. 290- 291

Estate of JOHN BROCKMAN, deceased, in account with Oswald Brockman, executor .. amount of sale of property of said estate, $2047.36½ .. settled 16th November 1832 by Thos. Coleman, Jonathan Graves, Benja. Coleman. At a court held .. 27th November 1832 .. returned and ordered to lie. At a court held 22nd May 1837 .. approved and ordered to be recorded.

pp. 290- 293

Estate of JOHN BROCKMAN, deceased, in account with Oswald Brockman, executor .. paid Mrs. Coleman .. paid Brockman Bell in right of his wife in lieu of a horse .. paid James Mallory in right of his wife for horse.. paid James Hawkins as a tuition for Hugh M. Brockman .. settled 5th February 1833 by John W. Sale, Jacob Graves, Jonathan Graves. At a court held .. 23rd September 1833 .. returned and ordered to lie. At a court held .. 22nd May 1837 .. approved and ordered to be recorded.

pp. 292- 293

The estate of THOMAS BROCKMAN, dec'd, in account with Oswald Brockman .. $249.27 Thomas Brockman's portion of John Brockman's estate now in hands of Oswald Brockman, the executor .. settled 25th March 1833 by Jacob Graves, Thos. Coleman, John W. Sale. At a court held .. 23rd September 1833 .. returned and ordered to lie. At a court held .. 22nd May 1837 .. approved and ordered to be recorded.

pp. 294- 295

The estate of CAPT. JOHN BEADLES, dec'd, to William Dulaney .. the sum of $164.33½ remains in the hands of Col. Dulaney .. settled 25th June 1830 by Joseph Eddins, Thos. Davis, William Sims. At a court held 28th June 1830 .. returned and not being excepted to was approved .. ordered to be recorded. A further settlement made by John N. Sorrille, Ro. Pritchett, William Collins. At a court held .. 27th March 1837 .. returned and ordered to lie. At a court held .. 22nd May 1837 .. approved and ordered to be recorded.

pp. 296- 299

Richard Richards and Richard Faulconer, executors to the estate of ANN FAULCONER, deceased .. one twelfth part of $1992 which is to be divided into eleven parts .. William Highlander's part in right of his wife, $126 .. Thomas Wright in right of his wife, Spencer Faulconer, Edward Beale, attorney for William Highlander .. Richard Faulconer's legacy .. George Faulconer per receipt .. Spencer Faulconer, attorney for Ambrose Faulconer .. cash paid William Faulconer .. settled 11th February 1837 by Benj. Sanders, Thos. Row, Richard Richards Jr. At a court held .. 27th March 1837 .. returned and ordered to lie. At a court held .. 22nd May 1837 .. approved and ordered to be recorded.

pp. 298- 299

WEEDON SLEET, deceased, administrator to estate of PHILIP SLEET, dec'd .. paid Rebecca Sleet per receipt .. settled 12th November 1836 by Thos. Row, Benj. Sanders, Thomas Robinson. At a court held .. 27th March 1837 .. returned and ordered to lie. At a court held .. 22nd May 1837 .. approved and ordered to be recorded.

pp. 300- 303

The estate of WILLIAM T. BURRUS, dec'd, in account with William S. Frazer, administrator .. settled by Tho. A. Robinson, James Shepherd, Mann A. Page, Reynolds Chapman. At a court held 27th February 1837 .. returned and ordered to lie. At a court held 22nd May 1837 .. approved and ordered to be recorded.

pp.   Joseph Apperson, administrator to the estate of PETER APPERSON,
304-   deceased .. property sold 14th November 1834 .. settled 11th February
305   1837 by Richard Richards, Benj. Sanders, Thos. Robinson. At a court
        held .. 27th February 1837 .. returned and ordered to lie. At a court
        held .. 22nd May 1837 .. approved and ordered to be recorded.

pp.   Estate of RICHARD B. WEBB, deceased, in account with Benjamin
304-   Hume, late Sheriff of Orange County .. received $97.10 from Metcalf
307   on account of estate who was agent of Rosanna Wright .. settled 20th
        March 1837 by Mann A. Page, James Shepherd, Thos. A. Robinson. At
        a court held 27th March 1837 .. returned and ordered to lie .. At a
        court .. 22nd May 1837 .. approved and ordered to be recorded.

pp.   An inventory of the estate of JAMES DANIEL, deceased, taken this
306-   20th day of April 1837 .. Sarah Daniel acting as curator of James
307   Daniel, dec'd, est .. no value of items or total value. Returned
        into court 22nd May 1837.

pp.   Will of JOHN TALIAFERRO. .. sell slaves (named) together with
307-   land purchased of Robert Cave lying and being in the county of Orange
308   .. money arising to pay my debts .. I wish my wife, Mildred M. Talia-
        ferro, to remain in full and peaceable possession of all the remainder
        of my estate .. after my wife's decease .. property to be sold and
        money arising from same to be equally divided between all my children,
        to wit, Ann Elizabeth Walters, Lucy H. Taliaferro, Martha M. Talia-
        ferro, Jas. C. Taliaferro and Mary L. Taliaferro .. appoint my wife,
        Mildred M. Taliaferro, executrix .. this 1st day of July 1834 ..
        Test   (signed)
            Joseph A. Mansfield, R. Thomas   John Taliaferro
        Codicil: grant to Mildred M. Taliaferro letters of administration
        without binding her to security ..
            At a court held .. 22nd May 1837 proved by Joseph A. Mansfield ..
            At a court held .. 26th June 1837 .. further proved .. ordered to
        be recorded .. motion of Mildred M. Taliaferro, the executrix .. with
        Joseph A. Mansfield, her security .. bond in the penalty of twenty
        five hundred dollars .. certificate was granted her for obtaining a
        probate thereof in due form.
            On Margin. Adm de bonis non granted Isaac Walters at May Court
        1849.

pp.   Appraisal of the estate of GEORGE NEWMAN, deceased .. value
308- $31.75 .. made by appraisers V. M. Houseworth, Bluford T. Williams,
309   A. Madison. Returned into court 27th June 1837.

p.   Inventory and appraisement of POLLY PRICE, dec'd, 15th day of
309   April 1837 .. valued at $14.87½ .. made by appraisers Robert Dedman,
        Danl. Young, Joseph Hilman. Returned into court 27th June 1837.

pp.   Joseph Jones, executor to the estate of ELIJAH JONES, deceased
310-   .. amount from sale of property, $678.56 .. amount from John Jones
311   agreably to the will for a cow and sow pigs, $10.00 .. made 5th May
        1837 by appraisers Richard Richards, Richard Richards Junr., Benj.
        Sanders, Thomas Robinson. At a court held .. 22nd May 1837 .. report
        returned and ordered to lie. At a court held .. 24th July 1837, ap-
        proved and ordered to be recorded.

pp.   Will of ALBERT G. AMOS. At a court held .. 24th July 1837 .. de-
311-   positions of Robert Amos and Joseph Thompson purporting the noncupa-
312   tive will of Albert G. Amos, deceased, are established by the court
       as the last will and testament of said Albert G. Amos .. direct that
       the small amount of property now in the possession of my father,
       Benjamin Amos .. be given to my sister, Janette Amos .. this 27th
       day of February 1837 ..
                                              Robert Amos
           Certified 24th June 1837 by James Thompson. Sworn before Robert
       W. Brooking, justice of the peace.

pp.   Will of GEORGE NEWMAN. .. give and bequeath to my son, James
312-   Newman, one half of the tract of land I purchased of William Winslow
314   (description) .. the other half of land I purchased of the said Wins-
       low, I give and bequeath to my son, Elias Newman .. I give and be-
       queath to my son, George Newman, all my land I purchased of George
       Hamilton lying in the county of Madison .. to my daughter, Elizabeth
       Winslow, late Elizabeth Newman, wife of Edward Winslow, all my lands
       that I purchased of Joseph Williams .. on the waters of Marsh Run
       .. (next four bequests grants negroes to each of his children) .. I
       lend to my wife, Ann Newman .. (negroes) .. I give to my son, George
       Newman, all my household furniture which I left in Madison County
       when I moved therefrom .. appoint my two sons, Elias Newman and
       George Newman, executors .. (undated) ..
       Teste   (signed)
           Joseph Cave, P. C. Cave   George Newman
           At a court held .. 26th June 1837 .. duly proved ..
           At a court held .. 24th July 1837 .. further proved .. and ordered
       to be recorded.

pp.   An inventory and appraisement of the estate of FORTUNATUS WINSLOW,
314-   deceased, made the 16th day of May 1837 .. total value $4431.12½ ..
316   including ten slaves with an appraised value of $1750 .. made by
       appraisers James Finks, William Dulaney, James P. Sims. Returned
       into court 29th August 1837.

pp.   The estate of ISAAC DAVIS JUNR. in account with the estate of
316-   DAVID WHITELAW, dec'd .. account begins 20th June 1825 .. to July 17,
321   1834 .. a ten percent commission allowed on $5717.25¼ .. settled
       30th January 1837 by James Beazley, Benjamin W. White, Edward G.
       Ship. At a court held .. 26th June 1837 .. returned and ordered to
       lie. At a court held .. 28th August 1837 .. approved and ordered to
       be recorded.

pp.   Sales of the estate of FORTUNATUS WINSLOW, deceased, made the
321-   2nd day of June 1837 .. Mary Winslow primary purchaser .. also James
325   Beadles, Henry Winslow, Noah Smith and others .. total amount of
       sale, $1386.44½. Returned into court 29th August 1837.

pp.   Reuben Lindsay, administrator of WILLIAM LINDSAY, deceased ..
324-   balance due estate, $199.78½ .. settled by William C. Moore Senr.,
327   George W. Morton, Jacob Graves. At a court held .. 26th June 1837 ..
       returned and ordered to lie. At a court held .. 28th August 1837 ..
       approved and ordered to be recorded.

p.   Settlement of A. (Andrew) Samuel's administratorship of his
326   father's (John Samuel) estate .. settled by Joshua Willis, Curtis
        Brockman, Wm. Mallory. At a court held .. 28th August 1837 .. re-
        turned and ordered to lie. At a court held .. 23rd October 1837 ..
        approved and ordered to be recorded.

p.   Settlement of Andrew Samuel's administration account of CATHARINE
327   SAMUEL'S estate .. settled by Joshua Willis, Curtis Brockman, Wm.
        Mallory. At a court held .. 28th August 1837 .. returned and ordered
        to lie. At a court held .. 23rd October 1837 .. approved and ordered
        to be recorded.

pp.   The estate of JAMES FARISH, deceased, in account with Wm. W.
328-   Jones, Executor .. $510.51 paid Robert Latham on the 15th September
331   1834 for the purchase of 50 acres of land by order of the decree of
        County Court of Culpeper for the benefit of James W. Farish, infant
        child of James Farish, dec'd .. $187.87 retained to myself in right
        of my wife, Elizabeth .. same amount paid Martin Slaughter and wife
        .. John Slaughter and wife, and Benjamin Farish .. appears to be a
        suit in County Court of Culpeper .. settled 28th December 1836 by
        G. W. Latham, Danl. Ward, Fred. Fishback. At a court held .. 28th
        August 1837 .. returned and ordered to lie. At a court held .. 23rd
        October 1837 .. approved and ordered to be recorded.

pp.   Thomas G. Garth, administrator to the estate of SAMUEL HAM, dec'd
330-   .. paid legatees, Frances Ham, Sarah Ham $377.25 each; Elizabeth
333   Collins, $321.54, Elijah Ham, $50, Elijah K. Davis for Achilles
        Rogers, $300, Elijah Ham for Vernon Ham, $50 .. amount still due
        legatees, $1165.26 .. settled 20th April 1836 by George S. Blakey,
        Granville Kennedy, Jacob Haines. At a court held .. 28th August ..
        returned and ordered to lie. At a court held .. 23rd October 1837 ..
        approved and ordered to be recorded.

pp.   An appraisement of the property of GEORGE NEWMAN SENR. deceased,
332-   at $19.37 .. made by appraisers V. M. Houseworth, Robert Newman,
333   Hugh Robinson. Returned into court 23rd October 1837.

pp.   Will of JOSEPH EDDINS. .. I loan to my beloved wife, Nancy Eddins,
333-   all my tract of land on which I live, all my negroes except Jenny,
334   all my stock, all my household and kitchin furniture, etc. .. if
        she married, my children has the priviledge of compelling her only
        to take use of one third part of the above property .. immediately
        after my death, my executor to sell .. Jenny .. to pay all my just
        debts .. after wife's death, property to be sold and equally divided
        among all my children, Susannah Eddins, Thomas J. Eddins, Simeon D.
        Eddins, Addison D. Eddins, William Eddins, Mary Eddins and Julian
        Eddins .. appoint my son, Thomas J. Eddins .. sole executor .. this
        21st day of September 1837 ..
        Acknowledged before   (signed)
            William Dulaney, Thos. M. Shearman   Joseph Eddins
        At a court held .. 23rd October 1837 .. duly proved .. ordered to
        be recorded .. on motion of Thomas J. Eddins .. with James G. Blakey,
        William C. Willis, Daniel Miller and Richard S. Boulware, his securi-
        ties .. bond in the penalty of sixteen thousand dollars .. certifi-
        cate was granted him for obtaining a probate thereof in due form.

pp.
335-
337
An appraisement and inventory taken at the late residence of JOSEPH EDDINS, deceased, the 15th of November 1837 .. 283 acres of land @ $15.07½, $4444.51½ .. five negroes, $2000.00 .. total value of appraised estate, $8589.51 .. made by appraisers William Collins, John G. Dulaney, William Sims. Returned into court 27th November 1837.

pp.
336-
337
Appraisal of the estate of the late WM. COX SENR. .. 3rd March 1837 .. total value $2971.00 .. Returned into court 27th November 1837.

pp.
337-
339
Will of JOHN WILLIAMS. .. I loan my wife, Mildred Williams, if she survives my decease .. all that part of my land whereon I now live which is on the north side of Marsh Run including my mansion house .. that my daughter, Polly Williams, may enjoy the same with her Mother .. balance of my land on south side Marsh Run to be rented .. money equally divided among my five children, Polly Williams, Elizabeth Parrott, Fanny Austin, Joseph Williams, William Williams .. appoint my two sons, Joseph Williams and William Williams, my executors .. this 18th day of October 1828 ..

In the presence of   (signed)
    Valentine Johnson   John Williams
    Robt. Mansfield, Joseph A. Mansfield

At a court held .. 27th November 1837 .. proved .. ordered to be recorded .. William Williams coming into court refused .. on motion of John Williams, the other executor .. with William Williams, Michael L. Eheart and Robert Thomas, his securities .. bond in the penalty of fourteen thousand dollars .. certificate was granted him for obtaining a probate thereof in due form.

p..
339
The estate of JAMES HANEY, dec'd, to Bazil Haney, administrator .. settled 18th September 1837 by John N. Sorrille, Th. G. Garth, John Shelar. At a court held .. 23rd October 1837 .. returned and ordered to lie. At a court held .. 25th December 1837 .. approved and ordered to be recorded.

pp.
340-
341
The estate of JEREMIAH WHITE, dec'd, in account with Daniel White, Executor .. met at house of Robert Cave 13th October 1837 .. find a balance of $2505.24 3/4 due estate or legatees of Jeremiah White, deceased .. settled by Robert W. Booking, Robt. Cave, William Eddins, William Wayland. At a court held .. 23rd October 1837 .. returned and ordered to lie. At a court held 25th December 1837 .. approved and ordered to be recorded.

pp.
341-
343
Will of ADAM EHEART. .. desire to be buried in my family graveyard .. bequeath to my sister, Mary Darnal, thirty acres of land on which she now lives adjoining the lands of Milton Wilhoit and Robert Brooking .. also two hundred dollars .. to my niece, Jinsey Darnal, two hundred dollars .. my sister, Sarah Eheart, three hundred dollars .. my sister, Caty Lucas, three hundred dollars .. my sister, Elizabeth Eheart, my musical instrument (piano) .. appoint my two friends, Ezekiel Lucas and William Wayland, executors .. this 29th day of November 1837.

Witnesses   (signed)
    John Pittman, William Eddins   Adam Eheart
At a court held .. 25th December 1837 .. proved .. ordered to be recorded .. on motion of (executors) .. with William Simons, William

Eddins and Thomas Yager, their securities .. bond in the penalty of six thousand dollars .. certificate was granted them for obtaining a probate thereof in due form.

pp.
343-
345

An inventory of the personal estate of JOHN WILLIAMS, dec'd, made by me as executor thereof on the 8th day of December 1837 .. total value, $7457 .. signed Joseph Williams .. appraisers Robt. W. Booking, William Martin, Joseph Snell. Returned into court 25th December 1837.

pp.
346-
347

Will of REUBEN CONWAY. .. I constitute and appoint my beloved wife, Lucy, executrix .. I subject all my estate to the payment of my debts .. one half of the balance (which still may be due) paid by the sale of negroes which I acquired by my wife .. I give and devise my beloved wife in full and absolute fee simple .. all the balance of the estate that came by her .. and after her death I give and devise that part of my estate given to my wife during her life to my own relations to be divided among them as the law directs .. this 23rd day of June 1837 ..

In the presence of   (signed)
   Reynolds Chapman   Reuben Conway
     A. Madison, James Shepherd
     At a court held .. 22nd January 1838 .. proved .. ordered to be recorded.
     At a court held .. 23rd April 1838 .. on motion of Lucy Conway, the executrix .. with James M. Macon, Conway C. Macon and Reuben Macon, her securities .. bond in the penalty of fifteen thousand dollars .. certificate was granted her for obtaining a probate ..

p.
347

We Catlett Rhoades, Daniel Young and Thomas Rhoades, appraisers of the estate of POLLY MACKINTOSH, dec'd .. appraise one colt to the value of twenty dollars .. 5th day of December 1837. Returned into court 26th February 1838.

pp.
347-
349

A list of the appraisement of the estate of GEORGE STUBBLEFIELD, deceased, taken on the 12th day of February 1838 .. total value, $2180.75 .. made by appraisers Jeremiah Pannill, George Pannill, Thomas W. Gray, Elhanon Row, D.S. for Thomas Row, S.O.C. Returned into court 26th February 1838.

pp.
348-
350

An account of the settlement of the administrative accounts of James G. Lindsay on the estate of REUBEN LINDSAY, deceased .. settled 18th January 1838 by William C. Moore, Thos. Coleman, John P. Coleman, Jacob Graves. At a court held 22nd January 1838 .. returned and ordered to lie. At a court .. held 26th March 1838 .. approved and ordered to be recorded.

pp.
350-
353

An inventory of the real and personal estate of JOHN TALIAFERRO, dec'd, made by me, executrix thereof on the 15th day of December 1837 .. value totalled, $3789.37½ .. William Eddins, Joseph Snell and William Martin viewed and appraised 24th December 1837. Returned into court 26th March 1838.

p.
352

We, William Smith, Hugh Robinson and Valentine M. Houseworth .. appraisers .. property belonging to ELIAS NEWMAN, deceased .. value not totalled .. sworn before C. C. Macon. Returned into court 23rd April 1838.

pp.   Will of NANCY LINDSAY, widow of William Lindsay .. direct my
353-   executors .. to sell all my estate .. with the exception of my
354   sorrel horse, saddle and bridle and two beds which I dispose of as
           follows. I give to Julia Mason, my housekeeper, my sorrel horse,
           bridle and saddle and one bed and furniture .. I give to Marcellus
           Shepherd, son of John Shepherd, late of Fredericksburg, Virginia ..
           I give to Proctor Bickers .. I give the balance of my estate to Helen
           Shepherd, daughter of James Shepherd of Orange County Courthouse,
           Virginia .. Alexander Shepherd, Marcellus Shepherd and George Shep-
           herd, sons of Joseph Shepherd, late of Fredericksburg, and James L.
           Robinson, son of Thomas Robinson of Orange County, Virginia .. ap-
           point William (son of John) my executor .. this 27th day of April 1838 ..
           In the presence of   (signed)
               James B. Moore, Frances Moore,   Nancy Lindsay
               Elijah Morton, William S. Reynolds
             At a court held .. 28th May 1838 .. proved in open court .. or-
           dered to be recorded .. Richard Richards .. with James Shepherd and
           Thomas A. Robinson, his securities .. bond in the penalty of four
           thousand dollars .. certificate was granted him for obtaining letters
           of administration with the will annexed ..

           (Compilers' note. The settlement of the estate of William Lindsay
           is detailed in their book, Pamunkey Neighbors of Orange County,
           Virginia.)

pp.   Appraisement of MAJOR WILLIAM'S estate, dec'd, this 26th May
354-   1838 .. value not totalled .. made by appraisers Daniel Landrum,
355   Henry C. Bell, John Huston. Returned into court 28th May 1838.

pp.   A list of the property personal and real belonging to the estate
355-   of the late REUBEN LINDSAY .. includes twenty-nine negroes with an
357   appraised value of $8350 .. Polly and Phillis no value shown .. made
           by appraisers C. C. Macon, Jno. H. Lee, John Willis, A. Madison.
           Returned into court 28th May 1838.

pp.   The estate of WILLIAM H. STANARD, deceased, to Newton Hume, ad-
357-   ministrator .. settled 21st April 1838 by William Dulaney, James
359   Beazley, Ro. Pritchett. At a court held .. 23rd April 1838 .. re-
           turned and ordered to lie. At a court held .. 25th June 1838 .. ap-
           proved and ordered to be recorded.

pp.   Settlement of the administration accounts of John W. Sale on
360-   the estate of CHARLES BOSWELL, deceased, made 22nd March 1838 .. set-
361   tled by Joshua Willis, Walter Gambril, Jas. G. Lindsay. At a court
           held .. 26th March 1838 .. returned and ordered to lie. At a court
           held .. 25th June 1838 .. approved and ordered to be recorded.

pp.   The estate of WEEDON SLEET, deceased, to Richard Richards Junr.,
360-   administrator with will annexed .. paid commissioners $6.00 for set-
364   ling up deceased guardianship of Sarah F. Wood, formerly Berry ..
           paid Philip Wood's receipts .. 27th March 1837, cash received from
           James Willis, guardian of Philip Sleet's children .. whole amount
           received, $889.39½ .. settled 21st April 1838 by Benj. Walker, Benj.
           Sanders, Thos. Row, Thomas Robinson. At a court held 23rd April 1838
           .. returned and ordered to lie. At a court held .. 25th June 1838 ..
           approved and ordered to be recorded.

pp. 364-367
1835. The administrator of the estate of WILLIAM STEPHENS, deceased. A list of sales, cash on hand and accounts received .. the account of George Stephens .. settled 23rd March 1838 by Geo. W. Shearman, James Wayt, John Graves. At a court held .. 26th March 1838 .. returned and ordered to lie. At a court held 25th June 1838 .. approved and ordered to be recorded.

p. 367
Commissioners Martin Baker, Robert King and Chas. Beale appointed to allot and assign to MARTHA KEY, widow and relict of WALTER KEY, dec'd, one half in value of the slaves of which the said Walter Key possessed .. as her dower .. (12 slaves) .. Returned into court 27th August 1838.

pp. 368-369
The administrator to the estate of GEORGE STEPHENS, deceased, on a former settlement which was made and returned into court .. made 23rd March 1838 by Geo. W. Shearman, James Wayt, John Graves. At a court held .. 26th March 1838 .. returned and ordered to lie. At a court held .. 25th June 1838 .. approved and ordered to be recorded.

pp. 368-373
The estate of MARTIN BAKER in account with William M. Baker, Executor .. paid Mrs. Maria Baker, 24th August 1836, $11.66 (and other payments shown) .. also shows payments to John M. Baker, George Parrott, Wm. M. Baker, Cleavers Baker .. settled 20th January 1838 by commissioner Richard M. Chapman. At a court held .. 28th May 1838 .. returned and ordered to lie. At a court held .. 23rd July 1838 .. approved and ordered to be recorded.

pp. 372-375
WEEDON SLEET, deceased, committee in account with ARCHIBALD PETTY (Lunatic) .. shows a balance due Archibald Petty of $606.58½ .. made 23rd day of June 1838 by Thos. Row, Benj. Sanders, Thomas Robinson. At a court held .. 25th June .. returned and ordered to lie. At a court held .. 27th August 1838 .. approved and ordered to be recorded.

pp. 374-375
The report that appears on page 367 concerning the division of the slaves of WALTER KEY, to his widow, Martha Key, is repeated.

pp. 375-378
An inventory of the personal estate of ADAM EHEART, dec'd .. 6th day of January 1838 .. value totalled, $3132.22, made by Ezekiel Lucas, William Wayland. Some prices annexed to report by Edward Cason, James White, Richd. Sims. Returned into court 27th August 1838.

pp. 378-380
An inventory of the bonds due the estate of NANCY LINDSAY, dec'd, of Orange County, Va. .. (four bonds) .. total $1226 .. and an inventory and appraisement of the estate of NANCY LINDSAY, dec'd .. including sale of 153 acres of land adjoining John W. Sale and others, $918 .. ten slaves with an appraised value of $4675 .. made 31st May 1838 by appraisers William C. Moore Senr., William S. Reynolds, Elhanon Row. Certified a true copy by Richard Richards. Returned into court 27th August 1838.

pp. 380-382
A list of the property belonging to the estate of JOHN LANCASTER, dec'd, 8th day of June 1838 .. value totalled $1056.37½ .. made by appraisers Vivion Quisenberry, Benjamin Wright, Joseph Hilman, John Herndon. Returned into court 27th August 1838.

pp.   A list of the appraisement of the estate of WILLIAM COLLINS,
383-   dec'd, taken the 2nd day of August 1838 .. value totalled $592.50 ..
384   made by appraisers Joseph Jackson, Robert Kindall, Wm. Stevens.
           Returned into court 27th August 1838.

p.   Sale made by George Newman, executor of GEORGE NEWMAN, dec'd,
384   on the 16th day of November 1837 .. on a credit of nine months ..
           Elias and George Newman only purchasers. Returned into court 24th
           September 1838.

pp.   A list of the property sold by George Newman, administrator of
384-   GEORGE NEWMAN, dec'd, January 13, 1838 .. on nine months credit. Re-
385   turned into court 24th September 1838.

pp.   Appraisal of the personal estate of SARAH COOKE, dec'd .. value
385-   not totalled .. made by appraisers William T. Davis, John S. Cowherd,
386   William J. Davis. Returned into court 24th September 1838.

pp.   A list of the personal estate of JOHN PENCE, dec'd, taken on the
386-   15th day of September 1836 .. Benjamin White, administrator .. total
387   amount of sale, $182.09 .. certified by Benjamin W. White. Returned
           into court 24th September 1838.

pp.   Will of SUSAN HOUSEWORTH. .. I give unto my children all my lands
387-   lying in Orange County .. I give my negroes to my children to be
388   equally divided among them .. I appoint my husband, Valentine House-
           worth, the guardian for all my children and that the court will
           allow him to act without security .. and that he shall give to his
           daughter, Martha .. eight hundred dollars out of the crops .. appoint
           my husband, Valentine Houseworth, executor .. this ( ) day of June
           1838.
In the presence of   (signed)
     John Walker   Susan Houseworth
     Sarah Beadles, Walter Houseworth
     At a court held .. 27th August 1838 .. proved .. James W. Walker
swore John Walker (his father) was dead ..
     At a court held .. 24th September 1838 .. further proved .. and
ordered to be recorded.
     In Margin. At a court held .. 27th January 1840 .. Valentine M.
Houseworth, the executor appointed in the last will and testament of
Susan Houseworth, being dead .. on motion of James Beadles .. with
Oliver Finks, James F. Finks and James M. Macon, his securities ..
bond in the penalty of twenty thousand dollars .. certificate was
granted him for obtaining letters of administration with the will annexed ..

pp.   A list of the names of those who purchased and the amount of
388-   property sold belonging to the estate of ANN LINDSAY, deceased, on
391   Saturday, the 25th day of August 1838 .. Richard Richards Junr.,
           William Cosby, John Robinson, Richard Rawlings, Robert Bowler,
           Charles Young, William Martin, Capt. Elijah Morton, William C. Moore,
           Jefferson Almond, Reuben Snell, George Cox, William C. Webb, Col.
           Elhanon Row, Wythe P. Campbell, Paul Verdier, Hezekiah Richards,
           Richard Bowler, Robert Kendal, Larkin Herndon, John Herndon, William
           S. Reynolds, Jonathan Johnson, Vivion Quisenberry .. Returned into
           court 24th September 1838.

pp.   The estate of Capt. JOHN BEADLES, deceased, to William Beadles,
391-   Executor .. settled 9th February 1838 .. by Ro. Pritchett, Newton
392   Hume, William Collins. Another account settled 10th June 1838 by
        John N. Sorrille, Ro. Pritchett, Newton Hume. At a court held ..
        23rd July 1838 .. returned and ordered to lie. At a court held ..
        24th September 1838 .. approved and ordered to be recorded.

pp.   Will of ELIZABETH COWHERD. .. I give all my estate .. to my
393-   mother, Lucy Cowherd, and my sisters, Lucy and Mary S. Cowherd ..
394   I bequeath my slaves .. to my two brothers, John S. and Francis K.
        Cowherd .. to each of the children of my deceased sister, Sarah
        Henshaw, one hundred dollars each .. not to be paid in any event
        until the death of my mother .. appoint my brother, John S. Cowherd,
        executor .. request security not be required .. this 15th day of
        September 1837.
        In the presence of   (signed)
            James Newman   Elizabeth Cowherd
            Peyton Grymes, Charles Scott
            At a court held .. 24th September 1838 .. proved in open court ..
        and ordered to be recorded.

pp.   The estate of EDWARD COLLINS, deceased, to Lewis D. Collins and
394-   George Morris, executors .. $909 amount of sale of Charles, the pro-
395   ceeds of the sale of whom were devised to Edward Collins' children
        by his last wife and which have paid to them .. At a court held ..
        27th August 1838 .. returned and ordered to lie. At a court held ..
        22nd October 1838 .. approved and ordered to be recorded.
            In Margin. account settled .. allowed five percent commission ..
        mentions sale of Charles .. due each legatee, $807.74½ .. Reynolds
        Chapman and Richard M. Chapman.

p.   Sale made by Lucy H. Conway, executrix of REUBEN CONWAY, dec'd,
396   of the following property, 5th October 1838 .. amount of sale not
        totalled .. included are notes, "10 sheep killed by dogs," and
        "8 hogs died" .. Returned into court 22nd October 1838.

pp.   Amount of the sales of THOMAS BURRUS, deceased, on the 15th day
396-   of November 1836, sold on a credit until the 15th day of November
398   1837, for all sums of five dollars and upwards under that sum cash
        will be required. Purchasers .. Lancelot Burrus, Alexander Peacher,
        Alexander Campbell, Reuben Thompson, Joseph Hilman, Horace Layton,
        William Austin, Daniel Young .. amount of sales, $1540.37½. Returned
        into court 22nd October 1838.

p.   Will of JOHN BROWN. .. after all my debts are paid, I give all
399   my property to my two sisters, Peggy and Nancy, to be equally divided
        between them .. after the death of either of my sisters, I wish the
        whole of my property to go to the survivor. I wish my two friends,
        Robert W. Brooking and William Wayland to be the executors .. this
        14th day of November 1830 ..
        Attest   (signed his mark)
            Alex. O. Bradford   John Brown
            Thomas Parrott, Thomas Watts Yager
            At a court held .. 26th November 1838 .. proved .. ordered to be
        recorded .. Robert W. Brooking refused .. on motion of William Way-
        land .. with Robert W. Brooking, his security .. bond in the penalty
        of five thousand dollars .. certificate was granted him for obtaining
        a probate thereof in due form.

pp.   The estate of JOHN FEARNEYHOUGH, deceased, in account with
398-   Michael L. Eheart, administrator .. 27th July 1837 paid $7.83 to
401   William Rhodes for the tuition of William and Lewis Fearneyhough ..
        paid $3.00 for the purchase of 3 hats for the children of John
        Fearneyhough, dec'd .. settled 25th August 1838 by Joseph Cave,
        William Eddins, Thos. M. Mansfield. At a court held .. 24th Septem-
        ber 1838 .. returned and ordered to lie. At a court held .. 26th
        November 1838 .. approved and ordered to be recorded.

pp.   Lancelot Burrus, administrator in account with the estate of
400-   THOMAS BURRUS, deceased .. legatees' amount, $882.73½ to be divided
403   by ten .. settled 18th October 1838 by Jas. L. Coleman, George W.
        Morton, Joseph Jackson. At a court held .. 22nd October 1838 ..
        returned and ordered to lie. At a court held .. 24th December 1838
        .. approved and ordered to be recorded.

pp.   The Estate of MOSES BLEDSOE, deceased, in account with Benjamin
404-   Bledsoe, executor .. 11th June 1835 paid $60 to John Bledsoe in full
405   of special legacy .. 7th February 1737, whole amount of sales of
        perishable property of the estate, $263.28 .. whole amount of sale,
        $1450.22 .. settled 13th October 1838 by Wm. S. Frazer, Philip Mal-
        lory, Elhanon Row, Catlett Rhoades. At a court held .. 22nd October
        1838 .. returned and ordered to lie. At a court held .. 24th Decem-
        ber 1838 .. approved and ordered to be recorded.

pp.   The estate of ABRAHAM EDDINS, deceased, to Alfred Eddins, ad-
406-   ministrator .. amount of sales, $3199.54 .. paid out per account,
407     $2113.43½ .. settled 11th October 1838 by Newton Hume, Daniel Miller,
        Ro. Pritchett. At a court held .. 26th November 1838 .. returned
        and ordered to lie. At a court held .. 24th December 1838 .. approved
        and ordered to be recorded.

p.   An inventory and appraisement of the estate of ROBERT LAYTON,
408   deceased, taken the 9th day of October 1838 .. total value, $64.25
        .. made by appraisers James G. Lancaster, Alexander Peacher, Richard
        Richards .. certified a true inventory by Elhanon Row, D.S. for Thos.
        Row, S.O.C. Returned into court 28th January 1839.

End of Orange County Will Book 8.

ABSTRACTS OF SUITS FILED IN THE SUPERIOR COURT OF ORANGE COUNTY, VIRGINIA

There are several suits in the loose papers regarding the children and other descendants of John Clarke who, according to a deposition of Reuben, one of his sons, died suddenly on the 4th of August 1831 in Orange County. With respect to his estate, these suits show that his grandson, John C. Wells, son of his daughter, Mary and her husband, Thomas Wells, was given administration of his estate. When John C. Wells died, before the suits were settled, his brother, Fontain Wells, became his administrator, and Lucy Clarke, one of John Clarke's daughters, became the administratrix of John Clarke's estate.

According to a suit initiated in the Orange County Court in October 1838 by Lucy Clarke, she says that her mother's name was Mary (who died intestate) and that John Clarke and Mary, his wife, had eleven children: John, Henry, William, Abner, Edmond, Reuben, Sarah (Sally), James, Jane, Mary and herself (Lucy). In another suit (there are at least four among the loose papers), Edmund Clarke also lists John and Mary's children. From these suits, the following are also mentioned, Sarah (or Sally) and Lucy being unmarried during these years.

Jane Clarke married Fleming Turner (who died before 1831). She was living in Buckingham County, Virginia, in 1838.

Mary Clarke married Thomas Wells. Their children were John C., Fontain, Fleming T., Thomas and Nancy (or Ann) who died before 1831), who married John G. Wright "and moved to the west." Ann and John G. Wright had a daughter, Susan Wright, who married ( ) Clemens, and a daughter, Julia Wright, who was unmarried in 1838.

William Clarke died before 1831. His wife is not named but his children are listed in two suits as John, James, Mary, Reuben, Nancy, Bathsheba, Virginia, Tabitha and Elizabeth Clarke. (In 1838, Nancy, Bathsheba, Virginia and Tabitha "were not residents of Virginia.") Elizabeth Clarke married William Carroll (license issued 20th August 1823 with Abraham Booten as surety). Elizabeth died before 1838 leaving a son, Franklin Carroll. Of the other children of William Clarke, Nancy Clarke married Hamlet Sandford and was a resident of Ohio in 1838; Bathsheba Clarke married Abraham Booten, who died before 1831. (The Orange County Marriage Register shows the issuance of a marriage license on 20th December 1819 and their marriage by John C. Gordon on 23rd December 1819.) Virginia Clarke married Thomas W. Nash. (A marriage license was issued 15th January 1824.) The suits show Benjamin Walker of Orange County qualified as the administrator of the estate of William Clarke.

In one suit, Reuben Clarke, a son of John and Mary Clarke, says that he managed his father's estate for about two years before his father died in August 1831, having taken over from his brother, James. He found the affairs of the estate in a very bad condition and much in debt, debts that his father believed had been paid. His father authorized him to sell their negroes to pay the debts. Reuben states that his sisters, Lucy and Sarah, had advanced money to their father. "They agreed to buy a negro girl apiece and pay him what price that the said negroes were valued over what they had loaned my Father. So Mrs. Weedon Sleet and Joshua Willis were appointed to fix the value which they did, and Lucy and Sarah gave their bond for about 220$dollars which they would owe on account of the purchase of the two negroes." In further explaining the transaction, Reuben says the bonds were credited with payments and applied to his Father's debts, but he failed to enter one payment because he was leaving home. While gone, "his father died on the 4th of August 1831." When he returned, he credited the bonds with the payment "seeing no injustice to the estate being done."

In the summer before John Clarke died, William S. Frazer, the Deputy Sheriff of Orange, came to his house with two executions, one in the name of Andrew Newman "for 101$2cents," and the other in the name of Thomas Sparks for "144$28cents." Both had interest payable and costs. Reuben says his father was much distressed and worried if he had enough negroes to satisfy his debts and work for him. His father asked his daughter, Lucy, if she would pay these executions, which she agreed to do, he giving her a bond to make her safe. She said she would have to collect some of the money from people in Madison County and the Sheriff agreed to wait. His father died before the money was collected.

Before an administrator was appointed, the Sheriff returned and required the executions be paid or he would have to sell the negroes. Rather than see the property "sacrificed," Lucy paid the executions. Whereupon the Sheriff said, "as she had money she had as well pay the taxes for that year." Reuben did not recall the amount but believed it to be between seven and ten dollars.

In an earlier suit, John C. Wells, the first administrator of the estate of John Clarke, sued Edmund Clarke, one of John's sons, for a debt John C. Wells contended Edmund Clarke owed the estate. The commissioner's report of July 2, 1837, summarizes the suit. It appears by a record copy that at the April Term of the court in 1829, John Clarke had come into court and acknowledged himself indebted to his son, Edmund, in the amount of $1870.34. Before a settlement could be made, John Clarke died, but at the September Term of the Court in 1832, Edmund Clarke recovered this amount from John C. Wells as administrator.

This suit depends on what Edmund Clarke had received from his father. His brother, John Clarke Junr., testified that Edmund had left his apprenticeship as a sadler and harness maker in 1797 and began working at his trade at his father's house; that he employed a man by the name of Dickerson as a journeyman; that both boarded with his father; that board never was paid; that his father had paid for wearing apparel for Dickerson who left in 1798; that his father bought materials for his brother to carry on his trade, in fact laid in materials for several years; that in the year 1803, his brother, Edmund, left his father's house but returned in 1805, and remained "until the late war," during which period his father bought materials for him out of the sales of the wheat crop, that when his brother had money and his father required the use of it, he had it.

In this suit, Edmund's sister, Lucy, relates the circumstances of his returning to his father's house in 1805 "as remaining there as a boarder until the close of the late war;" that her father bought materials for him to carry on his trade.

The Commissioner is concerned throughout that the Court has disallowed certain testimony, especially that of the arbitrators, Edward Cox, Tandy Collins and William Cox, who examined, settled and stated the accounts between John Clarke, the father, and Edmund Clarke, the son, on the 22nd of September 1821, and awarded to Edmund the sum of $1870.34. The Commissioner noted that "both parties were present during the whole examination of the papers and after the results were known, and what sum had been awarded, John Clarke expressed himself satisfied with the award and executed his

obligation for the amount awarded and that one of the referees wrote the
obligation at the request of the parties."

In a deposition of John Clarke Junr., the following was abstracted.
"About the year 1803 or sometime near that, Edmund Clarke left John Clarke's
house and went to live at William Clarke's, who kept a tavern at the place
called Collins' old tavern .. (after one year) William Clarke moved away
and Joseph Graham occupying the tavern, Edmund Clarke continued to live
with Joseph Graham and lived with him until the fall of 1805."

In another suit sworn to on 26th May 1835, by Lucy Clarke, and on 27th
May 1835 by Sarah Clarke, the names of the heirs and distributees of John
Clarke are listed as follows: John Clarke of Orange; Henry Clarke of Orange;
Edmund Clarke of Orange; Reuben T. Clarke of Orange; Jane M. Turner of
Rockingham; Sarah and Lucy Clarke, complainants, of Orange; James Clarke
of Orange; John C. Wells of Albemarle; Fountain Wells of Fluvanna; Thomas
Wells of Linchburg; Fleming Wells of Texas; William Payne and Mary, his
wife, late Mary Wells, of Kentucky; John Wright who intermarried with Nancy
Wells, since died, and his two children, Susan and Julia (out of state but
residence not known), Hanley Sanford and Nancy his wife, late Nancy Clarke
of Indiana; Tabitha Clarke of Indiana; Mary Clarke of Orange; John Clarke
of Fredericksburg; Abraham Booten and Beersheba, his wife, late Beersheba
Clarke, of Kentucky; Virginia Nash ————; and William Carroll and Elizabeth,
his wife, late Elizabeth Clarke, of Orange.

* * * * * * * * * * * * * *

In a suit in which John W. Sale is plaintiff and Josiah Samuel and
others are defendants, the family of Josiah is mentioned as Maria S., and
their children as Amanda, Ann, Dounda, Selina, Anthony, Emanuella and Lucy
V. Samuel. In a deed dated 17th August 1842, Josiah Samuel and Maria S.,
his wife, are shown "of the Town of Harrisonburg, County of Rockingham,
State of Virginia."

In other entries, Anthony Twyman and James Twyman are shown as being
from Madison County, Virginia; Watson Carr and Hugh Carr were believed to
be residents of Rockingham County, Virginia. In the year 1842, George Pannill is mentioned as the administrator of William Davis. On the 25th of
December 1841, James G. Lindsay is mentioned as the administrator of Mrs.
Frances Lindsay.

* * * * * * * * * * * * * *

At the August Term, 1835, in the Circuit Superior Court of Orange,
Richard H. Field presiding, Milton Huffman and his wife, Felicia, formerly
Felicia Ancel, and Edward Ancel filed suit against Robert Ancel, Lawrence
T. Dade and James Sims. The plaintiffs contend that some time in the year
1808, Robert Pearson died after having made his will which was proved and
admitted to record in the clerk's office of the County of Orange (Orange
County Will Book 4, pp. 303-304). In his will, Robert Pearson devised to
his granddaughter, Felicia Ancel (who afterwards married Milton Huffman),
and his grandson, Edward Ancel, a female slave named Nan, who was then in
the possession of their father, Robert Ancel, who had married Frances Pearson. The slave, Nan, had died but a son named Tom survived her, also in
the possession of Robert Ancel until sold to James Sims of Orange County
for seven hundred dollars.

The plaintiffs further charge that Robert Ancel had been appointed by
the Orange Court as guardian to his two children, Felicia and Edward, and
one Lawrence T. Dade was his security on his bond; that Dade has since
removed to Kentucky where he was living at that time. They contend their

guardian or his security has never delivered up to them the slave, Tom, the increase of the female slave devised to them, and that he has never made any settlement of his guardianship accounts of the estate of his wards.

In the testimony accompanying the suit taken at the tavern of James Sims in the town of Stanardsville and county of Orange on Friday the 9th of September 1836, Michael Ancel says that Robert Ancel married Frances Pearson and at the time of their marriage, Robert Pearson gave them a small negro girl by the name of Nan, who they kept for about twenty years. In response to a question as to how long Robert and Frances were married before Robert Pearson died, he answered, "about four years," permitting the assumption they were married in 1804.

In other depositions, the following is noted. Milton Huffman had a brother, Kerriah Huffman. In the deposition of Elizabeth Lucy taken the 3rd day of September 1836, she says Felicia Ancel Huffman lived with her grandfather from age three and a half until she married in 1824 and that Robert Ancel's father's name was Edward. In the deposition of John Goss taken in Albemarle County 26th September 1836, he recollects "distinctly" to have married Milton Huffman and Felicia Ancel some years ago, "say thirteen or fourteen or thereabouts in the presence of a respectable assembly at a house occupied by Joseph Gilbert." In the deposition of Weston Gilbert of Orange County taken the 27th of September 1837, he says Robert Ancel married second a "Miss Boswell," in the spring of 1835 "and moved in the fall of the same year to (Missouri)."

* * * * * * * * * * * * * *

In a Bill filed in November 1829, the parties in the suit were Margarett Davis, widow and relict of John Davis, deceased (estate appraisal recorded in Will Book 5, pages 56-58), against Edmund Row, administrator de bonis non with the will annexed of John Davis, deceased, Evan Davis, son of John and Margarett Davis, Lucy Davis, widow of Reuben Davis, another son of John and Margarett Davis, the original administrator of the estate of John Davis, deceased, and William and Elizabeth Davis, infant children of Reuben Davis, deceased.

John Davis died intestate before July 1, 1816, according to the Commissioner's report. His son, Evan claims he ran the farm as a manager for four years before his father's death after he attained the age of twenty one. Evan's claim for payment in the Commissioner's report is for the years 1811 through 1814. In her Bill, Margarett Davis states her husband possessed a small tract of land in Orange County and six negroes besides a little perishable property, leaving to inherit his estate two sons, Reuben Davis and Evan Davis. Reuben qualified as administrator of the estate, dividing the negroes among himself, his brother, Evan, after affirming his mother's dower. He sold the perishable estate but made no assignment of land. Not long after, Reuben was suddenly killed by lightning before he settled his accounts and Margarett Davis is in court to obtain a settlement by Edmund Row, who had taken out letters of administration on the estate of John Davis, deceased. She argues she suffers from want of a settlement to the extent that being aged, poor and feeble, she is unable to support the negroes that were allotted to her as her dower negroes and wishes to surrender them and let them be divided at once between Evan and Reuben's two children, Elizabeth and William Davis. There is no final settlement by 1843, and it appears from an entry dated 4th May 1841 that Margarett has died.

* * * * * * * * * * * * * *

A suit brought by the Mutual Assurance Society of Virginia against fire on buildings, which was incorporated by an Act of the General Assembly of Virginia the 22nd of December 1794, in order to alleviate the calamities of such unfortunate persons as may suffer the ravages of fire, traces property insured by the company in the Town of Columbia in the County of Fluvanna. The original insurer was Duncan McLachlan, who insured three buildings on his lot No. 79 on the main or St. James Street in the Town of Columbia, 26th of April 1805. The executor of Duncan McLachlan was John Quarles who, according to his will, sold the property, the purchaser being David Ross of Richmond the 27th of May 1811. The said Ross conveyed the property to one Jacob Meyers in trust for his son, D.W.R. Meyers, then an infant. The deed of conveyance is dated 5th of July 1811. On the 8th day of August 1823, James Byars Junr., a special agent of the said Society, made an evaluation of the property. On the 23rd day of November 1827, the said David W. R. Meyers, having come of age, conveyed the same to Eliza Woolfly of the Town of Columbia. When she died (date not shown), she left as her sole heirs two sons, John and Henry Woolfly, to whom the title of the said lot descended. John died first, under age, leaving his brother, Henry, his sole heir. Soon afterwards, Henry died and from him the title to the said lot descended to his maternal aunts, Mary, wife of Joseph Stevens, and Jane, wife of Thomas Newman, and Nancy Hackney. Mary Stevens and Jane Newman gave depositions that they sold their rights to Nancy Hackney. The Assurance Society was suing because the premiums had not been paid from 1821 until the 1st of April 1843 (the total being $109.44), which was awarded in the final decree.

* * * * * * * * * * * * * *

In a suit filed the 4th of October 1838 in which Minor Rucker is the plaintiff and Benjamin Burton, surviving Executor of May Burton, deceased, who was the original Executor of John Rucker, deceased, Mary Graves, widow of Waller Graves, deceased, and the heirs of Willis Rucker, deceased, are defendants. The Bill was amended 2nd December 1841 because the names of additional distributees had been learned. Many of the depositions in this suit provide genealogical information on several generations of the family of John Rucker of Orange County and his descendants.

In the suit (Minor Rucker is the son of Joel Rucker and grandson of John Rucker), the children of John Rucker and Mary, his wife, are shown as: Joel, Franky, Milly, William, Jeremiah, James, John, Mary, Molly, Nancy and Burton.

Minor Rucker in his Bill states the children of Joel Rucker were himself, Blyfil and Elzy, who survived his father but has since died leaving a widow, Mary Rucker, and their children, Joseph and Edward Rucker and Kitty, who married James Tompkins. All the heirs of Elzy Rucker live outside of Virginia.

In an affidavit of John Duncan and John Black, both citizens of Madison County, Kentucky, on the 25th January 1828 in the Town of Richmond, said they were well acquainted with Joel White and Franky, his wife, now both deceased, Henry White, their son, and his wife, both deceased, had one child, a daughter, Florina. The children of Joel White and Frankey (daughter of John Rucker) were Henry, John, William, Durrett, Polly, Florina, Betsy, Milly, Phoebe, Nancy, Fanny and Lucinda, who is dead, leaving no children. All the rest are alive and have children living.

Galen White (unidentified), guardian of Florina White, appointed Richard White of Orange County, Virginia, his attorney the 30th of January 1828. Galen White had been appointed guardian to Lucinda and Florina White, heirs of Joel White, deceased, in Madison County, Kentucky, May Court, 1816.

In the affidavit of Durrett White and Yelverton Payton and Milly, his wife, late Milly White, heirs of Joel White and Franky, his wife, deceased, they appoint William Thornton their attorney. They were of Madison County, Kentucky, and the paper is dated 11th October 1826.

The deposition of William Rucker was taken on the 24th day of December 1840 at his house in Monroe County, Missouri, in which he states he sold his interest in his father's estate (John Rucker, deceased) to Minor Rucker sometime between 1821 and 1824.

A paper filed from the Madison County, Kentucky Court dated the 5th day of May 1823, shows the dismissal of William Barrett, guardian of Emily Rucker, orphan of Jeremiah Rucker, and Emily, being over the age of four-teen years, was admitted to court and chose William Thornton as her guardian, Joseph Miller his security. At another court in Richmond, Madison County, Kentucky, the 5th of July 1824, Thomas Rucker, orphan of Jeremiah Rucker, being over fourteen years and under twenty one years, had William Thornton appointed by the Court to be his guardian, Joseph Miller his security. On the 16th of November 1826, in Madison County, Kentucky, Susannah Barrett certified there were only six children of Jeremiah Rucker, deceased. In Madison County, Kentucky, an affidavit dated 16th day of October 1826, is made by Milton S. Rucker and Valencourt Foster and Alevit, his wife, late Alevit Rucker, and Talton W. Oglesby and Antonet, his wife, late Antonet Rucker, all heirs of Jeremiah Rucker, deceased, of the county of Madison and state of Kentucky .. appoint William Thornton of the same county and state their attorney. In an affidavit of William Miller and Lucy (or Louisa), his wife, made in Garrard County, Kentucky, appoint William Thornton their attorney. The paper is dated the 2nd of November 1829, and Lucy is described as an heir of Jeremiah Rucker.

A deposition of William Thornton was taken at the house of Abel Marley in the Town of Fayette in the county of Howard in the state of Missouri on the 24th day of August 1840.

The deposition of John B. White, taken the same day, notes that Reuben E. Gentry married his sister, Elizabeth, daughter of Joel and Fanny White, the legal heirs and representatives of John Rucker of Orange County, Virginia, and the receipts of Richard, Joel W., Reuben Jr., William Gentry and Jane Ramy were given to Minor Rucker .. further states that John Crook married his sister, Riney White and not John Brooks as described in Minor Rucker's Bill .. and that the receipts of Richard P. Crook, William W. Crook and Elizabeth Trice and John Trice, her husband, were given by me to Minor Rucker .. and further the deponent knows those to be the heirs of Riney Crook, deceased, who are the heirs of Joel and Fanny White, deceased, and they the heirs of John Rucker, deceased, of Orange County, Virginia .. and the deponent further states that John Tooley married his sister, Phebe White and James Tooley married his sister, Nancy White, both daughters of Joel and Fanny White .. the deponent further knows that James and Nancy are both dead and that John Tooley was appointed and is guardian for his own children as well as those of James and Nancy Tooley.

John Tooley submitted an affidavit dated 18th August 1838 from Charleston County, Missouri, in which he acknowledges receipt of money from Minor Rucker for the heirs of Phebe Tooley, deceased, who was an heir of Joel and Frankey White, deceased, of Madison County, Kentucky, and said Franky White was an heir of said John Rucker, deceased. He also acknowledges receipt of money for the heirs of Nancy Tooley, deceased, who was an heir as above.

In a paper dated 28th day of June 1824, Burton Rucker of the County of Bibb and state of Alabama appoints Willis Brown his attorney.

In an affidavit dated 17th October 1826, the following appears. Jefferson White and Lucinda, his wife, late Lucinda Fox, and Emily Fox, daughters of Mary Fox, deceased, and who was one of the children and heirs of John and Mary Rucker, deceased, of the county of Madison and state of Kentucky, do hereby .. appoint our trusty friend, William Thornton .. our lawful attorney.

On the 23rd of October 1824, Thomas Fox, in Madison County, Kentucky, certified that there were only eleven children of Joel White and Franky, his wife, and that one of them by the name of Lucinda had departed this life without issue and that there are only two heirs of my wife, Mary Fox, deceased, who was one of the above eleven children of Joel and Franky White, deceased.

In a receipt dated 17th April 1833, in Ruckersville, Virginia, W. B. White certifies he received from Joseph Rucker the full legacy of Mildred Rucker Minor "of John Rucker, dec'd, for her interest in her grandmother's estate." W. B. White married Mildred. In the deposition of Richard Durrett taken in Greene County, Virginia, the 30th April 1840, he states that William B. White of Georgia, who married Milly Rucker of the above-named state, did send by me to Minor Rucker, late of Orange County, Va., a receipt written for an interest in grandmother's estate through mistake instead of grandfather's.

From Elbert County, Georgia, an affidavit dated 16th July 1827, there appears the statement that "we, Milly Rucker, widow and relict of John Rucker Junr., deceased, William H. Alston in right of his wife, Elizabeth, formerly Elizabeth Rucker, daughter of the said John Rucker, deceased, and Milly Rucker and Amanda B. Rucker, daughters also of the said John Rucker, deceased, appoint John S. Foster .. their lawful attorney.

On the 15th May 1822, John R. White of Charleston County, Missouri, wrote a letter to James Collins of Orange County, Virginia, transmitting his affidavit and that of William White made jointly appointing Collins their attorney.

George M. Head (referred to in Minor Rucker's Bill as Marshall Head) was of Albemarle County, Virginia, when he made a bond dated 25th February 1813 to May Burton. In the obligation he mentions his wife, Milly Head, and the witnesses are Nancy Rucker and Lucinda Head.

A deposition of John Head made 22nd December 1840 in Randolph County, Missouri, he states he was present in Orange County, Virginia, in 1819, when Willis Rucker, then living in Georgia, in Elbert or Wilks County, sold his share in his father's (John Rucker) estate to Minor Rucker.

* * * * * * * * * * * * * * *

In a Bill (possibly filed in 1834), Peyton Grymes and Harriet, his wife, late Harriet Dade, administrator and administratrix of Francis Dade, deceased, are plaintiffs and William Dade is defendant. The plaintiffs contend that in 1809, when Francis Dade arrived to the age of twenty one, his guardian, William Dade, was indebted to Francis in the sum of £ 190.12.8½. The plaintiffs charge that William Dade executed a deed of trust whereby he conveyed to Philip Slaughter for the purpose of securing a debt of $1000 due by him to Lawrence T. Dade and other bonds to secure his debt to his ward, Francis, as well as to his sister, who was the wife of Edwin Conway.

The plaintiffs charge William Dade had paid his debts except the $1000 due Lawrence T. Dade and the balance due Francis. When Francis died, Harriet qualified as his executrix, and afterwards married Peyton Grymes.

* * * * * * * * * * * * * * *

The last will and testament of William H. Martin, was duly recorded in Orange County Court after he died in December 1832. His children were Lucinda Martin, who married Ichabod Mallory. They had two sons, Philip M. Mallory and William P. Mallory before Lucinda died (before 1834); Mallory Martin; Jane Martin who married William B. Arnall September 10, 1809 and who had at least seven children, two of whom were Mary and John Arnall (Jane was granted a separation from William B. Arnall in 1834); Joannah Martin who married Benjamin C. Bickers; William Martin; Thomas Martin. Mallory Martin and John Woolfolk were appointed executors in the will but only Mallory Martin qualified. Benjamin C. Bickers, William and Thomas Martin, and Ichabod Mallory were the securities in his executorial bond. Subsequently, by an order of the Orange County Court, Ichabod Mallory was released from his said securityship by the entering of one, Tartan Smith, as security in a new bond according to law. (Tartan Smith was the son of James Smith, who died in Orange County in December 1822, and whose will is in Will Book 6, pp. 60-62.) By September 30, 1837, Thomas and William Martin, Benjamin C. Bickers and Joannah, his wife, Jane Arnall and Tartan Smith had departed the Commonwealth.

In a suit filed in 1833 in the Orange County Superior Court of Law and Chancery, Ichabod Mallory, as heir and distributee of his deceased son, Philip M. Mallory, and as administrator of the same, and as guardian to his son, William P. Mallory, were plaintiffs against Mallory Martin, executor of the will of Robert H. Martin, the father in law of Ichabod Mallory and grandfather of Philip M. and William P. Mallory. Ichabod Mallory contends that in his last will and testament William H. Martin directed all of his estate to be sold and the proceeds, after paying his debts, to be divided equally among all his children. He contends that Mallory Martin's executor's account had an amount of money, $3808.40, which should be divided among the heirs and distributees. He further contends that all the children of William H. Martin except his wife's, Lucinda, two sons, had received their share but Lucinda's children had received only $254.60. He contends that each child should be entitled to one seventh of the $3808.40.

Of particular concern to Ichabod Mallory was the fact that the executor, Mallory Martin, was in the process of moving from the Commonwealth to settle elsewhere; that he had sold all his land in Orange County and had advertised a public auction to sell his personal estate except what he planned to carry with him. He notes that Benjamin C. Bickers, a security, "being while here in low circumstances" already had moved to the west; that Tartan Smith, the most solvent of the securities, was preparing to move with the executor, Mallory Martin, on Sunday, September 28, 1834; that William Martin was nearly insolvent and Thomas Martin was possessed of scanty property, "wholly inadequate to make good even the smallest sum," Ichabod Mallory believed was due him. Under these circumstances, Ichabod Mallory seeks an injunction against their departure from the Commonwealth until they give sufficient security "for the payment as well of what may be due Ichabod Mallory and due his son, William P. Mallory, and doing whatever else the court may in this behalf decree; that a complete settlement of the executor's accounts in that capacity may be had before a commissioner of the court and justice done to all the legatees of the testator, William H. Martin.

A writ of Ne Exact was executed on the 2nd of October 1834 upon the body of Mallory Martin, who thereupon entered into bond with Lewis B. Williams, his security. Thomas F. Coleman, Deputy Sheriff, Thomas Coleman, Sheriff of Orange County.

On the 2nd of October 1834, the Clerk of the Orange Court commanded the Sheriff, without delay, to cause Mallory Martin to give sufficient bail as security in the sum of seven hundred and sixty dollars, "that he will not go or attempt to go out of the limits of this Commonwealth, and in case the said Mallory Martin should refuse to give such bail or security, then you are to commit him to the jail of your county, there to be kept in safe custody until he shall do so of his own accord . . . ."

In the final decree, Ichabod Mallory, for his son, Philip M. Mallory, received $187.50 with interest from 1 January 1836; the same for his son, William P. Mallory, and the other legatees and distributees, Thomas and William Martin, and Benjamin C. Bickers in right of his wife, Joannah, received $49.73 with like interest; Jane Arnall received $93.62 with like interest; and Mallory Martin retained the balance of the assets of the estate in his own right and as a legatee and distributee being one sixth of the sum. Mallory Martin was ordered to pay out of his own goods and chattels the plaintiff's costs by him expended in the suit.

* * * * * * * * * * * * * *

In a suit filed 7th January 1833, a daughter of William H. Martin, Jane Martin, was plaintiff with Mallory Martin, her next friend, and William B. Arnall, her husband, was defendant. On May 3, 1833, she was permitted to change her next friend to Benjamin C. Bickers. Jane notes in her suit that she married William B. Arnall "in the year eighteen hundred and (blank)." (The marriage record of Orange County shows she married him on the 10th September 1809.) At the time she filed her Bill, she claims her husband was living in Hanover County; that despite her efforts to be a dutiful wife, he filled her with fear of personal violence. She challenged an investigation into her deportment and charged that her husband "for years past treated (her) in a manner not only not becoming a husband but the bare recital of which she is persuaded will not only awaken the sympathies of the court for her sufferings, but present an unanswerable claim upon its justice for relief from the pressure of that marital power which has been used in time past so as only to make her unhappy, painful as it is to lift the veil from the faults of one who was once her friend, she owes it to herself and her children and their happiness to do so . . . ." She further charges her husband "has given himself up to the most disolute, abandoned and depraved habits, is scarcely doing any business and is worth nothing save an interest in the estate of her father, William H. Martin, deceased, amounting to nearly eight hundred to a thousand dollars, which he has not yet received from the executor of said estate."

Jane Arnall further charges that her said husband, William B. Arnall "has never furnished her with any of the necessaries of life during the past two years; that by reason of his cruel and unkind treatment and because he has not provided for her the ordinary necessaries of life, she has been compelled to throw herself upon the charity of her friends for a bare subsistence, and is reduced to want, which he has left her and is now living with another woman in the County of Hanover in adultery . . . ." She requests the court to grant her a divorce "a mensa & thoro" from her husband and decree her perpetual separation from and protection against him, and restore to her all the rights of property conferred on him by marriage and dispose of the children so as to secure to her the management and education of them and "in the meantime grant her alimony or an allowance for herself and children" and restrain her husband by injunction from selling any of the said property devised by her father's will . . . ."

During the course of the suit, Mary Arnall, a daughter of William B. Arnall and Jane (Martin) Arnall, gave testimony (3 July 1833). When Mary was asked if she ever knew her father to abuse her mother, she answers, "yes, by language most abusive and threatening to take her life." She also testifies that her father beat her mother in her presence and treated her mother cruelly; that she had not seen her father "for three years next Christmas." When asked how many children there were, she answers, "seven, there are five with her now, two have gone to trades."

Also one of their sons, John M. Arnall, gives testimony answering the same questions as his sister.

A deposition of Garland B. Taylor was taken on the 30th of July 1833 at the tavern of Richard Rawlings at Orange Courthouse. He states "that in the year eighteen hundred and thirty two, he lived in the County of Hanover within one mile & half of William B. Arnall," who was renting a house from Edmund Minton, in which house he kept a woman named Frances Southard as his wife; that Arnall told him he slept with her and that she was with child by him." Taylor testifies that he sold William B. Arnall coffee, sugar and bacon and "whilst there he treated this woman as his wife & she treated him as her husband."

An injunction was awarded Jane (Martin) Arnall in April 1834 against Mallory Martin and John Woolfolk, executors of William H. Martin, presumably to preclude any payments to William B. Arnall.

* * * * * * * * * * * * * *

In a suit filed before the 28th October 1833, Jeremiah Walker and Rachel, his wife, Evalina and Virginia Ann Jones, infants of tender years of Catharine Jones, their next friend, are plaintiffs and John Shelor, Catharine Jones and Nancy Powell are defendants. The plaintiffs are suing to get John Shelor, who qualified as the executor of his father's (John Shelor) estate, to settle his accounts and pay over the bequests as specified in the testator's will. In the course of setting out the Bill, the plaintiffs state that Catherine was one of the daughters of John Shelor, deceased, that she married Edmond Jones, that they had two daughters, Evalina and Ann Jones, and that for some time before her father's death, Catharine lived with her father apart from her husband, Edmond. The Bill mentions that another daughter of John Shelor, deceased, Nancy, married James Powell, and "she lived at the date of the will and still does live in the remote west." Another daughter, Rachel, a plaintiff, married Jeremiah Walker. John Shelor in his response to the Bill states that his father died in the month of April, "yet the apples and hay being crops which make themselves were devised with the land not being ripe or secured, he had advised that as such they were assets in his hands." He further answers that "the quantity was small only furnishing enough to make fifty to sixty gallons of brandy and seven or eight wagon loads of hay. The then Rachel Shelor continued to reside in the house of John Shelor, deceased, until Christmas and was supported from the property and used the apples during that time, and the hay was fed to the horses which aided or were used in securing the crops growing and grown upon the land."

* * * * * * * * * * * * * *

In a suit in which the plaintiffs are not named except that the oratrix is the administratrix of James Taylor Junr., deceased, her former husband, Margaret Sims, widow of Jeremiah Sims, is being sued. (On 6 December 1789, Margaret Taylor married Jeremiah Sims, performed by the Rev. George Eve.)

Jeremiah Sims had died intestate "many years anterior to the year 1827;" that Margaret qualified as the administratrix of his "large real and personal estate in Orange County." The suit was filed to have Margaret settle the estate. The Bill names the children, heirs and distributees of Jeremiah Sims and Margaret, his wife, as Elizabeth, "who married Joseph Kirtley;" Lucretia, "who married James Oliver;" Nancy, "who married Jefferson Jarrell;" William, James, Jeremiah, Mary and Clarrisa Sims.

* * * * * * * * * * * * * * *

A suit filed in the Circuit Superior Court, Orange County, in 1836.

To the Honorable Richard H. Field, Judge of the Circuit Superior Court of law and chancery for the County of Orange, Humbly complaining sheweth to the court your oratrix, Dolly P. Madison, in her own right and as executrix and devisee of her deceased husband, James Madison; that her testator departed this life on the 28th June 1836 having first duly made and published his last will and testament which has been duly proved and recorded together with a codicil thereto, by which said will your oratrix was left sole executrix thereof and duly qualified as such and taken upon herself the burden of the execution thereof. By one of the clauses of the said will (a copy whereof is herewith exhibited), it is provided as follows, to wit:

"I devise to my dear wife during her life the tract of land whereon I live as now held by me, except as herein otherwise devised, and if she shall pay the sum of nine thousand dollars within three years after my death, to be distributed as hereinafter directed, then I devise the same land to her in fee simple. If my wife shall not pay the said sum of money within the period before mentioned, then and in that case it is my will and I hereby direct that at her death the said land shall be sold for cash or on credit as may be deemed best for the interest of those entitled to the proceeds thereof. If my wife shall pay the said sum of money within the time before specified as aforesaid, was to become entitled to the fee simple in the said land, then I bequeath the said sum of money to be equally divided between all my nephews and nieces which shall at that time be living and in case of any of them being dead leaving issue at the time living, then such issue shall take the place of its or their deceased parent." In the codicil aforesaid, it was provided, "It is my will that the nine thousand dollars to be paid by my wife and distributed among my nephews and nieces may be paid into the Bank of Virginia or into the circuit superior court of chancery for Orange within three years after my death."

Your oratrix further shews to the court that immediately after the decease of her husband as well for the purpose of securing to herself the benefit of the devise in said clause above recited as to carry into effect without delay the benevolent purposes of the testator towards his relations, she provided the sum of nine thousand dollars and deposited the same in the Bank of Virginia at Fredericksburg with a view to be distributed as directed by the testator, and supposing it to have been the intention of the testator that she should be relieved from the burden and responsibility of distributing it enclined to the Board of Directors of said office of the Bank of Virginia extracts from the testator's will and requested them to receive the deposit for distribution as therein directed. The said Board however declined this task but agreed to receive the money on deposit to the credit of your oratrix and to pay the same upon her checks to the parties entitled as they might be presented. Your oratrix thereupon deposited the money to her own credit and was about proceeding to notify those whom she supposed entitled, that she was ready to pay them their share upon the principle of distribution which she supposed proper under the will; when she understood there was some conflict of opinion as to the proper construction of the will as to the persons entitled to take, which instead of making 31 shares would exclude some that your oratrix presumed was intended by the testator to be embraced within the provisions. In consequence of this difficulty which she was advised she was under no obligation and which she feels entirely incompetent to decide and especially as the Bank of Virginia has refused to accept the deposit otherwise than as above stated. Your oratrix has been advised to request this honorable court to take control of the said fund now in Bank and distribution thereof according to the rights of the parties, the facts out of which these rights are to be ascertained and the above question as well as any others that may arise upon the above clauses of the will to be determined are these:

Mr. Madison had six brothers and sisters to wit: Francis Madison, William Madison, Ambrose Madison, Nelly Hite, Sarah Macon and Frances Rose; all of whom had children (who were the nephews and nieces of course), who either were living at the death of the testator and are now living, or died before the testator having children now living.

Stock 1. Francis Madison's children were 1. Conway Madison, now living in Alabama; 2. Catlett Madison; 3. Nelly Wood who died before Mr. Madison leaving six children of whom all died before Mr. Madison without issue except two: Margaret, wife of ———— Tappan & Joseph Wood (of Tennessee), 4. Fanny, now the wife of Thompson Shepherd; 5. Catherine, wife of Spotswood Taliaferro; 6. Elizabeth Shepherd, widow of Andrew Shepherd; 7. Mary Smith, who died before Mr. Madison, having two children, viz. to wit: Walton Smith, Mississippi & Nancy Buck, wife of John Buck.

Stock 2. William Madison's children who were living at the testator's death & now are dead having children then living. 1st. Rebecca Chapman, wife of Reynolds Chapman; 2. Robert L. Madison, who died before Mr. Madison leaving 3 sons: infants, viz. T. Cooper Madison, William & Robert. 3. Ambrose Madison. 4. Letitia Slaughter, wife of D. F. Slaughter, died before Mr. Madison leaving two sons, viz. infants, Edwin Slaughter and Philip Slaughter; 5. Eliza Willis, wife of Lewis Willis, died before Mr. Madison leaving one daughter, Frances Willis, an infant.

Stock 3rd. Ambrose Madison died before testator leaving one child, viz. Nelly C. Willis.

Stock 4th. Nelly married Isaac Hite, her children are two, viz. James M. Hite of Frederick County and Nelly, who married ———— Baldwin & died befor testator leaving 7 children, viz. Eleanor C., wife of ———— Davidson (later shown as Edward J.); Mary B. Baldwin, Ann Baldwin, Isaac Hite Baldwin, James M. Baldwin, Robert Stuart Baldwin, all living.

Stock 5. Sarah Macon whose children living at the death of the testator and still are viz. Conway C. Macon, James M. Macon, Lucy Conway, wife of Reuben Conway, Ambrose Macon, Henry Macon, Reuben Macon besides one or more children who died before testator without having children.

Stock 6th. Frances wife of Robert Rose, deceased, her children are viz. Ambrose Rose of Alabama, Nelly Newman, widow of ———— Newman, who died before the testator; Robert Rose, Alabama; James Rose, Alabama; Erasmus Rose; Henry Rose, Frances & Samuel, the last two believed to be infants.

Then it will be seen that there are twenty five nephews and nieces who are living at the death of the testator and who are still living; that there were six who died before the testator, leaving children then living

& living when your oratrix was ready to pay the nine thousand dollars deposited in Bank and which she is now ready to pay as soon as it is ascertained who are entitled. Indeed she is now willing and intends to go on to pay the surviving nephews and nieces the sum they will be respectively entitled to on a division of the whole into 31 parts which will be their full proportion if the children of the above named six deceased nephews & nieces be entitled, as they insist they are and who it is contended by the surviving nephews and nieces not entitled to any participation in the said fund and some of whom claim to hold your oratrix responsible if she shall allow them any portion of the same and therewith to throw the risk and responsibility of this controversy upon your oratrix, who is no way interested in it except to have the fund properly paid according to the will of the testator and so as to perfect her fee simple to the estate devised to her.

Your oratrix further shews to the court that since the death of Mr. Madison, Thompson Shepherd, who is entitled in right of his wife to one share, has taken the oath of an insolvent Debtor whereby the said share is vested in the Sheriff of Orange County, George Morris, who executed the process under which he swore out and it is insisted by the said Sheriff that he is entitled to said share for the benefit of the creditors and the said Shepherd and wife still claim to be entitled to receive the same.

All of which is contrary to equity and good conscience and tends to the manifest wrong and oppression to your oratrix, and for as much as she is remediless in the premises save by the interposition of this honorable court where matters of this sort are properly cognizable and relievable. To the end therefore that the said Conway Madison of Alabama, Catlett Madison of Madison County, ---- Tappan and his wife, Margaret & Joseph Wood, both of Tennessee; Thompson Shepherd & Fanny, his wife; Spotswood Taliaferro and Catherine, his wife, all of Madison; Elizabeth Shepherd of Culpeper; Walton Smith of Mississippi; John Buck and Mary, his wife, of F'burg; Reynolds Chapman & Rebecca, his wife; Ambrose Madison of Orange; T. Cooper, William & Robert Madison, infant children of Robert L. Madison, deceased; Edwin Slaughter and Philip Slaughter, infant children of Letitia Slaughter, deceased; Nelly C. Willis of Orange; James M. Hite and the children of Nelly Baldwin, deceased, viz. ---- Davidson and Eleanor C., his wife, Mary B., Ann, Isaac H., Cornelius, James M., & Robert S. Baldwin, all of Frederick County, except Nancy, who is absent in foreign parts; Conway C. Macon, James M. Macon, Reuben Conway and Lucy, his wife, Ambrose Macon, Henry Macon and Reuben Macon of Orange; Ambrose Rose, Hugh Rose, Nelly Newman, Robert, James, Erasmus, Henry, Frances & Samuel, all of Alabama, and the two last being infants, and George Morris, Sheriff of Orange County, may be made parties defendants have the said infants by guardian to be appointed by this court to defend them, and may true and perfect answers made to the premises; that this honorable court will take into its custody and under its control the said sum of nine thousand dollars and distribute the same or direct its distribution among those entitled under the true interpretation of the will; that your oratrix may be declared to have complied with the conditions in the will which entitles her to a fee simple estate in the land in which the testator resided & that she may have such other and further relief as is consistent with Equity and the nature of the case may require may it please the court to grant the Commonwealth's most gracious writ of subpoena.

- - - - -

Notes of the Sheriff on one subpoena:

Copies of the within delivered to Mrs. Davison, wife of Edwd J. Davison, for herself and husband, he being from home, & she a free white person over the age of sixteen years.

Copy delivered Ann Baldwin & copies left with Mrs. Davison for Robert & James M. Baldwin, they being from home (Mrs. Davison being also a member of the same family).

Cornelius Baldwin is dead.

James M. Hite lives in Clarke County.

Mary B. Baldwin & Isaac H. Baldwin are non-reisents of Virginia.

Griffin Frost, D for
M. Taylor, Shff. Fred'k Cty.

- - - - -

To the Hon. Richd. H. Field, Judge of the Circuit Superior Court of Law and Chancery for County of Orange. The petition of Mrs. Dolly P. Madison respectfully represents that she filed her Bill in this honorable court setting forth that her deceased husband, James Madison, had devised her a large real estate upon condition that she paid to his nephews and nieces within three years the sum of $9,000, which payment was to be made by depositing the money in the Va. Bank or in the chancery court of Orange. Your petitioner stated also the difficulty she had encountered in an effort to deposit the money in the Bank and also that controversies had arisen as to the persons entitled to distribution of the fund. In consequence of these difficulties, your petitioner filed her said bill concerning those claiming a division of the fund and praying the court to decide who are entitled to participate and to direct its distribution. Your petitioner has proceeded to pay many of the legatees the sum to which they are entitled and she herewith exhibits the receipts of fifteen of said legatees for the sum of $290.32 each and one legatee for $290.00, which sums amount to $4644.80, leaving in the hands of your petitioner the sum of $4355.20, and she prays she may be authorised and directed by the court to pay the same into court or to deposit the same to the credit of the suit in which her said bill is filed in the Bank of Va. at Fredericksburg or wherever else the court may order so that all possible difficulty or doubt may be removed as to her having complied strictly with the condition on which the estate devised her by her deceased husband was to be complete and absolute.

And your petitioner will ever pray

D.P. Madison
Executrix & Devisee of
J. Madison, dec'd

- - - - -

Receipts or checks made by D. P. Madison (most are numbered), one unnumbered to Ambrose Madison, $290.32, dated Aug. 30, 1836; another unnumbered, a receipt of James M. Hite for $290.00, received Oct. 11th 1836. The others, all for $290.32, are numbered.

No.			
	2	Received October 4, 1836	Reynolds Chapman
	3	Received October 5, 1836	William Madison Jr.
	4	Received October 13, 1836	William A. Macon
	5	Received October 13, 1836	Lucy H. Conway
	6	Received October 14, 1836	Henry Macon
	8	Received October 15, 1836	Nelly C. Willis

No. 9 Received October 15, 1836   Elizabeth Shepherd, by James,
                                        Francis M. Shepherd, legal attorney
                                        for Elizabeth C. Shepherd
     10 Received October 17, 1836   James Madison Macon
     11. Received October 17, 1836   Reuben Macon
     12 Received November 5, 1836   Erasmus T. Rose
     13 Received October 31, 1836   Conway C. Macon
     14 Received October 31, 1836   Catherine B. Taliaferro
     15 Received October 31, 1836   Frances T. Shepherd
     16 Received December 14, 1836   Catlett Madison

- - - - -

Circular
Montpelier, September 17, 1836

Sir

By the will of Mr. Madison, his widow is directed to deposit $9,000
in the Bank of Virginia within 3 years after his death "to be equally divided between all my nephews and nieces which shall at that time be living
and in case of any of them being dead leaving issue at the time living,
then such issue shall take the place of its or their deceased parent."

As one of the legatees under this clause of Mr. Madison's will, you are
hereby notified that the deposit has been made and the Bank having declined
the task of distribution, Mrs. Madison will check for the separate amounts
due, but a question having arisen among some of the legatees as to the construction of the clause, she will limit the amount to be paid to each to
the share produced by a division of the whole sum among 31 nephews and
nieces including those now living and those who are dead leaving issue now
living, but the payments to the latter will be suspended 'till the decision
of the chancery court is had whether they are entitled to the money or not.

Where personal appliation for the check is inconvenient it should be
made by formal power of attorney legally authenticated.

- - - - -

A Sheriff's Note:
A copy (of the subpoena) delivered to Edwin and Philip Slaughter on the
17th of November 1836. Executed upon Edwin Slaughter and Philip Slaughter
on the 17th of November 1836 by delivering to each of them a copy hereof.
                              Tandy G. Morris D for
                              G. Morris, S.O.C.

- - - - -

A portion of an amended bill:
. . . . your oratrix, Dolly P. Madison, executrix and devisee of James
... Madison, dec'd, that some time during the last year she filed her bill
of interpleader in this court to which she made one Conway Madison a party
defendant, believing that he was then alive, in which fact she has since
learned that she was mistaken and now by way of amendment to her said bill
by leave of the court first had and obtained, she respectfully represents
that the said Conway Madison departed this life before her testator and
devisor, leaving a widow and six children, viz. Winna Madison, his widow,
Mary, Frances, James, William, Eugenia E. and Elizabeth Madison, two of
who, viz. Mary and Frances Madison, are of age & the others infants of Tender years as she has been informed and so charges. She prays that (those

named) be made parties defendants to this bill and her original bill here-
inbefore referred to . . . .

- - - -

A partial decree provides that the infant children of Ambrose L. Rose,
dec'd, Frances T. and Jane N. Rose, are entitled to their father's share
of $290.32.

- - - -

Affidavit of John P. Todd
Orange County to wit:
John P. Todd this day appeared before me, a justice of the peace for the
count, and made oath that he is satisfied from information derived from
Winny Madison, the widow of the late Conway Madison, who was a nephew of
the late James Madison, that Mary, Frances, James, William, Eugenia E. and
Elizabeth Madison, the children of the said Conway Madison, reside out of
the state of Virginia.
In testimony whereof I hereto put my hand this 3rd day of May 1837.
                                                     John F. Taliaferro

- - - -

There are three newspaper clippings notifying absent defendants of the
suit and the need to appear. Each appeared in the POLITICAL ARENA, "a
newspaper printed in the Town of Fredericksburg," bearing dates 25 November 1836, 27 January 1837 and 30th June 1837, each certified by Wm. M.
Blackford, Editor.

- - - -

There is a final decree in draft form appearing to confirm the payments
noted before but no papers indicating the payments for the balance ($4355.20).

- - - -

John G. Holladay, Esqr.   Columbus, Mississippi
Dear Sir: December 20, 1837
Your letter of the 28th ultimo was received this morning. No guardian
has yet been appointed for the children of my deceased friend, Ambrose L.
Rose Esqr., and none will be unless the business in Virginia requires it.
Mr. Rose devised the whole of his estate (which is small) to his wife,
Elizabeth K. Rose, who was also appointed by the will sole executrix and
has qualified as such in the probate court of this county. The will speci-
fies "both real and personal estate of any nature and kind whatsoever and
wheresoever his will to speak from the time of his death as to his real
as well as his personal property," which is a good will under the statutes
of this state.
He left two children, both daughters, the elder, Frances T. Rose, aged
eight years 9th July 1837, and the younger, Jane N. Rose, aged four years,
24th August 1837. They are both alive. No mention however is made of
them in the will, but if the money in Virginia you consider as coming to
them or not, Mrs. Rose will take out letters of guardianship and send you
as a power of attorney to receive the money. Be pleased to advise me on
the subject and direct in what manner the power of attorney is to be authenticated.
Your own judgment, on which we have every reliance will be your guide
concerning the business touching Genl. William Madison's accounts.
                                        Respectfully
          * * * * * * * * * * James T. Harris

In a suit in which George G. Taliaferro and Sarah, his wife, late Sarah Jenkins, George G. Jenkins and Robert T. Jenkins, by George G. Taliaferro, his guardian, represent that Thomas Jenkins, the father of Sarah, George and Robert, died about the year 1822, having made a will in which he appointed his wife, Elizabeth, executrix. Elizabeth Jenkins died the following year without having sold any or a very small portion of Thomas Jenkin's estate. They state that shortly after Elizabeth's death, administration of the estate was granted to Charles Taylor. He returned an inventory and sold a portion of the estate before he died in 1826 or 1827. The plaintiffs charge that the settlement of the estate recorded in court was not the account of Charles Taylor but that portion Richard Chapman made for Taylor. The plaintiffs further charge that the granting of the administration of the estate of Thomas Jenkins to his son, William T. Jenkins in 1829 was "wholly irregular and illegal." In the Bill, the plaintiffs name the children of Thomas Jenkins and Elizabeth, his wife, as Sarah, wife of George G. Taliaferro; George, Robert, William T., Edward, Charles T. and James M. Jenkins.

The papers in this suit contain the division of the slaves of Doctor Charles Taylor. The sum of $7865 was divided into nine parts: William Milburn, Thomas Jenkins, Robert Taylor Junr., Charles Taylor, Catlett Conway Junr., Martha S. Taylor, George Francis Taylor, Matilda R. Taylor and Evelina M. Taylor.

* * * * * * * * * * * * * *

Suit filed in 1839.

To the judge of the Circuit Superior Court of Law and Chancery for Orange County, Your complainants, John White and Lucy, his wife, late Lucy Adams, respectfully shew that the said John made a contract with one John Brown of Orange County in exchange their interest in the estate loaned to Nancy Adams (Lucy White's mother) during her life by the will of her husband, for a tract of land of about 95 acres lying in Orange County to which said Brown claimed title. William Adams, the father of your complainant, Lucy, by his will of record in Orange County, gave certain portions of his estate to his widow, Nancy, during her life and at her death directed it to sold by his Extr and the proceeds equally divided among his children, Robert, William and Polly Adams, Nancy married to John Herndon, Catherine to William Jones, and your complainant Lucy White, and it was your complainant's interest in this property under the will of her father which was the subject of this contract. Brown was to make your complainant, John White, a good title to the tract of ninety five acres which he gave in exchange for the aforesaid interest. Your complainants executed a deed to John Brown for their interest in the estate loaned to Mary Adams for life dated 5th Jany 1830, and also a Deed of Trust on the tract of 95 acres, copies of these deeds and William Adams' will are filed with this bill as part of it.

Your complainants, who are totally ignorant of the proper mode of transacting such business, executed these deeds at the instance of Brown in whom they confided, who told them it was the proper mode of doing the business, and they expected Brown to make your complainant, John White, a deed to the tract of land of ninety five acres and conveying a good title to it, but after being fraudently obtained, the deeds aforesaid of your complainants, he wholly failed and refused to convey the said land to your complainant,

John, & they then discovered that he had not a good title to the land himself and so could not make a good title to his vendee according to his
contract.

Your complainants then informed Brown that as he had not complied with
the contract and was unable to do so that they considered themselves ab-
solved from it and that they would have nothing further to do with it and
refused to take the land. Your complainants are further informed and
charge that Brown has since been in the habit of claiming ownership over
said land by cutting timber on it and otherwise showing that he considered
it his property. Nevertheless they find that Brown has had these deeds
recorded, and on death of Nancy Adams, the widow, which occurred in January
last, he set up a claim to your complainants' interest in the property
which she held under her husband's will, and yet persists in it.

Your complainants allege that Brown has never paid one cent or conveyed any property to them, or either of them, in consideration of their
interest so conveyed to him, Brown, as before stated, they have literally
received nothing for it, but were deceived & defrauded into the execution
of said conveyance and also into the execution of the aforesaid deed of
trust for which also they have received no consideration whatever.

Your complainants further shew that on the death of the widow (the
executor of William Adams being dead), administration de bonis non with the
will annexed of William Adams was committed to Richard Richard Sr., and
also administration on the estate of Nancy Adams, and in on or both of these
characters (they know not which) he has sold all the property left by the
widow as well what she held for life under her husband's will, as her own
absolute estate proper and now hold the proceeds in the form of bonds.
Your complainants contend they are entitled to participate in the final
---- as if the aforesaid contract and deeds had never been made but the
said John Brown claims under said deeds all their interest in it. Your
complainants claim that part of it given to your complainant, Lucy, by
her father's will; they claim one sixth of Nancy Adams' estate because she
died intestate, and your complainant, Lucy, is one of the six distributees,
and they claim one seventh of that portion given by the will of William
Adams in right of your complainant, Lucy, as one of his distributees.

William Adams Jr., left Virginia some years ago before his father's
death and the latest account received from him was in June 1822 -- the old
man died in 1826 -- the legacy to his son, William, and he being now un-
heard of for seven years is in law pronounced to be dead, and your complainant entitled in right of said Lucy to one seventh of his estate & he
being one of the 7 distributees. If your complainants are mistaken in this
and the legacy of William Adams is a lapsed legacy then as to it the old
man died intestate and your complainant, Lucy, being one of his distributees
they are entitled in her right to one 7th of it. All the children of William Adams Sr. are those named in his will and they are also all the children of his widow, Nancy Adams. In consequence of the pretensions set up
by Brown under said deeds, the aforesaid Richards will not pay any thing
to your complainants under the order of a court of equity . . . .

Not shown in the bill but shown in the list of parties and in the sum-
mation to describe defendants is Elizabeth, wife of Washington Howard.
Elhanon Row was the attorney for John White and wife. In the final decree,
suit of plaintiff dismissed and they were ordered to pay defendant's costs.

William Adams Jr. left Virginia some years before the death of his
father and the last intelligence received from him, and the last information showing he was still living was a letter written by him to his father
from Adams County, Mississippi dated 3rd June 1822. A copy of this letter
(taken by Edmund Row, the executor, from the original in his possession)
is filed with this bill. Edmund Row held in his hands William's portion
of the proceeds of the sale of his father's estate awaiting his call. After the lapse of more than seven years from the receipt of this letter,
William's mother, brothers and sisters, believing him dead, and being
advised that the law so presumed, claimed of the said Edmund Row a distribution of the fund among them, they being entitled thereto as his heirs
at law and distributees. Row disputed their right to it and they instituted
a suit in chancery of the county court of Orange against him to establish
it. This suit was never decided, but during the pendency, Row being satisfied that they were entitled to the principal of the fund (but still denying
their right to interest on it, and claiming that the cost of the suit
should be paid out of the fund) paid over to the parties without any ----
if the court authorizing it, such amount as he considered them entitled to
and then left the state for Mississippi where he died.

The complainants were not satisfied with the distribution which Row made
of that fund but as he left no estate in Virginia and there are no avail-
able means of prosecuting the claim against him, the suit was dismissed;
nor is it the purpose of the complainants now to ask any relief in that
matter, but merely to shew how that part of William Adams' interest in his
father's estate was disposed of . . . .

                                                    John Z. Holladay
Filed April 1839   Pltfs Atty

The answer of Edmund Row, the executor, is dated Sept. 26, 1839, and
details efforts to locate William Jr. with no results. Included is a
paper noting that at a monthly court held on twenty eighth of January 1839,
Edmund Row has died and Richard Richards granted letters of administration.
(This is part of a suit brought by Washington Howard and Elizabeth, his
wife, late Elizabeth Adams.)

Copy of letter from William Adams Jr. to his father, William Adams, dated
June 3, 1822, Adams County, Mississippi.

Dear Father:
This being the third time that I have wrote to you since I landed in
this country and this morning I were in Natchez, call'd at the post office
enquired if there were a letter for Wm. Adams Jr., the answer was there
is not, certainly it bears heavy on my mind knowing that I have left my
nearest and dearest relations so long a distance. I received a letter to
my first in the latter part of last September which was much satisfaction
to hear the family were in better health than they had been for a long
time stating in all possibility Polly would get well again. I am now writing dr Father dr Mother brother and sisters to you all hoping that you may
receive this letter and that it may find you all in health & a longing
desire for the pardon of the many sins that we all are liable to through
Jesus Christ. My health I do not know that I have any right to complain
of but cannot serve my maker as I ought to do. As it is your wish that I
should write lengthy, it appears that my mind is full but some times as if
I could say little. But I will go on to say there are farmers in this coun-

try that make from thirty to forty thousand dollars in a year for their
crop of cotton, and overseers get from five to eighteen hundred dollars a
year. There is no man that will be accepted for an Overseer without he
can read write and know some thing of figures because every days picking
are to be weighed after dark, the name of each negro set in a line against
his cotton. I have been Overseer for Col. P. Hoggatt for five months.
I am sorry to state that my dear and only brother has not a sufficient
knowledge of figures to be an overseer in this country in forwarding the
work to each days picking. The principal crop in this country is cotton.
A great variety of vegetables come in early to market, corn roasting years
plenty this time, bacon from six to seven cents a pound, corn thirty seven
& half cents per bushel, flour from three to five dollars per barrel though
the planters raise no wheat and very little corn or bacon, it nearly all
comes from Kentucky and the adjoining states, whiskey very cheap from twenty
to thirty cents per gallon. I have been in the state of Louisiana and am
much pleased so far as I have seen. I expect to travel three hundred miles
near about next Christmas to Red River. You desired me to let you know
what part of the country I like best, the country where I am at present.
The people in this country make use of the rain and river water most of
which are injurious to their health. There are very few springs or wells
in this country. Father I hope to receive a letter from you in great speed.
It appeared in your letter that you had a desire to know how my horse performed. I swaped my horse with John Chewning near Fredericksburg, Va.,
got a bay mare she carried me nearly eight hundred miles, her back got so
badly scalded with the saddle I had to trade her & give twenty dollars to
boot. Dr Mother I being so well acquainted with the tenderness of your
heart that I cannot help thinking about the distance we are apart. In the
next to me add a line if you please. My love to you all wish to be remem-
bered to uncle Quisenberry and family. There are many things I would wish you
to write concerning crops, the price of produce, etc. Also how the girls
come on getting married if I never see any of you on this earth I hope to
find you with the Lord where the righteous dwell. I must conclude my subscribing myself. Your son,
                                              William Adams Jr.

   Dr Brother. I shall never persuade you to come to this country it is
far from being healthy though I should be glad to see you here lands sells
for different prices from two to one hundred dollars per acre if I ever
come back to Va again I expect to come by water for the fatigue of traveling
by land are so great and expensive.
                                 Your brother   W A

   In the final settlement, legatees received William's portion.
            * * * * * * * * * * * * * * * *

   In a bill filed 1st October 1834, Elizabeth L. Terrill, executrix of
Robert Terrill, is the plaintiff and Elizabeth F. Coleman, her daughter,
an infant, by Thomas Coleman, her guardian to defend her in this suit,
Elizabeth Terril in her own right and as Executrix of James Coleman, are
defendants. The plaintiff states that "some time in the year 1825" James
Coleman (her first husband) died, possessed of a considerable real and
personal estate which he devised in his will to be equally divided between
his wife and infant daughter. As Elizabeth L. Coleman, she claims she
had made considerable progress in paying her husband's (James Coleman) debts
when she married Robert Terrill (license 2nd January 1827), who became

entitled to the administration in right of his wife and took possession of
the remaining estate of James Coleman. He did not make a division of the
estate but continued to pay the debts until his death "which occurred some
time during the present year."

The papers in this suit show a survey in settlement in which Elizabeth
Terrill is assigned Not No. 1, 193 acres, and Lot No. 2, containing 312
acres with the mill lot of four acres assigned to Elizabeth F. Coleman. The
193 acres was the dower land of Elizabeth Coleman, mother of James Coleman.

In another suit, in the deposition of John Terrill taken 20th April 1838,
he mentions her father, Joseph Coleman, and her brother, Reuben L. Coleman.
In the deposition of George W. Coleman, taken at the house of Elizabeth L.
Terrill, 20th April 1838, he refers to her as "my sister."

* * * * * * * * * * * * * *

In a suit in which Charles Quisenberry and Antonia Adeline, his wife,
formerly Antonia Adeline Brent, are plaintiffs, they argue that they executed a bond to Miss Mary H. Brent, sister of Antonia Adeline; that Mary
died in 1836 in the county of Nelson; that her brothers and sisters are
Antonia Adeline, John, Alexander and William Brent. They argue that Frederick Peyton of Nelson County exhibited a paper in the Nelson County Court
which was executed in Orange County purporting to be the last will and
testament of Mary H. Brent, by which her estate was given to Hellin Peyton,
Henry Peyton, John Brent, Thomas Henry Quisenberry (an infant child of the
plaintiffs who is since dead), Frederick Peyton and Nancy Peyton. When the
will was admitted to record, Frederick Peyton qualified as executor. The
plaintiffs charge that "the said writing or supposed will (which will be
exhibited as soon as procured) is not the will of Mary H. Brent because it
was procured by fraud or undue influence or both and because Mary H. Brent
at the time of the said supposed will was executed was incapable in law of
disposing of her property by reason of imbecility or want of a disposing
mind . . . ." (This paper is all there is in the file of this case.

* * * * * * * * * * * * * *

In a suit in which Nancy Burrus is represented by her next friend, William Stevens, she states that in the year eighteen hundred and twenty three,
she married Joseph Burrus, her present husband, now in the county of Orange,
and in her Bill sworn to the 30th day of January 1837 contends "notwithstanding her dutiful conduct as a wife and her conjugal fidelity, in short
notwithstanding a course of deportment on her part into which she chal-
lenges an investigation, and as to which she defies any just reprehensions,
her said husband, Joseph Burrus, has for years treated (her) in a manner
not only not becoming a husband but the bare recital of which she is persuaded will not only awaken the sympathies of this court for her sufferings
but present an unanswerable claim upon its justice for relief from the pressure of that marital power which has been used in time past so as only to
make her unhappy instead of for her protection and comfort." In her Bill,
she mentions her father, William Terrill. She asks that the court grant
"a divorce a mensa et thoro from her said husband."

In a deed of trust referred to in the Bill, the children of Joseph Burrus and Nancy, his wife, are shown as Nancy, Martha Ann, Frances, Thomas
Foster, William T. and Catharine S. T. Burrus. The eldest is twelve years
of age.

* * * * * * * * * * * * * *

On a single piece of paper with no other notations, the following appears:
John M. Hume
Newton Hume
Aziel Simpson & Polly, his wife
Hugh B. Stanard and Maria, his wife (formerly Maria Taylor)
Eliza Taylor
Franklin Hume
Charles Oscar Hume   John Hume   Ellen Hume
Ann Maria Hume   Harriett Hume
John Spaulding & Elizabeth, his wife, formerly Elizabeth Simpson
William Simpson
Henry Lewis; Mary Ann; Francis; Charles; Sarah Jane & Lucinda Simpson.
                * * * * * * * * * * * * * *

In a suit, James Sleet and Rebecca, his wife, and Andrew Bourne and Ann,
his wife, exhibit their Bill of Complaint against Patrick Petty and John
Mallory, administrators de bonis non of George Petty, deceased, the same
Patrick in his own right, John Boston and Frances, his wife; Weedon Sleet
and Patsy, his wife; Reuben Clark and Elizabeth, his wife; Peyton Keith and
Sally, his wife; George Petty, George M. Petty, Benjamin F., Alfred, Jar-
rell and Barbara Ann Petty, infants under the age of twenty one years by
John Stanard assigned to defend them in this suit; William Morton, Jonathan
C. Gibson, executors of William Mallory, deceased; Thomas Newman; Curtis
L. Brockman; Benjamin Hume, Sheriff of Orange County to whom was committed
for administration the estate of Elizabeth Petty, deceased, who was an
original administratrix of George Petty, deceased; and aforesaid Patrick
Petty, who was an original administrator of George Petty.
When Patrick Petty died intestate, the County Court of Culpeper ordered
Richard Tutt, Sheriff of said county, to take the estate to administer
according to law.
On 30th September 1828, John Stanard, marshal of the court, was appointed
guardian of the infants. On 7th October 1828, there is the notation in
the proceedings that Ann Sleet had married Andrew Bourn (the marriage re-
cord shows that Andrew Bourn married Ann Sleet, widow, with Weedon Sleet
as surety, on the 5th of October 1826). In the proceedings of 26th October
1828, the record shows Philip Sleet has died; that the defendants, Reuben
Clarke and Elizabeth, his wife; Dabney Morris and Polly, his wife; George
Petty, George M. Petty, Benjamin F. Petty; Alfred Petty, Jarrell Petty and
Barbara Ann Petty are not inhabitants of the Commonwealth.
                * * * * * * * * * * * * * *
In a suit in which there was a final decree dated 5th October 1839,
James Michie Junr. and John C. Webb are plaintiffs against Elliott Jones.
In the Bill, the heirs of Elliott Jones are shown as his widow, Elizabeth
Jones, who has since intermarried with William Sims, and nine children, to
wit: Elizabeth, who married John Farneyhough; Sarah, who married with Eze-
kial Herndon; Evelina, who married with Zachariah Garton; Jane, who married
with Henry B. Blake; William, Paschal, Susan, Pamela and Meredith Jones,
who are under the age of twenty one years.
                * * * * * * * * * * * * * *

In a Bill filed 24th December 1832, George Proctor says he married Frances Grady, daughter of William Grady, deceased, who departed this life intestate leaving a little property which was sold, the personal by his administrators, William and Alexander Grady, and the land by commissioners.
                * * * * * * * * * * * * * *

In a suit brought by William Quarles, he explains that Thomas Mitchell
made a bequest of ₤ 2000 to Thomas Johnson in trust for Barbara H. Johnson.
If she survived her husband, Francis Johnson, she was to receive the trust;
if her husband survived her, her children were to receive the trust. Thomas Johnson refused to take "upon himself the burthen of the said trust,"
and William Quarles was appointed by the court, a function he performed
for nearly fifteen years "to the satisfaction of all concerned in the
business." William Quarles notes that Elizabeth died and her husband survived her; that she had left two sons, Alexander H. Johnson and Francis
Johnson Jr. William Quarles states that he had grown old and infirm and
was incapable of managing the said fund as he used to do; that he has applied to the parties interested to release him from it; that they are all
anxious to do so and he asks the court to appoint some fit person to suc-
ceed him, suggesting Francis Johnson Junr. was such a person. In his deposition, Alexander H. Johnson tells the court he has no objections to the
appointment of his brother, and the court approves.

                    * * * * * * * * * * * * * *

In a suit brought by James Barbour, the following was made by John Miller on the books of the former surveyor of (Orange) county in the following
words and figures:
24th of November 1802 then did Major John Miller enter & locate 200
acres of land in Orange County at the Great Mountain on a land office
Treasury Warrant No. 16363 issued the 12th day of May 1783 to Wm. Clark,
Assignor, to John D. Grymes, Assignor, to Daniel Woolford, adjoining John
McMullen, John Page, Craigs, Jeremiah Beazley, at the head of Gum Swamp by
note from the said Daniel Woolford to said John Miller dated the 29th of
September 1796. Reuben Lindsay, S.O.C.
Another entry in the surveyor's books: 12th August 1792, then did John
Miller enter & locate 250 acres of land adjoining to J. Holsapple Entry
Richard Payne and Kirby Duglass on a Warrant No. 21222. A copy Reuben
Lindsay, S.O.C.
In his Bill, James Barbour states that he purchased of William Johnson
a certain parcel of land lying in the county that the said William had
succeeded to as one of the heirs of the late Benjamin Johnson. James Bar-
bour states he has had peaceable possession of the land in question and
nothing doubting his title when a certain (Richard) Rawlings pretends to
claim the same by a conveyance from the Patentee, Michael Ott.
At a court held for Orange County at the court house on Monday the 22d
day of October 1804, James Barbour and Lucy, his wife, are plaintiffs, and
William Johnson and Frances T. Johnson, infants represented by William
Mallory, their guardian, are defendants. In the Bill, the division of the
estate of Benjamin Johnson is set out. James Barbour and Lucy, his wife,
received one third; William Johnson one third; Frances T. Johnson one third.
James Barbour and Lucy received the tract of land called Carter's in which
is included the tract of land Col. Johnson purchased of divers persons according to two plats returned by Valentine Johnson, the one plat called
Capt. James Barbour's plat of the river land which, according to estimation, contains nine hundred and forty five acres and one quarter, and one
other plat called Capt. James Barbour's plat of the Goodrich tract containing by estimation eighty six acres and a half which land we estimated
at four thousand four hundred and eighty five pounds, twelve shillings.
To William Johnson, the tract called Barbour's tract, it being the tract

of land upon which Major Ambrose Barbour lived, the tract of land called
the Mill Tract, the tract of land called Goldson's, and tract of land purchased by the late Col. Johnson of Richard Payne, and a tract of land called
the Patent land, it being land lately taken up by Col. Johnson; the tract
of land called the Mill Tract is that upon which Colo. Johnson's father
lived and died (the amount of land in each tract is given); Frances T.
Johnson received a tract containing by estimation five hundred and twenty
seven acres and one quarter, a tract of land called Lucas's land (182 acres);
John Cave's tract (332 acres), the tract of land the late Colo. Johnson
purchased of Benjamin Cave (35 acres), and a tract called Jarrell's (310
acres). In a deed accompanying the suit, it shows William Johnson and Alice,
his wife, of Madison County, sold land in Orange County to James Barbour.

* * * * * * * * * * * * * *

In a suit filed in November 1837, Susan Nelson, formerly Susan Robinson,
who sues by Catherine Robinson, her mother and next friend, James Nelson,
her husband, contending in her Bill that about the month of October 1821
"while she was a very young girl being only fourteen years of age, she
intermarried with James Nelson, then and now a resident of Orange County."
In a few days after the marriage, his conduct became neglectful, his
language abusive, and in less than twelve months he used personal violence
towards her. Although she tried "to mitigate the severity of his conduct,"
his severity increased, and she often "suffered cold for want of a fire."
In her Bill, she says she had two children, one previously born being dead,
and the other has remained with his father. (In a deposition, this child's
name is shown as William Henry Nelson. We have been told by Mr. Herbert
E. Ryle of Upper Marlboro, Maryland, that William Henry married Frances
Carlton in Boone County, Kentucky. Their daughter, Virgie Nelson, married Willie Clyde Ryal (a distant cousin of Mr. Ryle.)

* * * * * * * * * * * * * *

In a deed of trust between Newman Faulconer and Maria, his wife, dated
28th day of July 1832, and John Woolfolk of the second part, and Reuben
Newman, Joseph Hiden and Owen Snider of the third part, there is a description of a house that Newman Faulconer agrees to build. A building of brick
twenty feet front on the street, two stories high, above ground and running
back more than twenty five feet, and said house to have no windows or doors
on the side opposite his, the said Joseph Hiden's tavern, and but two windows and no door in the North end of said house, and the said Joseph Hiden
is to have the privilege of removing the house now on said lot and if he
should build adjoining said Newman Faulconer's herein before described to
have liberty to join his wall with said Newman Faulconer's by paying the
said Faulconer half the price of the wall thus joined .. and Joseph Hiden
agrees to sell to Newman Faulconer a lot of land adjoining Edwin Nichols
beginning at the corner of the said Nichols and Hiden on the street and
running along the street twenty feet thence back parallel to said Nichols'
house as far as said house runs.

* * * * * * * * * * * * * *

John Moore petitions the court as executor of Alexander Holmes, deceased,
and one of the securities of Reuben Terrill for his administration of the
estate of William Terrill Junr., deceased, and Thomas Coleman, surviving
administrator of the estate of Wilson Coleman, deceased, another security
of the said Reuben Terrill's administration. John Moore states that when
William Terrill Junr. died, he was possessed of a considerable estate,

"far more than sufficient to pay all his debts." He states that upon the death of William Terrill Junr., Reuben Terrill, his brother, took administration upon his estate with John Moore and Wilson Coleman as his securities. Wilson Coleman has since died and John Moore, Thomas Coleman and Lucy Coleman, since deceased, became administrators of his estate. John Moore charges that Reuben Terrill "has largely wasted the estate of his intestate, William Terrill Junr., and is considerable indebted to other as administrator .." John Moore charges Reuben Terrill has "recently made a pretended sale" of all his estate to James Terrill, his brother, for an amount James is in no position to pay. He further charges that James Terrill has conveyed all the estate he had "pretended" to have purchased to Jackson Morton in trust for Reuben Terrill, Elizabeth Terrill, Nancy Terrill, William Terrill, Catherine Terrill, David Terrill and George Terrill, infant children of the said Reuben Terrill. On a scrap of paper dated 11th March 1823, Reuben Terrill's wife is shown as "Sukey."

* * * * * * * * * *

In a Bill filed in 1833, Solomon Sholes, Charles Geer and Elizabeth, his wife, and Fanny Sholes, an infant by said Geer her next friend, are plaintiffs and David Sholes is defendant. The plaintiffs state that David P.P. Sholes died intestate leaving a considerable real and personal estate, a widow, Nancy Sholes, and six children, viz. three (a son, David, and two daughters named Margaret or Peggy and Mary or Polly, now the wive of William Taylor and Benson Henley or Henry) by a former wife or wives, and three (Solomon Sholes, Elizabeth Sholes, now wife of Charles Geer, and Fanny Sholes), by the said Nancy, his last wife. When David P.P. Sholes died, his son, David, took possession of the estate, sold the perishable property and divided the proceeds of the sale and the slaves between himself and his two sisters, contending that Solomon, Elizabeth and Fanny were illegitimate because David P.P. Sholes and Nancy were never married. The plaintiffs contend that David P.P. Sholes went to Rockingham County, married Nancy, returned to Orange, where they lived together as man and wife for seventeen years, during which time the plaintiffs were born. The plaintiffs outline what each of his step-sisters and David received in the division. The estate of David P.P. Sholes was appraised on the 2nd day of March 1822 and valued at $1201.55. In February, 1834, the plaintiffs were residents of Rockingham County. In an undated bill, it is noted that David Sholes has died and administration of his estate committed to George Morris, Sheriff of Orange County, as well as the unadministered estate of David P.P. Sholes.

* * * * * * * * * * * * * *

In a bill filed in August 1835, James Stone states that Elijah Powell of the county of Madison, state of Virginia, died intestate without issue, leaving Phoebe Powell, his wife, and Ambrose Powell, his brother, his only next of kin him surviving. The Bill further shows there were two deeds of gifts recorded in the Clerk's Office of the County Court of Scott in the state of Kentucky, in which Ambrose Powell gave and conveyed to his children and grandchildren "all his right title and interest" in the estate of Elijah Powell, deceased, as follows. To his daughter, Sally Crawford, and to his sons, Reuben, Colby, Willis and Fielding Powell, one each sixth part thereof; to his son in law, Honor Powell, one twelfth part thereof, and to the children of his daughter, Mildred Powell, deceased, the wife of the said Honor Powell, the remaining twelfth part. Her children are named as Achilles, Benjamin, William, James, Francis and Ann, who are citizens of the state of Kentucky. The bill notes that the defendant, Fielding Powell, resides in Orange County, Virginia.

* * * * * * * * * * * * * *

In a suit brought by Paul Verdier against Eliza T. Taylor, administrator of George C. Taylor, deceased, and Francis Walker, injoining them from proceeding on a judgment they had obtained on a bond which he had executed to the said Eliza for purchases at the estate sale, contending what George C. Taylor owed him exceeded the value of the bond.

The deposition of Reynolds Chapman (who was Orange County Clerk from 1801-1844) taken the 23d of May 1839 (being the Tuesday after the fourth Monday) at the tavern of Richard Rawlings at Orange Court House in the county of Orange: "he (Chapman) came to live in the office of the late George C. Taylor (Orange County Clerk from 1798-1801), the intestate of said Eliza T. Taylor, who was the clerk of the county court of Orange, in the early part of October, he thinks the 4th of the month, in the year 1799; that said George C. Taylor boarded deponent with Paul Verdier, who then kept a tavern at Orange Court House from the time deponent came to live with Taylor till the office was moved from the courthouse which was as well as deponent recollects in the latter part of winter or early spring of 1800; that deponent's washing was done at the Verdier's; that when deponent came to live with Taylor, he found Charles Bell in the office as an assistant of Taylor and boarding with Verdier and continued to board with Verdier and to act as an assistant of Taylor till the removal of the office from the courthouse, that he presumes Bell's board was also to be settled by Taylor."

Reynolds Chapman testifies further "that the office was kept in a house belonging to Verdier when he first entered the office and they continued to occupy the same house as an office till their removal before referred to, and that Charles Bell and deponent slept upon a bed belonging to Verdier the greater part of the time they remained at the courthouse . . . ."

Reynolds Chapman testifies further that "George C. Taylor generally dined at Mr. Verdier's tavern when he was in the neighborhood; that said Taylor was very liberal, indeed extravagant, in his expenses and that he was severely pressed for money from deponent's first acquaintance with him until his death."

In the deposition of Thomas Row taken the 8th day of July 1837, he says "that he was a member of the Orange Court at the time that Geo. C. Taylor was elected clerk of said court & that on the day of the said Taylor's election, he invited the whole court & it is believed the Bar also to a sumptuous dinner at the tavern of Paul Verdier at which dinner it is also believed by the deponent most of the members of the Bar & Court attended & deponent would also say that the said Taylor was very liberal in treating his company at said dinner .."

In the deposition of William Newson Senr. taken the 30th day July 1837, he says he "was in the habit of keeping bar and doing business with Paul Verdier from the time he, the said Verdier, purchased the Orange Hotel in 1799 for many years on court days and all publick days; deponent knows that George C. Taylor was in the habit of frequenting the said Verdier tavern and had with him a large tavern account, and deponent believes was in the habit of borrowing small sums of money of said Verdier .. that said Taylor

was in the habit of frequenting the said Verdier's tavern with his horse,
attending balls, barbecues, etc., and that he was very liberal and in the
habit of having a large bar account and treating his friends freely and to
the best of the deponent's recollection and belief never paid any part of
his account .."

* * * * * * * * * * * * * *

In a Bill sworn 23rd October 1837, George A. Gentry and Jane Estes,
formerly Jane Ogg, widow of Samuel Estes, and Susan Ogg are plaintiffs,
who contend that some years before John Ogg had died leaving a will whereby
he appointed C. Parrott his executor, who renounced his executorship, and
his widow, Sarah Ogg, qualified as his administratrix, and gave bond with
David Goodall as security. The plaintiffs contend David Goodall sold the
property and collected the debts due the estate and "finally absconded
from the Commonwealth of Virginia;" that the said Sarah died about the year
1828, insolvent, her estate was committed to the Sheriff of Orange County,
William T. Burrus, who also had died and the estate committed to Thomas
Row, the Sheriff.

* * * * * * * * * * * * * *

In a suit filed by George Newman, he contends that George Newman, his
father died in the year 1837 having first made and published his last will
and testament; that by his will he had devised his real estate to his four
children, James Newman, Elias Newman, himself (George Newman), and Elizabeth Winslow; that although he appointed himself and his brother, Elias,
as executors, only he (George) qualified. In his Bill, George states
that his brother, James, died during the lifetime of his father, intestate,
and without issue, and that Elias died a short time after his father, intestate, and without issue.
    In the will of George Newman (the father) he refers to "my daughter,
Elizabeth Winslow, late Elizabeth Newman and wife of Edward Winslow .."
In her deposition, Elizabeth contends her brother, George, is the debtor
to the estate of their father instead of being a creditor as he claims.

* * * * * * * * * * * * * *

In a suit filed by Elizabeth (Newman) Winslow, the same genealogical
material appears. In the papers in the will of George Newman Senr., he
give's his wife's name as Ann, and the names of his grandsons as Thomas
T., George A., and James F. Newman, who would have had to have been the
children of George Newman, Junr., since his other two sons, James and Elias,
died without issue.

* * * * * * * * * *

In a suit in which Daphne, Philip, Harrison, William, Mary, free persons
of colour, sue in forma pauperis, contend that Robert Campbell, also a
free man of colour, the husband of Daphne and the father of their children
departed this life intestate "sometime lately (spring 1834) in the county
of Orange where he resided; that Richard Richards qualified as his administrator in the county court of Orange and holds and threatens to sell your
complainants as slaves of the said Robert Campbell into bondage." The
plaintiffs contend "that they are the bastard issue together with the said
Robert Campbell of one Daphne Campbell by the same or different fathers,
also a free woman of colour." The petitioners advise that the said Daphne
is the common mother of them all.
    "Your complainants would however present their claim to freedom in a
dowable aspect. They would show to the court that the said Robert Campbell

purchased your complainant, Daphne, many years ago and has always since lived with him having by her as his wife your other complainants as his children always treating and regarding your complainants as children and wife as aforesaid."

In the deposition of Benjamin Walker, he says Robert Campbell was always known by the name "Bob;" that he purchased Daphne and her son some years before his death and they lived in the neighborhood.

Reuben T. Clarke deposed and said that Robert Campbell had written a will and "emancipated the appellants as his wife and children, and directed his land and other property to be sold and the money applied after paying what he owed, to purchasing a jersey, wagon or cart, to remove them to a free state;" that a short time before his death Robert Campbell asked him to write another will. When Reuben Clarke met him on the road one day he asked him why he needed another will and was told he had "burnt the old will," but Reuben Clarke never wrote another will.

In the deposition of Thomas Harwood taken at the house of Jamison Corbin in the town of Falmouth and county of Stafford on the 26th day of April 1836, he responds, "I know his mother to have been a free woman and that her name was Hannah Campbell." When asked if he knew if Hannah's mother was a free woman, he says he knows nothing of her. The questioner suggests Hannah's husband was known as Crooked Joe and Harwood replies he knew him and says "he was the husband of Hannah Campbell and the reputed Father of all her children .. they lived near me for many years." In answer to a question, he names Hannah's children as "Bob, Rebecca, Bill, Summerville, Phil, Ann, Joe and one other by the name of Patsey."

William S. Frazer says in his deposition that he knew Robert Campbell before he purchased Daphne of John Fisher, who considered her the wife of one of his slaves, Robert White.

Owen Cooper says John Fisher sold Robert Campbell a slave, Daphne, and her son, Phil or Philip. Martin Slaughter and John H. Lee were assigned Counsel for Daphne and her children. In the deposition of Robert H. Hope in the town of Falmouth, he says the mother of Hannah Campbell was Nancy Campbell, "a free woman who lived & died in the town of Falmouth." In the deposition of Joseph Ennever of Falmouth, he says he was acquainted with Robert Campbell from 1792 or 3 until he left about the year 1806 or 7. He says Robert's mother was Hannah Campbell and his father was reputed to have been Crooked Joe; whom Hannah purchased and whose name was Joe Lomax.

In a long recapitulation of the events and depositions, especially the deposition of Benjamin Walker, the court refuses to accept his deposition as the last will and testament of Robert Campbell. Daphne and her children prayed for an appeal to the next Circuit Superior Court. There is no information in this file as to the final settlement.

* * * * * * * * * * * * * * *

In a suit for divorce brought by ---- Adams from his wife, Martha Ann, of the County of Orange, he contends that they have three children and in the year 1843 moved to Gordonsville where he carries on his trade as a carriage maker. To his "great mortification and distress, he heard sundry rumors implicating the virtue of my wife; that for some time he was indignant at them and determined to resort to the law to vindicate his reputation against what he thought unfounded calamny, but unfortunately circumstances soon afterwards transpired which convinced him all the suspicions with regards to her were true." He charges that his said wife "during her

residence in Gordonsville was frequently seen in positions with other men
than her husband which no woman can be seen or be without the loss of her
character; that she was seen once or more to meet and go to meet her para-
mours at the distance of a mile or more from the place at which she resides.
Finally, he charges that she left the house of your complainant and went
to the city of Richmond and openly took up residence in a house of ill fame
in which she committed all the vices incident to such places of infamy and
depradation...."

In the deposition of Benjamin Boughan taken at the Bell Tavern in Richmond on the 3rd day of July 1845, he says he knew Martha Ann and went on
to relate what he considered something "amiss in her conduct."

"The last Saturday of last August I undertook to watch the lady and in
the first place she started from my house to go to my neighbors, Mrs.
Bowers, but did not go immediately there. I watched her as far as Mr.
Ancker's store where she went in and remained some time, and what she did
in there I do not know being then out of my sight. When she came out, I
saw her go to the Capitol Square where she took her bonnet off and washed
her face. From there she went with a man who met her on the Square up the
street leading from the Washington Tavern to the suburbs or edge of the
city. She stood there and talked about five minutes and then returned to
Broad and H Streets where, after she gave him a slight slap upon his face,
he left her. Then she came around by the Odd Fellow Hall and went in a
Confectionary under it, and I left her there and went to the old Market,
and there staid until she passed, and she passed me there and took up Valley
Street as far as the Church, and she went from that street by the old Pine-
apple Church down the street leading to Franklin Street and came down again
to the Old Market house, and from thence to Main Street. She went up Main
Street a short distance to a store where she remained by a few minutes.
When she came out she went down Main Street considerably below the Union
and then I put myself in the way where she could see me, and after she saw
me she turned short around and went up to Mrs. Bowers . . . . Some few
weeks after that I understand she was in town again (after having gone to
Gordonsville) and was informed that she was at Widow Night's, and a young
man named John Bennett went to see if she was there, and she had left there
as this young man said, and he found her at Martha Stevens, and a few eve-
nings after that her husband and father came down to my house and then went
up to the Cage and got Captain Jenkins and some of his men .. we took her
out of Martha Stevens, a common house or house of ill fame, and we tried
to get a room in a tavern but being unable to do so we went down to the
Cage and there she remained all night."

In the deposition of Captain Jenkins, he states that "sometime during
the last Fall, I do not know the day, I was applied to by Mr. Adams, the
husband of Mrs. Martha Ann Adams, together with an old gentleman said to
be her father, to give them some information as to how she could be found
for her father stated to me that he understood she was in a common house
in this place. I then stated to them that I was particularly engaged,
having the watch to set, to call at the watch-house in about half an hour
and I would then let them know whether I thought there could be anything
done or not. They then informed me that she, the said Martha Ann Adams,
had come to Richmond on a visit and they had been informed that she was
in a common house in this city, and they wished me to take her in charge.
I told them that I had no right to do so but if they thought proper to take
her in charge themselves I would go with them and thought I might perhaps

find her. They asked me to do just what I thought was right. I went with them to Martha Stevens, who keeps a notable common house or house of ill fame. We went into the back yard and up a pair of steps to a door which led into a room on the second floor. I knocked at the door and was answered by someone within; I asked if I could see Martha Stevens. At that time I heard someone coming down the steps and the door opened by a strange female to me, who had a candle in one hand; I stepped in suspecting who it was and placed myself in such a position as to prevent any retreat either up the stairs or through the passage. At that moment, the father cried out my child! and seized her. The father and daughter both shed tears bitterly. The first thing I recollect the father said after they got over their agitation was "My daughter, how could you have treated your mother and Mr. Adams in this way. If it don't kill your mother, I think it will be the death of me! She replied that 'I know that I have done wrong but it is done now and can't be helped.' About that time, Martha Stevens came into the room and I enquired of her if she, Martha Ann Adams, brought anything with her when she came there. To which she, Martha Stevens, replied that she brought her trunk with her and had received another one since, and that if we would go up stairs with her into her room or the room she occupied, we could get all that belonged to her. We then went up stairs into this room and she, Mrs. Adams, gathered her things, clothing and the like. At that moment I enquired of Mr. Adams and her father where they were going to remain until the cars started the next morning. They both told me they were strangers in town and did not know how to act in such a case and they would be much obliged to me if I would tell them what was best for them to do, and how they should act. I advised them to try to get lodgings as near the Depot as they could. From Martha Stevens', I accompanied them to the Swan Tavern where they failed to get lodgings, from there to the Washington Hotel. There I went in and saw the landlord myself. After informing him under what circumstances I had brought him that company, he also declined to receive them. I then told them I did not think they could get lodgings anywhere if the circumstances were made known to the keeper of any respectable house, and as I was concerned in the matter I could not consent for anyone to take them in unless I made the facts known. They seemed to be very much at a loss at what to do and upon seeing their embarrassment, I told them that if they thought proper to go to the Watch-house, they could remain there until time for the cars to leave in the morning, being satisfied they could not be able to get any place else to lodge that night. They accepted the offer and went with me from the Washington Hotel to the Watch-house where they remained until daylight in the morning. After getting there I understood that she had some children in Richmond that they wished to carry home with them. I then advised Mr. Adams to go and bring the children there and to engage a hack to carry them up to the cars in the morning. He presently started off for that purpose and left his wife and father at the Watch-house. Some time after Mr. Adams was gone, his wife looked very earnestly at her father and asked him why did he come after her? He replied, 'My dear child for the purpose of carrying you home with us in hopes to reclaim you. Your mother is willing to forgive you and so is Mr. Adams, and I will take you as a child again, if you will do as you ought to do from this time.' She looked down for a few moments, raised her head, and looking her father in the face replied it is useless. You may carry me home now but I will come back for I won't stay there or in that neighbourhood. Her father asked her why. She replied that she would not then be respected as other females were, and how could she go to some church or meeting-house, the names of which I do not now remember, and see other females looked upon differently to what I should be. And I will come back to Richmond where I can enjoy myself more in one week than I can in the old neighbourhood in a whole year. Her father then observed, 'Martha, you are a member of the church and your character I am afraid is gone; now I want you to tell me if you have ever been guilty of such bad conduct before you visited Richmond.' To which she replied, 'Yes, I have.' Her father observed in the name of God how came you ever to be guilty of such conduct. She answered it is done and over. The old man turned his head from her and I believe shed tears freely. I presently observed, "Mrs. Adams did I understand you to say that you are determined to return to Richmond?' She answered me yes, and I will do it. I then told her that after seeing so much of the spirit of forgiveness extended from her father and husband, if she did come back to Richmond under such circumstances I would take her up as soon as she got here. She looked at me and laughed and replied you will not know where to find me. To that I remarked, you might have supposed I would not have known where to find you tonight but you see I did find you and can always do so if you step in Richmond. She then remarked there were other places that I can and will go to for I am determined not to stay home. About that time Mr. Adams came in and said he had engaged a hack and that the children would be there after a little while.

"I then left them all in charge of the house keeper at the Cage until I took a round through the city to see the different watchmen, and when I returned to the Watch-house, I found Mr. Adams and her father sitting before the fire. I asked where Mrs. Adams was to which the housekeeper replied that he had made her a palet in one of the rooms in which she was locked up. Just at daylight the hack came and Mr. & Mrs. Adams and the children together with the baggage went up in the hack. Her father and myself walked on behind. The old man seemed to be greatly distressed and had but little to say on the way to the Depot. When we got to the Depot, it was some time before the cars were ready to start. I told Mr. Adams where to get his tickets, he accordingly obtained them. Mrs. Adams and the children were put into the car. I then took leave of Mr. Adams and his wife's father, they thanking me very much for the services I had rendered them to which I told them they were welcome and that I wished it might be for the best. And I have not seen or heard one word from any one of them until this evening when Mr. Adams called on me to make this statement.

The divorce was granted 9th October 1845.

* * * * * * * * * * * * * *

In a suit in which Walter Key and Martha, his wife, are plaintiffs, their Bill shows that Martha is the widow of John Daniel. The suit is over the sale of a horse by Henry Mitchell to satisfy a debt of Edmund Henshaw. The plaintiffs contend that they are entitled to any assets derived from the estate of Henry Mitchell before another could make a claim. In the Bill, one son of Henry Mitchell is named, Benjamin. Another son, William, makes a statement sworn to 26th day of October 1842, in which the question is asked: "Was your father interested in old Mr. Lucas's estate and if so to what extent?" William answers, "He married a daughter." In answer to another question, William says he was born according to the register in the year 1799 and in the month of May. He says his brother, Benjamin L. Mitchell, lived with their father until 1821 and then went to live with James Barbour Junr. In a paper dated 22nd September 1845, this suits abates as to the plaintiff, Walter Key, and defendant, Edmund Henshaw, by their deaths.

* * * * * * * * * * * * * *

The suit of John Boston and Charles Dean against William Porter, John Taliaferro and William M. Chapman is in regards to a judgment against plaintiffs in favor of William M. Chapman on a bond executed by plaintiffs for $25 to William Porter who assigned the bond to John Taliaferro, who assigned same to William Chapman. The bond was executed for certain legal services to be rendered by William Porter whom plaintiffs allege never performed the services and if forced to pay the judgment it would be a payment without consideration.

The Bill was sworn in court 25th May 1830, and removed to the Circuit Superior Court for trial 26th September 1842. By this time, John Boston had died and was represented by Alexander A. Boston, his administrator. John Taliaferro also had died (before August 24, 1841) and Mildred M. Taliaferro, his executrix, became the defendant.

The depositions of Alexander A. Boston taken 23 July 1832, contains the following: "It is admitted that John P. Boston, whose deposition has been taken in this cause, is the son of John Boston, the father and intestate of Alexander A. Boston, one of the plaintiffs in the cause, and that John Boston died without a will. Alexander A. Boston."

In a deposition taken 18 July 1842, William H. Terrill states he was twenty six years old.

In a letter written 10 March 1841, Joseph A. Mansfield to Reynolds Chapman, he refers to "my sister," and finds her willing to proceed with the case." He probably was referring to Mildred M. Taliaferro, the defendant.

* * * * * * * * * * * * * * *

Georgiana Taliaferro sues the estate of her late brother, Lawrence Taliaferro, for payment of the hires of her negroes from 1812 to 1826. In her Bill, Georgiana states that her brother died intestate without issue. (In his deposition taken 28th November 1836, John Guard says Lawrence moved to Culpeper County in 1822.) In the final decree, 29th April 1837, Georgiana was awarded $1633.03 with interest from the 1st of January 1827 until paid and her costs.

* * * * * * * * * * * * * * *

The following summons was found in the suit of King against Parrott.

Summons to William Parrott, late Sheriff of Orange County, to whom was committed for administration the estate of Julius King, deceased, Joseph Cave, James G. Blakey and Robert Miller, securities for the said William Parrott. Benjamin Hume, late Sheriff of the county of Orange, to whom was committed for administration the estate of John Mallory and Moses T. Harris, administrator of Tandy Bowcock, deceased, which said John Mallory and Tandy Bowcock were also securities for the said William Parrott as sheriff as aforesaid .. to answer a bill .. against them .. by John Hansford and Sally, his wife, late Sally King; John W. Evans and Nancy, his wife, late Nancy King, and John King .. 9 August 1834 .. Executed on all parties October 6th 1834. Curtis Wilhoit, D.S. for Thomas Coleman, S.O. C.

* * * * * * * * * * * * * * *

In a suit, John Boston states that Ann Boston, his sister, late of the county of Orange, deceased, died some years hence intestate leaving considerable personal property consisting of slaves with John Boston and his sister, Elizabeth Waugh, late Elizabeth Boston, now a widow, together with the children of William Deane, who intermarried with Sarah Boston, deceased, her distributees; that in the month of September in the year 1826, being subsequent to the death of the said Ann Boston, Gowry Waugh and George Deane qualified in the Superior Court for Orange County as her administrators, executing bond with John Deane, William Deane, Basdel Haney, Arrit Sullivan, Alexander Waugh and George Newman securities; that they, the said administrators have since their qualification been in possession of the said slaves and have received the hires and profits thereof without having rendered any account of their administrationship. The plaintiffs are asking for a settlement.

In his Bill, John Boston said that Sarah Deane, the wife of William Deane, died many years since and before the death of the said Ann Boston, leaving ten children to wit: Charles, George, Mary (who has since intermarried with William Deane), Elizabeth (who has since intermarried with Basdil Haney), John, Ann (who has since intermarried with Edward Sullivan) and Sarah, together with Reuben, Francis and Robert B., who are infants.

In a decree, Alexander A. Boston is shown as the guardian of Robert B. Deane. On the face of a summons is written -- "George Newman is the son of Alexander; William Deane is the son of John."

After the Bill was introduced, it appears Ann married Joseph Baker (the will says she married Edward Sullivan). Another paper requests the Bill be amended making Joseph Baker, who has intermarried with (blank) Sullivan, widow of Arrit Sullivan, deceased, a defendant. In another paper, Arrit appears as Evritt. In a newspaper clipping, the name is Edward Sullivan and Ann, his wife.

A pencil notation after the name of Sarah Deane appears "mar'd Hinkle Jarrell."

* * * * * * * * * * * * * *

The following was found on a sheet of paper with no apparent reason for being in the file.

State of Virginia, Orange County, to wit: Be it known that before me (blank) a justice of the peace in and for the said county, personally appeared Richard Hackney and made oath under forms of law that he is the identical person named in an original pension certificate in his possession which I hereby certify the following to be a true copy.

War Department

Revolutionary Claim

I certify that in conformity with the laws of the United States of the 7th June 1832, Richard Hackney of the State of Virginia, who was a private in the War of the Revolution is entitled to receive Forty Dollars per annum during his natural life commencing on the 4th of March 1831, payable semi-annually on the 4th of March and 4th of September in every year.

Given at the War Office of the United States this 13th day of June One Thousand eight hundred and thirty three.

Examined and Countersigned   John -----
    I. L. Edwards   Acting Secretary of War

That he now resides in Orange County and has resided therein for the space of two years past and that previous thereto he has resided in Fluvanna County.

* * * * * * * * * * * * * *

In a suit filed in 1838, Lindsay v. Lindsay, Landon Lindsay, Lunsford
Lindsay, John S. Lindsay, Ludwell Lindsay, Lancelot Lindsay, Levingston
Lindsay, children of Caleb Lindsay, deceased; John Roach, Robert Roach,
George Mason and Polly, his wife, late Polly Roach, John Stringfellow and
Sally, his wife, late Sally Roach, which said John Roach, Robert Roach,
Polly Mason and Sally Stringfellow are children of Elizabeth Roach, deceased,
sister of William Lindsay, deceased, Richard Robinson, Walter Robinson,
James Robinson and John F. Almond and Mary Ann, his wife, are children of
Nancy Robinson, deceased, daughter of the said Elizabeth Roach, deceased,
John Lindsay and Larkin Lindsay, sons of James Lindsay, deceased, who was
a brother of the said William Lindsay, deceased, Polly Wright, William
Lindsay, Elizabeth Lindsay; Mary Brockman, a sister and devisee of the
said William Lindsay, against

William Roach and Thomas Robinson, administrators de bonis non with the
will annexed of William Lindsay, deceased, the said William Roach in his
own right and the said Thomas Robinson, administrator of his deceased
wife, Nancy; Frances Lindsay, widow of Reuben Lindsay, deceased, and James
G. Lindsay, Joseph Allen Mansfield and Susan, his wife, Robert Cave Jnr.
and Sally, his wife, Evaline Lindsay, Julia Lindsay and George C. Lindsay,
the last three being infants; John Lindsay (son of Joshua), Taylor Lindsay,
Joshua Lindsay, the heirs of Reuben Lindsay, deceased (sons of Joshua),
John A. Patrick and S., his wife, and Francis Stubblefield and E., his
wife, heirs of Joshua Lindsay, deceased; Caleb Ware, --- Gentry and Susan,
his wife, formerly Susan Ware, --- Gentry and Eliza., his wife, formerly
Eliza. Ware, Lindsay Ware, James West and Sally, his wife, formerly Sally
Ware, William Ware, --- Smith and Jane, his wife, formerly Jane Ware, and
--- Samms and Charlotte, his wife, formerly Charlotte Ware; Thomas Row,
Sheriff of Orange County, committee administrator de bonis non with the
will annexed of Caleb Lindsay, deceased; Benjamin Hume, late sheriff of the
county of Orange and committee administrator de bonis non with the will
annexed of Lewis Lindsay, deceased, and Richard Richards, administrator
with the will annexed of Nancy Lindsay, deceased, defendants, in Chancery.

The plaintiffs this day filed their Bill against the defendants, and the
defendants John Lindsay (son of Joshua), Taylor Lindsay, Joshua Lindsay,
the heirs of Reuben Lindsay, deceased (son of Joshua), John A. Patrick and
S., his wife, and Francis Stubblefield and E., his wife, heirs of Joshua
Lindsay, deceased, Polly Wright, William Lindsay and Elizabeth Lindsay,
children of James Lindsay, deceased; Caleb Ware, --- Gentry and Susan, his
wife, Lindsay Ware, --- Gentry and Eliza., his wife, William Ware, ---
Samms and Charlotte, his wife, James West and Sally, his wife, --- Smith
and Jane, his wife, not having entered their appearances and given security
according to the Act of Assembly and the Rules of this Court, and it appearing by satisfactory evidence that they are not inhabitants of this
Commonwealth, on the motion of the plaintiffs by counsel, it is ordered
that the said defendants (last named) do appear before the justices of our
said county of Orange at the court house on the fourth Monday of February
next and answer the Bill of the plaintiffs, and that a copy of this order
be forthwith inserted in some news paper published in the town of Fredericksburg for two months successively and that another copy thereof be posted
at the front door of the court house of this county.

* * * * * * * * * * * * * *

TAYLOR. Maria 166; Martha F. 31,
74; Martha S. 2, 161; Matilda
R. 2, 31, 70, 74, 161; Mary C.
74; Pernello E.H. 9; Robert 23,
25, 32, 41, 61, 71, 89, 127;
Robert Jr. 2, 6, 15, 46, 61, 70,
74, 76, 88, 101, 113, 130, 161;
S.G. 55; Sally (Wood) 13; Sarah
T. 31; Sary 5; St. Clair 90;
William 2, 20, 169; Major William
42; William D. 25; William F.
9*, 11, 47.

TERRILL. Ann 71; Buckner 18, 60,
89, 120; Catherine 15, 159; Claibourne 15; David 169; Edmond 16,
31, 36, 47, 70, 71; Elizabeth 15,
71, 107, 109, 112, 169; Elizabeth L. (Coleman) 164, 165; Frances 71; George 15, 71, 169;
Goodrich 108; Heeling 3; James 8,
69, 71, 74, 107, 108, 113, 117,
129, 169; Capt. James 40; Jane
13, 15; Jane (Morton) 15; John
7, 16, 19, 37, 41, 57, 68, 69, 71,
74, 77, 92, 95, 107, 108, 112,
117, 120, 131, 165; Mary Ann 13;
Nancy 15, 31, 71, 124, 129, 169;
Oliver 1, 3, 13, 28; Polly 71;
Reuben 71, 168, 169; Robert 1,
26, 107*, 112, 164; Robert Jr.
13, 16, 81, 97, 103, 109; Sarah
15; Sarah M. 29; Susan 13;
Susan (Middlebrook) 68; Susan Ann
(Grasty) 108; Susannah (Morton)
15, 169; Uriel 16, 24, 28, 101,
103, 107; Dr. Uriel 13, 28;
William 71*, 74, 81, 108, 110,
117, 165, 169; William Jr. 168,
169; William H. 15, 176;
William L. 12.

TERRY. John 130; Lucy (Oaks) 111,
130.

THOM. Reuben T. 14, 23.

THOMAS. B. Jr. 103; Catherine 4;
Edward 4; Henry 4*; John 22;
Lucy 4; Mary 4; Nancy 4; R. 122,
135; R. Jr. 26; Robert 138.

THOMPSON. David 94; Eliza 120;
Elizabeth 18; Frances 90, 106;
Henry 23, 25, 42, 56; James 90*,
92, 125; Jane 90; Joseph 136;
Lucy 18; Martha 90; Mary 56;

THOMPSON. Reuben or Reuben L. 18,
24, 38, 58, 66, 79, 82, 94, 120,
143; Sally 18; Saley (Lindsay)
7, 18; Samuel 18*, 24, 38, 58, 120;
Samuel Sr. 18; Sarah 90, 120;
Suckey 18; Susan 120; William
18, 120, 150.

THORNTON. Anthony 12, 37, 38, 40,
57, 60, 82, 85; Boswell 127;
Daniel 1, 41, 69, 98, 105*, 106,
108, 125; Daniel M.F. 114; Elizabeth 77; Elizabeth (Wright) 98,
123; George 13, 27; George W. 9,
10, 22; Henry R. 10, 22; Jno. T.
26, 56, 81; John 31, 46; Lucy W.
10, 22; Luke 1, 31, 41, 69, 89,
92, 108, 125; Luke T. 105; Mary
10, 22; Mary G. 10, 22; Melinda
(Wright) 98; Nancy (Twyman) 12;
Sarah 69; Seth B. 10, 22; Thomas
13, 69, 76*, 77; Thomas S. 60,
63, 82; William 31, 151.

THROOP. Thomas 179.

TINDER. Anthony 66, 85, 102, 115,
122.

TODD. John P. 159.

TOMPKINS. James 149; Kitty (Rucker)
149.

TOOLEY. James 150; John 150; Nancy
(White) 150; Phebe (White) 150.

TREVILLIAN. Eliza W. 45.

TRICE. Elizabeth (Crook) 150; John
150.

TRIMBLE. Major David 121.

TULLOCK. William 101.

TURNER. Fleming 145; Jane (Clarke)
145, 147; John 19.

TUTT. Richard 166.

TWYMAN. Alfred J. 116; Anthony 147;
Elijah 12; Elizabeth 23; Frances
12; Francis 12; Iverson 12; James
147; James Winston 121; Jonathan
12, 24, 100, 101, 110, 124, 125;
John 12, 23; Judah 12; Mordecai 12;
Nancy 12; Paschal 12, 126, 128,
132; Robert Davis 121; Samuel 12*,
40; Sarah 121; Sarah (Davis) 121;
Thomas 23; William 23; William
Horace 121.

TYLER. Richard 48.

URIEL. John 1.

Heritage Books by Ruth and Sam Sparacio:

Abstracts of Account Books of Edward Dixon, Merchant of Port Royal, Virginia, Volume I: 1743–1747

Abstracts of Account Books of Edward Dixon, Merchant of Port Royal, Virginia, Volume II

Albemarle County, Virginia Deed and Will Book Abstracts, 1748–1752

Albemarle County, Virginia Deed Book Abstracts, 1758–1761

Albemarle County, Virginia Deed Book Abstracts, 1761–1764

Albemarle County, Virginia Deed Book Abstracts, 1764–1768

Albemarle County, Virginia Deed Book Abstracts, 1768–1770

Albemarle County, Virginia Deed Book Abstracts, 1776–1778

Albemarle County, Virginia Deed Book Abstracts, 1778–1780

Albemarle County, Virginia Deed Book Abstracts, 1780–1783

Albemarle County, Virginia Deed Book Abstracts, 1787–1790

Albemarle County, Virginia Deed Book Abstracts, 1790–1791

Albemarle County, Virginia Deed Book Abstracts, 1791–1793

Augusta County, Virginia Land Tax Books, 1782–1788

Augusta County, Virginia Land Tax Books, 1788–1790

Amherst County, Virginia Land Tax Books, 1789–1791

Caroline County, Virginia Appeals and Land Causes, 1787–1794

Caroline County, Virginia Committee of Safety and Early Surveys, 1729–1762 and 1774–1775

Caroline County, Virginia Land Tax Book Alterations, 1782–1789

Caroline County, Virginia Land Tax Book Alterations, 1792–1795

Caroline County, Virginia Land Tax Book Alterations, 1795–1798

Caroline County, Virginia Order Book Abstracts, 1765

Caroline County, Virginia Order Book Abstracts, 1767–1768

Caroline County, Virginia Order Book Abstracts, 1768–1770

Caroline County, Virginia Order Book Abstracts, 1770–1771

Caroline County, Virginia Order Book, 1764

Caroline County, Virginia Order Book, 1765–1767

Caroline County, Virginia Order Book, 1771–1772

Caroline County, Virginia Order Book, 1772–1773

Caroline County, Virginia Order Book, 1773

Caroline County, Virginia Order Book, 1773–1774

Caroline County, Virginia Order Book, 1774–1778

Caroline County, Virginia Order Book, 1778–1781

Caroline County, Virginia Order Book, 1781–1783

Caroline County, Virginia Order Book, 1783–1784

Caroline County, Virginia Order Book, 1784–1785

Caroline County, Virginia Order Book, 1785–1786

Caroline County, Virginia Order Book, 1786–1787

Caroline County, Virginia Order Book, 1787, Part 1

Caroline County, Virginia Order Book, 1787, Part 2

Caroline County, Virginia Order Book, 1787–1788

Caroline County, Virginia Order Book, 1788

Culpeper County, Virginia Deed Book Abstracts, 1795–1796

Culpeper County, Virginia Land Tax Book, 1782–1786

Culpeper County, Virginia Land Tax Book, 1787–1789

Culpeper County, Virginia Minute Book, 1763–1764

Digest of Family Relationships, 1650–1692, from Virginia County Court Records

Digest of Family Relationships, 1720–1750, from Virginia County Court Records

Digest of Family Relationships, 1750–1763, from Virginia County Court Records

Digest of Family Relationships, 1764–1775, from Virginia County Court Records

Essex County, Virginia Deed and Will Abstracts, 1695–1697

Essex County, Virginia Deed and Will Abstracts, 1697–1699

Essex County, Virginia Deed and Will Abstracts, 1699–1701

Essex County, Virginia Deed and Will Abstracts, 1701–1703

Essex County, Virginia Deed and Will Abstracts, 1745–1749

Essex County, Virginia Deed and Will Book, 1692–1693

Essex County, Virginia Deed and Will Book, 1693–1694

Essex County, Virginia Deed and Will Book, 1694–1695

Essex County, Virginia Deed and Will Book, 1701–1704

Essex County, Virginia Deed, 1753–1754 and Will Book 1750

Essex County, Virginia Deed Abstracts, 1721–1724

Essex County, Virginia Deed Book, 1724–1728

Essex County, Virginia Deed Book, 1728–1733

Essex County, Virginia Deed Book, 1733–1738

Essex County, Virginia Deed Book, 1738–1742

Essex County, Virginia Deed Book, 1742–1745

Essex County, Virginia Deed Book, 1749–1751

Essex County, Virginia Deed Book, 1751–1753

Essex County, Virginia Land Trials Abstracts, 1711–1716 and 1715–1741

Essex County, Virginia Order Book Abstracts, 1695–1699

Essex County, Virginia Order Book Abstracts, 1699–1702

Essex County, Virginia Order Book Abstracts, 1716–1723, Part 1

Essex County, Virginia Order Book Abstracts, 1716–1723, Part 2

Essex County, Virginia Order Book Abstracts, 1716–1723, Part 3

Essex County, Virginia Order Book Abstracts, 1716–1723, Part 4

Essex County, Virginia Order Book Abstracts, 1723–1725, Part 1

Essex County, Virginia Order Book Abstracts, 1723–1725, Part 2

Essex County, Virginia Order Book Abstracts, 1725–1729, Part 1

Essex County, Virginia Order Book Abstracts, 1727–1729

Essex County, Virginia Order Book, 1695–1699

Essex County, Virginia Will Abstracts, 1730–1735

Essex County, Virginia Will Abstracts, 1735–1743

Essex County, Virginia Will Abstracts, 1745–1748

Fairfax County, Virginia Deed Abstracts, 1799–1800 and 1803–1804

Fairfax County, Virginia Deed Abstracts, 1804–1805

Fairfax County, Virginia Deed Book Abstracts, 1799

Fairfax County, Virginia Deed Book, 1798–1799

Fairfax County, Virginia Land Causes, 1788–1824